T0265654

WEST

Comrade, look not on the west:
'Twill have the heart out of your breast;
'Twill take your thoughts and sink them far,
Leagues beyond the sunset bar.

A. E. Housman

WEST

TALES OF THE LOST LANDS

MARTIN WALL

AMBERLEY

First published 2023

Amberley Publishing
The Hill, Stroud
Gloucestershire, GL5 4EP

www.amberley-books.com

British Library Cataloguing in Publication Data.
A catalogue record for this book is available from the British Library.

ISBN 978 1 3981 1019 9 (hardback)
ISBN 978 1 3981 1020 5 (ebook)

1 2 3 4 5 6 7 8 9 10

Typesetting by SJmagic DESIGN SERVICES, India.
Printed in the UK.

Contents

Foreword

From a small boy peering through the window of the tired family saloon across the ridges of the Long Mynd and Wenlock Edge I was drawn ...
    east to the iron and the fire, the furnace and the ore ... And west to the verdant, the black mountains and the white castle.
    What is it in the dying of the light? The faint echo across a bend in the river, the not quite lost memory of broken treaties and parleys

    of timeless deceptions.

Back and forth across the Saxon dyke our fathers' fathers moved...
    Border people live with the rub of change in their language, their inflections, their humour and superstitions ... this is the land I love.
    This weird corner of ... England? But is it England? I stand aside as Martin Wall illuminates and weaves in conversation and narrative. He explores our Mercia, the former Anglo-British kingdom ... A land rich in treasures and celebrated poets and bards ... saturated in song. Here he reveals at a giddy spin a melange of Black Country industrial fallout that spills across the ancient border of the last princes of the Cymru.
    All 'this and that' coupled with a poignant, deeply personal clutch of tales.
    He calls this latest work a 'spiritual hitch hike' where normal laws of time are suspended. All at once we enter a realm of cultural studies, anthropology, theology ... At others we are catapulted into fictional other worlds populated by spirits who only ever lived in Martin's imagination. They take their place among the 'real' historical figures to enhance our total experience of time and place.

7

Through this personal odyssey runs the timeless presence of the river-goddess, Sabrina fair, the slender ribbon over which his story travels ...

Martin Wall offered works of exotica and colour with great detail and eloquence in the past ... And now he offers a love letter to a lost land.

Enjoy these tales and set your gaze westward.

Robert Plant
2023

Introduction

It is a hard thing for a bard to lose his muse. Everything you were, are, could ever be, tossed to what Langland called the tarts of fate, a cacophony of pain, that once was bliss. Why? The writer Philip K. Dick tried to explicate the process in his *Exegesis*:

> Absolute suffering leads to – is the means to – absolute beauty. Neither absolute should be subordinated to the other. But this is not how it is: the suffering is subordinated to the value of the art produced. Thus the essence of horror underlies our realization of the bedrock nature of the universe. (*The Exegesis of Philip K. Dick,* Jackson, P. & Lethem, J. Eds. Gollancz, London, 2011).

The Bible simply says, 'For in much wisdom, there is much grief.' None of this is of any concern to her.

She has always been here, as long as the land rose from the sea, the waters sprang from the earth. On odd occasions, for no reason other than that it pleases her to do so, she may reveal herself. I stayed with a group of friends once at Trefeglwys in mid-Wales. I had a knee operation coming up, and so could not join in the hill-walking expedition, but suggested that since the source of the River Severn (or Hafren) was quite nearby, that might be a good walk for the group to take – and around the hearth we discussed the ancient goddess, Sabrina, after whom the great river is named.

In the morning after breakfast, my friend and I drove independently to Dolgoch Falls, and returned somewhat later than the rest of the party. They had not been too impressed with my suggested walk, they all said. For the most part it had been a grim trudge through dense plantations of coniferous trees, occluding any panoramic views. Beyond that, a desolate bog extended, and somewhere amidst this ooze and mud, the gurgling spring that ultimately disgorged itself into the *Mor Hafren* or Bristol Channel, was secreted away.

It was a disappointing experience for the walkers, on the whole, but there had been one highlight of the pilgrimage. A little in front of the party, a young girl strode on ahead. She was not well-equipped for such a walk, in such desolate country. She was, in fact, dressed in an Italian national football outfit, and carried nothing with her. It was noted by all who saw her that she was exceptionally pretty and looked as if she may be Italian. Eventually, and after much searching, my friends located the source of the river, a treeless waste, with views for many miles around.

But the girl in the Italian football kit was nowhere to be seen, and it was considered by my friends that she could not possibly have made the return walk on the single track through the Hafren Forest without her being observed by the group. Was this a manifestation of Sabrina the river-goddess of the Romano-Britons? Could a group thought-form, a so-called *egregore*, have manifested itself in the form of a pretty young girl in a remote Welsh forest? You may smirk – and if you do – this may not be the book for you.

Well, what sort of book is it then? As Jaquetta Hawkes (1910-1996) said of her own history *A Land* (1951); 'It is an uncommon book, difficult to put into the usual categories.' It is a tribute to a lost time and a lost land, the Britain of my youth, now disintegrating before our eyes, a 'personal odyssey through the decaying landscape of my past'. John Knowler, in his brilliant anecdotal history, *Trust an Englishman* (1973), described himself as being part of 'the generation that didn't show up'. I can readily identify with his sentiment of simply wanting to tell the tale of where he had been, and what he had been doing.

It is a dreamscape, a crypto-history, a psycho-geography. It is a misremembered history – an occidental hauntology, an 'English hiraeth'. It is an expiation and a celebration, a memoir and a prophesy – but above all, ironically, a reorientation – the word orient meaning 'east'. Yet this is a book about the occidental – the west, and especially concerns a fraternity of clerks – a fraternity entirely of my own imagining – whose mission throughout all ages has been to honour the Lady Sabrina and her myriad sisters, the living goddesses who enchant the land.

They are all men, and almost all men of the west. Some are world-famous, others forgotten or obscure, but all were responding to a mysterious telluric energy that infuses these Lost Lands. Alfred Watkins, who first postulated the existence of 'ley lines', is one famous example of someone who has experienced what James Joyce called an 'epiphany' in this landscape, but there are a host of others.

Some are real, others imaginary, my brotherhood knows nothing of academic propriety or temporal chauvinism. They include a Roman cavalryman forgotten to history, and an anonymous monk of Wenlock Priory; Walter Map, Layamon, Sabine Baring-Gould, A.E. Housman, Francis Brett Young, and J.R.R. Tolkien, Simon Evans, Archie Hill, Bruce Chatwin and Stephen J. Yeates – among others. There is another, rather obscure writer involved. Me. For this is a journey not only through occidental space, but also through time, my time in particular. Stories of a quest to glimpse the muse, if only for a precious moment more, in the Lost Lands of the west.

1

Heledd's Lament

The first ship turned towards the west,
Over the sea, the running sea,
And by the wind was all possessed
And carried to a rich country.

Philip Larkin

Paradoxically, my journey into the west began in the east, the East
Midlands anyway, Nottingham to be precise. How I came to be there
is another story, but there has always been a subconscious literary
interest behind my various itinerant wanderings, and that was true
of Nottingham in a way. The first words I read aloud, to my mother
while she was doing the ironing, were from *The Adventures of
Robin Hood*. I was a big fan of Alan Sillitoe as a young man, and
ironically I found myself living in the very streets which he describes
being demolished in his *The Death of William Posters* (1965).

The high-rise council flats which had replaced the terraced streets
and their pubs were now about to be demolished in their turn thirty
years later. I lived in these by then rather notorious flats, in an area
helpfully described by *The Guardian* as 'Crack City'.

I am still a Sillitoe fan, and once met him briefly. I deliberately
shook his hand. I happened to know that he had shaken hands with
Robert Graves when he visited the great poet in Majorca, where
he hoped to learn the secrets of the muse from Graves, who knew
her intimately in his day. Graves, as a schoolboy, had ridden on
his bicycle to see the elderly Thomas Hardy at Max Gate, and had
shaken *his* hand.

A mind which is amused by such literary trivia was bound, in the
end, to write this book. I read Sillitoe's *Raw Material* (1987) again

recently after thirty years, partly in search of a suitable style for the more personal elements of this project, which should become quite evident as we proceed. I was transported back to my own days in Radford.

I lived just off Canning Circus, in a high-rise block called Highurst Court, known to local wits as 'High-risk Court'. The descendants of Robin's outlaw band lived now not in the forest of Sherwood, but in the ghetto, and the area was simply left to eat its own smoke during the Thatcher years, when I was there, just in the aftermath of serious rioting. My flat was pretty high-up, and from the balcony I could see right over the city to the south-west, and Ratcliffe-on-Soar Power Station.

As my circumstances became more and more desperate, like Frank Dawley in Sillitoe's novel, I knew that my only hope of avoiding homelessness, possibly prison, was to leave. Looking towards the power station, I drew a line in my mind beyond that – to my boyhood home, the West Midlands.

I had a vivid dream one night of a place I had not seen for over twenty years – a place nearby where I now live, in fact. So there was certainly *something* at work in my unconscious steering me west. But my main hope back then, was to move to London, and so I went for an interview for a job down there. I was not selected, and unfortunately came down with an awful 'flu type infection on the train home.

The illness lasted three weeks, and my electricity was due to be cut off for non-payment. The only facility left to me was a telephone, and one morning it rang. It was my mother. An agency had contacted her, trying to locate me, because there was a job available in Worcestershire. She knew I was in a bad way, and suggested I take up the offer of work and stay at the parental home. Christmas was approaching, and with it my mother's birthday, and so with a heavy heart I left Nottingham and returned to my homeland in the west. I knew somehow that I would not come back.

I began work within a week or so, for the Psychiatric Emergency Services. Initially, my 'patch' was confined to north Worcestershire, the hill-country. I do not drive due to disability, so my boss advised me to use my bus pass to get around all the main facilities in the area and familiarise myself with the hospital wards, specialist housing projects and so forth, during the first week.

There was a considerable local infrastructure (at least back then) because a huge old asylum, Barnsley Hall, was just being closed. After many years in the inner city the gentle hills and woods of the region were a pleasant change, and I didn't know it then, but I was to be in the service for the next ten years. I had no inkling whatsoever that this relocation had any special spiritual meaning for me – but that would soon change.

Although I knew the area passably well, it seemed oddly unfamiliar to me at first. I was originally from South Staffordshire, the 'Green Borderlands' to the west of the Black Country, and had not had much to do with neighbouring Worcestershire since I left school. I have had a lifelong interest in folklore and mythology and so I was on the lookout early on for resonant places in the landscape. Some of my clients lived in the hill-villages and so I planned my visits so that I could intercept the last bus on my way home. As summer came on, I would stroll down St Kenelm's Pass to a pub in the Clent Hills where there was a convenient bus stop.

One day I visited St Kenelm's Well at Romsley, and it was there that I had my first intimation of some mysterious entity which wished to communicate itself to me mediated by *signs* embedded in the landscape – provided I was prepared to take the time and trouble to interpret them. This was a definite spiritual force of some kind, and quite a compelling one. I felt bound to respond to it, in much the way Philip K. Dick felt he must following the same kind of experience, which he records in his *Exegesis*, the possibility of what he called 'A manifold of partially actualised realities, existing tangential to this one'.

One evening I bumped into an old college friend I had not seen for over twenty years. I asked what she was doing with herself now and was surprised when she told me she was a professional spiritualist medium. Apparently, she had gone to some seances where she had demonstrated such exceptional natural ability that she had gone on to train as a medium. She volunteered to give me a free consultation, and since I had just experienced a very painful period in my life, I agreed to go along one Saturday morning to the room she hired for her work. I had grown up in the very village where we met, and it was the first time I had been in the building since it was the village shop in my boyhood. Memories came flooding back, and rather ironic ones. My mother had certain clairvoyant abilities and had been friendly with the shopkeeper and his wife. When my mother went into hospital to have a cyst removed, the childless couple minded me for a few hours while my father visited her at the hospital.

On one occasion my mother repaid their kindness by providing them with just such a consultation as I was about to attend. I had similar abilities, but repudiated them following a religious experience, so I had not had anything to do with spiritualism for many years. I was open-minded but wary, knowing how easy it can be to 'lead' the subject. The interview was tape-recorded. Some questions seemed to lead nowhere, but eventually I was asked if the name 'Alice' meant anything to me.

Alice was my maternal grandmother's name. Some of what she had to say seemed quite accurate, especially about my father's poor health. Then, my friend seemed to lapse into a sad reverie. I was such a fool, she said, to have ended a love affair, and endured a broken-heart – why had I not had more faith in the power of life and love? All this was, unfortunately, very accurate. Then, she said, I would soon become a writer! This was preposterous, for I could not type back then and had no inclination. But my friend was adamant. I would publish a book, and then many more would follow. I had no right to withhold them from the world, and although I might have a variety of day-jobs, ultimately I was a writer.

That was my purpose in returning here, she said, back to my real roots. I left after about an hour, leaving what I could afford, somewhat confused, unclear about what the whole thing meant. At any rate, within the year our team-clerk at work was made redundant. All staff were required to learn to type their own correspondence etc. and I soon started writing, at first as a 'blogger' on Julian Cope's *Modern Antiquarian* website.

What emerged, I soon realised, were communications from a mysterious inner-world, a shadowland or parallel landscape – and the revelation that the outer landscape is a sort of palimpsest. If the over-script of modernity could be *consciously* mentally erased, and the original under-script of our ancestors revealed beneath – then perhaps the meaning behind the mysterious message would be revealed once more?

The more I visited St Kenelm's Well, the greater the intensity of these inner revelations became, but to get to their deepest meaning, I needed to deconstruct a legend. Another thing gradually became clear. The origin of these communications was a living goddess.

For those unfamiliar with the territory, I can do no better than to quote the ground-breaking archaeologist and ethnographer Marija Gimbutas:

In Neolithic Europe and Asia Minor (ancient Anatolia) – in the era between 7,000 B.C and 3,000 B.C – religion focused on the wheel of life and its cyclical turning. This is the geographic sphere and the time frame I refer to as Old Europe. In Old Europe, the focus of religion encompassed birth, nurturing, growth, death, and regeneration, as well as crop cultivation and the raising of animals. The people of this era pondered untamed natural forces, as well as wild plant and animal cycles, and they worshipped goddesses, or a goddess, in many forms.[1]

Such a society worshipped the female energy, and the destructive male or 'yang' energies we are so familiar with in our own times were subordinated to the will of the goddess. The indigenous tribes of this Old Europe were farmers, and in the main they kept peace with each other. Socio-economic arrangements were egalitarian and inclusive, and this civilization produced great art.

Their experience of the world was so vastly different to ours – their consciousness so radically different – that it is extremely difficult to convey in words. In truth, to really know the ineffable quality, the sublimity of this consciousness, an actual experience of its power is necessary. Providing the reader has the time and resources at their disposal, it is perfectly possible to visit remote regions where Tantrik practices very similar to those postulated by Gimbutas are still taught. We see all this, unfortunately, through the prism of our own fractured culture, and so the thousands of ceramic representations of the goddess in our museums are usually labelled as 'fertility figures'. But the goddesses represented much more than fertility.

For Gimbutas they 'unveil a natural and sacred sexuality neglected by modern culture'. The goddess, she thought, 'personified every phase of life, death, and regeneration. She was the Creator from whom all life – human, plant, and animal – arose, and to whom everything returned. Her role extended far beyond eroticism.'

So sacred was she, that her physical form became intermeshed with the landscape, she and the land were a single entity. The sympathetic magic familiar to the ancients perceived 'terraforms' in the landscape suggestive of female breasts, such as the Clent Hills, for instance, and if sacred springs were located atop them, the holy well was, in their minds, an outpouring of life-giving nourishment for the tribe – her people.

But on certain holy days – such as the Tibetans still celebrate to this day – the goddess would take on *human form* as a selected maiden became indwelt by the spirit of the goddess and performed a sacred dance – the *Vajrayogini*. The concept of sexual sin or obscenity as being associated with the male or female body was unknown to them, and these festivals were a blissful celebration of the ecstatic joy of love.

But this ancient culture was threatened by invading newcomers from the Steppes of central Russia – the so-called 'Proto-Indo-Europeans', or less fashionably now, 'Aryans'. The 'Kurgan hypothesis' promulgated by Gimbutas proposed that a people who raised burial-mounds in the Pontic-Caspian Steppe region of Russia and the Ukraine, who tamed wild horses and equipped themselves with edged weapons, had migrated into Old Europe. They were a warrior people, male-dominated, and abhorred the goddess-worshipping aboriginal religion.

The megalithic monuments of their predecessors were violated, destroyed or usurped for their own use, usually rebuilt in a cruder form. Old European menfolk were gradually exterminated, but most young females were retained for breeding-stock. All traces of the great temples and settlements of the indigenous peoples were erased. The shock must have been just as great as the arrival of the European peoples was to the Native Americans more recently.

The Great Goddess had been cast down, she who embodied everything sacred and holy. The awe she inspired is evident even as late as the twelfth century A.D. Graves quotes from an English herbal:

> Earth, divine goddess, Mother Nature, who dost generate all things and bringest forth ever anew the sun, which thou hast given to the nations; Guardian of the sky and sea and all Gods and powers; through thy influence all nature is hushed and sinks to sleep ... Again, when it pleases thee, thou sendest forth the glad daylight and nurturest life with thine eternal surety; and when the spirit of a man passes, to thee it returns. Thou art rightly named Great Mother of the Gods; Victory is thy divine name ... Thou art mighty, Queen of the Gods. Goddess, I adore thee as divine, I invoke thy name; vouchsafe to grant that which I ask of thee, so shall I return thanks to thy godhead, with the faith that is thy due.[2]

Graves, somewhat controversially, suggested that far from being totally eradicated, the culture of goddess-worship was simply driven underground, surviving in a bowdlerised form in the medieval witch-cult, among other secretive organisations. This is not, I think, a notion which should be blithely dismissed, as some contemporary academics have been inclined to do since the great poet's passing in 1985.

So now, I was on the alert for 'signs', and over the years as my responsibilities increased, my patch extended into large parts of West Mercia. At weekends I spent my spare time out on the border with Wales, and sometimes visited the land of the Red Dragon for longer holidays. My intuitions became stronger the further west I went.

In Wales, especially near waterfalls, they were at their most intense. I could sense the presence of the *Tylwyth Teg* or 'Fair Folk' of my ancestral culture – and as I will relate, strange things occurred sometimes. I felt a similar kind of atmosphere in the west of Ireland, and I reasoned that the survival of the spirit-beings must be contingent on remoteness, a certain type of topography with mountains and water (especially waterfalls) – but also on proximity to the sea, the 'shores of the utmost west' of the famous hymn.

Another favourite haunt was Glastonbury in the south-west, but gradually my interest focused on a region the Welsh call 'The Lost Lands'. In the 1960s the 'Lost Lands Liberation League' advocated the restoration of the border counties of England such as Shropshire, Cheshire, Herefordshire, and Gloucestershire – roughly the area of the old Welsh Marches – to an independent Welsh state.

As we will see, this campaign is far from dead. This corresponds to the region with which this book is concerned, a book about what it means to be 'lost', and to experience the loss of entire cultures.

In his *Morte d'Arthur,* Tennyson describes that epic moment as Arthur is conveyed on a barge by fairy women to Avalon, the Celtic Other-world in the west:

> The old order changeth, yielding place to new
> And God fulfils himself in many ways
> Lest one good custom should corrupt the world ...

This story is a universal one, for each one of us must yield too, and adjust ourselves to disillusionment, sickness, bereavement – and finally, death. On the day the muse deserted me, I stumbled cursing into the west, knowing there could be no going back to the old days, the old ways. *'The old order changeth, yielding place to new.'*

It is the oldest of stories, and the saddest, repeated time and again throughout century upon century of history. But it is always more catastrophic when one's own personal order is being supplanted. Personal though this catastrophe was, I intuited that it portended a greater atomisation of human consciousness, as if my own personal distress contained a cipher for the malaise of the entire race – a sort of latter-day shamanism.

Perhaps I was right, because within a year the world succumbed to a devastating pneumonic virus which paralysed all social, political, cultural and economic institutions on a global scale which – combined with environmental degradation, war and financial collapse – seems set to catapult us back into the Dark Ages. Who was she, this 'Black Isis', who unleashed Nature's revenge?

In my culture, we call her 'the Lady', or Nimue, or Viviane, 'She of Many Names'. She it was who exacted an oath from Arthur, that during his enchanted reign both Christianity and the 'Old Faith' should be tolerated equally. She is bewitchingly beautiful, and mercilessly cruel.

As I related in the introduction to my previous book *The Magical History of Britain*, I have always had a strange relationship with the 'Lady of Nemi', Diana, and *Nemetons*, or enclosed sacred spaces – indeed, I grew up in one. Diana was a goddess with a special interest in the island of Britain. She had prophesied that Brutus, grandson of Aeneas of Troy, would find a blessed land in the western ocean and become its sacred king, and that his heirs would rule thereafter from a great city called *Troia Nova* or 'New Troy' – modern London, which would eventually become the greatest city in the world.

She also prophesied to her daughter, Nimue, that the greatest magician in Britain, Merlin, would become infatuated with her, revealing all his recondite knowledge. The first time he saw her, he was stricken, transfixed, enthralled.

The other time she came, it was just the same – a deadly plague raged, but only in the west. The 'Saxon Devils' had no contact with the Eastern Roman Empire, and so were preserved from the terrible pestilence. Their settlements in the east of the island were uninfected. But for the Britons of the Celtic-speaking west, the 'Yellow Plague' in the 6th century A.D. announced the denouement of their resistance in what is now England.

I say 'what is now England' because from my earliest childhood I intrinsically knew that I had been born in a *liminal* place, geographically, politically, culturally, and spiritually. I was taught early on not to describe myself as English, but as British, a practice I continue to this day. The accident of Christ being born in a stable did not make Him a horse. I was also taught early on to distrust the *consensus gentium* and to analyse anything taught by educational agents about our heritage with great care, lest it misrepresent our history.

One part of my family had been transplanted from Brecknockshire by the Earl of Dudley to open up deep-mining at Baggeridge Colliery in south Staffordshire. I knew as a boy that my ancestor John Hughes, a famous mining-engineer and Mayor of Dudley during the Boer War, had been among these Welsh settlers, but his descendants inter-married with the Wall family – indigenous 'Welshry' – as the Normans called Brythonic people in the western forests.

If anything, they were more militantly 'Celtic' than my grandmother's side, who were Celt-Iberians, Silurians, with curly raven-black hair and swarthy complexions. They were among the first new settlers in these islands following the retreat of the ice sheet 11,500 years ago, returning from a natural refuge in what is now the Basque region of Spain and France. My father and his sister could have visited villages in the Pyrenees and people would have taken them for natives.

There was a corresponding idealisation of Wales, and at every opportunity we headed west for holidays. I was told to 'make myself at home', and to proudly proclaim my Welsh ancestry to any local boys who dishonoured me. Outside a pub in Rhyl in the 1960s, this quaint notion was soon put to the test when Welsh lads attacked some 'scouser' kids; the Black Country boys pitched in on their side, but I felt oddly uneasy about fighting against my *own* people, so the inner tension was present in me even then.

My father had the idea that the village we eventually moved to, Kinver in Staffordshire, was in fact quintessentially Celtic, and as we explored the surroundings of our new home he would explain the ancient Druidic origins of the hill-fort at Kinver and so forth in some detail. I listened attentively, but although it was true that half of my classmates at primary school were named Harris, Jones, Hughes, Roberts, Price, Powys, Evans, Williams – the village had been so completely anglicised for so many centuries that all trace of the Celtic past had been eradicated, except for its name.

But my father explained that we in the 'Lost Lands Liberation League' did not seek a merely political liberation – but a spiritual one. The spirits of the ancestors were still here, in the land where they lay buried. We must honour them or lose our spiritual entitlement to the land.

I was left in no doubt that this was no mere whimsy on his part. The Prophesy of Merlin did not require any political campaign in order to fulfil itself. All that was required, was a stubborn refusal to give-in – only those who struggled all their lives, were 'indispensable ones'. I imagined Arthur's cavalry, riding out over Kinver Edge to do battle with the heathen Saxons, and in the early 1970s a Welsh TVseries called *Arthur of the Britons* fed my young imagination all the more.

I was always reminded that the name I had chosen for myself – Martin – was the anglicised version of *Myrddyn* the Brythonic 'Myrddyn Wyllt', a bard who was the inspiration for 'Merlin'. The entire island was originally known as *Clas Myrddyn* – 'Merlin's Enclosure', or 'Merlin's Precinct' or 'Sanctuary'. By choosing my name, I had sealed my fate; I must play my part in the 'Matter of Britain' in my turn, even as the dusk began to fall. A superb novel by Rosemary Sutcliff, *The Lantern Bearers* (1959) seemed to transport me into a different, Arthurian, time-zone, but not just in the historical past.

Somehow, the story seemed to pre-figure a similar dystopia and collapse to come in the future. This catastrophic worldview was encouraged by my father, who constantly expected a complete social and political meltdown at any moment, followed by anarchy. My mother was somewhat less pessimistic, quite cheerful in fact, but never really contradicted this paradigm, and treated any deviation from it as a form of disloyalty to my father, who exercised his authority like some ancient potentate.

They were not Church people at all, but they were not anti-Christian either. Theirs was what might be called a personal theodicy, in which this world was simply the 'Vale of Soul-making', as the poet Keats called it, but this emphasis on the 'formation' of the soul had very much more ancient origins, among the Druids, for example.

In this philosophy, evil was not something to be shunned, but rather accepted as a necessary correlative of good. I have come to see that this was actually a quite dangerous hermeneutic error, but unfortunately, I did not resile this position until quite serious damage had already been done. I was simply taught that the forces of evil were growing at such an exponential rate, and the entropy of our senescent culture so pronounced, that a global catastrophe was inevitable.

Many others at this time shared such views, by the way, and they were not especially eccentric. The Cuban Missile Crisis occurred shortly after I was born and the world was on the brink of nuclear annihilation all through my youth. My parents' decision to retire from society in virtual isolation was in part based on

Kinver Edge Rock Houses.

Unreconstructed Rock Houses, Kinver.

this suspicious view of the world, which I think derived from their own experiences of growing up in the Great Depression and Second World War. Another such world crisis would, my father always taught, mean the disintegration of the entire political and social apparatus. Then, and only then, we could emerge to claim our rightful inheritance – the 'Sovereignty of Britain'. All other concerns were of no consequence to us.

As soon as I was able, I began to explore the world beyond our woodland home by walking atop the cliffs of the nearby sand-quarry to take a path through Gibbet Wood to Gibbet Lane, which led directly into Stourbridge. From the prehistoric fortifications atop the Ridge, which formed the county boundary looking east, I could see the unbroken urban sprawl of the Black Country stretching endlessly into the distance. I knew that I wanted to explore the large towns and cities of Britain, places I had only seen on maps. The west seemed boring, rural, unexciting.

The Stewponey & Foley Arms pub, then a well-known local landmark (immortalised by Sabine Baring-Gould's novel *Bladys of the Stewponey*), stood at the busy road-junction near my home. From there it was possible to hitch-hike in every cardinal direction, north, east, south and west. I tended to hitch rides either north or east, and even before I left school I had travelled quite far afield. In the years to come, I was to visit most parts of England, Wales and sometimes France and Ireland using this method – until it became virtually impossible after 2001.

Initially, my main reason for doing this was to visit megalithic monuments, and to check possible ley-line alignments between them (I was a devotee of Alfred Watkins, whose *The Old Straight Track* (1925) was an early influence on me). Later, when I had entirely 'dropped out', as they used to say, I became interested in the operations of 'random' chance after reading *The Dice Man* (1971) by George Cockcroft (under the pen name 'Luke Rhinehart'). This aspect also fascinated me, and over a period of 20 years I travelled many tens of thousands of miles by this means and could appear levelling a thumb or bearing a destination sign anywhere in the island.

This experiment in space, time and chance, had some interesting consequences, because over the years some very extraordinary coincidences occurred. Not only this, but I really did have very powerful spiritual experiences at various megalithic monuments, and in particular near Arbor Low Henge in the Derbyshire Peak, at Summer Solstice 1991. Following these experiences, I became convinced that not only was there once a psychical-energetic or spiritual identification with the land, as Alfred Watkins had proposed – but that this connection could be re-established, if only we made a supreme conscious effort.

These ideas were actually experienced more as emotions or 'feelings', rather than intellectually informed or rationally reasoned-out. I was then a very wild, some would say mad, individual, at the margins of respectable society – perhaps beyond that. But, for all that, these experiences were, in their own way, quite 'real', and sometimes occurred in the presence of companions.

My conclusion, after decades of research, was that spiritual experiences, magic, and supersensible entities were certainly valid and reasonable psychological constructs. But in exploring these realms, I had let all other matters deteriorate: health, wealth, relationships, status, had all been sacrificed. Eventually, I made the decision (influenced by a kindly probation officer) to rehabilitate.

After many years study with the Open University, I was accepted for training as a social worker. My training, and then my job, took me all over England, and gradually my former interests and history faded into the background until I received that phone call from my mother – and set my face towards the west.

We first moved to Kinver when I was five years old. I was immediately aware of a strange atmosphere there, as if one had walked into an abandoned house. One had the feeling that the owners of the house could suddenly come home at any time. This was in the 'Swinging Sixties', before the Local Government Act of 1972 reconfigured the county boundaries, sundering the Black Country from its 'Green Borderland', as Elihu Burritt described it.

During the 1960s, slum-clearance in adjoining urban areas meant that many young families were re-settled by the local authorities in Kinver, including ours. Although we were from a rural, not an urban slum (our cottage had been condemned), many locals treated all newcomers with suspicion and barely concealed hostility. Even after half a century, I have never felt quite at home there, though I made some good and kind friends.

My parents, who were very sensitive to what would then have been described as 'bad vibes' immediately sensed this miasma, and what made matters more difficult was my father's anti-social personality and foul temper (which regrettably, I inherit) especially when he had been drinking. He was anathematised by his mother, and written-out of her will, a cruel blow since he was the eldest of her two children – she also had a daughter and the siblings despised each other. My grandmother was permitted to visit me once a week, since I was her favourite grandchild, the apple of her eye, but the visits often ended in the most furious rows, and this was very upsetting for me.

Although our new house was literally that, and well-built with all modern conveniences, my father hated it, and my mother felt the same way. They were both very private people and couldn't adapt to living in a close-knit village. My childhood had already been extremely traumatic before we moved, but one day as I was walking home through the snow, I stepped into a concealed drain-cover which had been vandalised.

The ceramic pipe inside had been shattered, and a jagged shard sliced my right leg open at the knee. God only knows how, but I managed to walk into the house, and sat down opposite my father who was reading his paper. I mumbled something about cutting my knee, and he glanced up.

I saw his face turn instantly white. When I looked down, my right leg (I was still in short-trousers) was cut-open down to the bone like a slab of meat. We had no car or telephone so my mother rushed to comfort me while my father ran into the village for Dr Phipps, our GP. They returned about 15 minutes later in Dr Phipps's car and they raced indoors. By now the pain had hit me, and I was screaming so that the whole street heard.

Between them they made a sort of tourniquet out of tea-towels. I remember the doc's words to this day; 'Little boy, this is going to hurt you more than you've ever been hurt, but it might save your leg, so if you need to scream – scream!' The procedure was admirably performed, and the scream duly let out. I happened to sit on a bench outside St Peter's Church quite recently and discovered that it was dedicated to the memory of Dr Glyndwr Phipps and his wife, now long-since deceased. That I could still walk at all was entirely due to his considerable medical skill.

Then, at last, the ambulance came. Dr Phipps came with us in the ambulance, because I was drifting in and out of consciousness from blood loss. The last thing I heard was the ambulance crew discussing the chances of preventing an amputation at the knee. They did not sound too hopeful. I remember thinking, 'You're wrong! I'll be OK ...' before I briefly recovered consciousness on my way into theatre for surgery ... and then, blackness and void again. I awoke to find my father's hand on my brow. 'You've still got two legs my lad,' he said, his eyes watering. I laughed, still under the influence of the anaesthetic. 'I've been in a place with tall giraffes,' I replied.

I was confined for quite some time, and hostilities between my parents and grandparents were mercifully suspended for a while. They visited often, always bringing gifts of chocolate and elaborately illustrated history books. I was not given any books at primary school. Because I lived on a council estate the teachers assumed I was either a dunce or illiterate. The headmistress was a Dickensian caricature who personally hated me, physically and verbally punishing me for any perceived infraction of her Victorian mores. The forbidding building, which I still walk past on most days, was a Gothic horror.

'Nice' boys, who could not read, would often ask me what the words in their book said, and it was common knowledge among all the other children that I could read much more advanced books. One of my classmates was called upon to read aloud one day but could not read the book selected. The teacher pointed to me, and in a fury shouted, 'I bet even *he* could read this!' The children sniggered, and so despite being a 'rough' boy, she asked me to read aloud from the book, which to her astonishment, I did quite easily. The rest of my schooldays were very much of a piece.

I was always a lone wolf. An only child, it is just in my nature. I eventually recovered, and on my seventh birthday a dream came true when my parents unveiled a shiny new bicycle. Soon I was free to explore the landscape outside the village, and the neighbouring villages over the county border in Worcestershire, just a mile away. These early explorations gave me my first faint hint of a lifelong fascination with the history, landscape and literature of the western Midlands. These impressions culminate in this book, which I hope I may complete, before joining my people in *Tir Na nOg* – beyond these Lost Lands.

How did the west come to be 'lost'? I have written extensively about this process in previous books, but for the purposes of this work, a brief recapitulation of the last days of the western British kingdoms will prove germane. If the poet and philosopher Charles Williams was correct in his hypothesis, then; 'Strictly speaking, past, present, and future are relative and provisional terms ... existence operates in timelessness: the past and future are happening ... we may warily hope that Herod does not slaughter the innocents, nor Salome demand the Baptist's head.'[3] As Anne Ridler observed, 'There is no such word as *too late*: all times, like all fortune, must be good.' The reason for this is that, as our Celtic ancestors intrinsically understood, 'The past, present, and future are intertwined.'

Through the operations of what Williams called 'Substitution' and 'Exchange', our potentially boundless, 'co-inherent' existence offers a 'liberation from the tyranny of time'. A talent for mining the secret seam of meaning hidden in the landscape, observing the goings-on of its inhabitants seen as a continuum, as it were, with analeptic events at one end of the cycle, and proleptic at the other – was exactly what I had accidentally discovered during my protracted confinement as a boy.

History was not enough. What I really desired was *time travel*. It was simply inadequate to just read about historical events. I needed to go to where 'events' had happened, to immerse myself in the place, and by a kind of spiritual osmosis, to literally *see* those events in my mind, rather like spiritualist mediumship. Interestingly, what was 'seen' often differed from received documentary and archaeological wisdom. Of course, as a youngster I had no way of understanding what I was doing – but I soon found a kindred-spirit in Rosemary Sutcliff. I have mentioned *The Lantern Bearers*, for which she won the Carnegie Medal, but in all her novels this 'immersive' approach was her method, portraying 'history as it must have been'. This obsession with history was my only strong suit at school, but a corollary of my private studies was that I became quite competent at English, Geography, and what used to be called 'Divinity' as well. In all other areas, such as Mathematics and Science, I was not only bone-headed, but also bone idle.

When I was at last liberated from the Transylvanian Infant School, my education improved somewhat, when I began Junior School. I was already marked from the beginning, of course, but Mrs Watson, the headmistress and Rector's wife, at least tolerated me. She had a penchant for producing lavish plays on historical themes. One such project was a production of *Beowulf* which even included a simulacrum of an Anglo-Saxon longship. Some of the teachers were spiteful, however, and one of them reported me to Mrs Watson for pointing out errors in the design of some of the costumes. For this helpful advice, I was excluded from the play, but it was obvious to the headmistress that I was, in fact, correct.

From that time I was more or less left alone to do my own thing. Mr Morgan, who ordered books for the school library, always ensured that I could add any that took my fancy. For four years, there was comparative happiness. In 1972 we finally moved out of the village, and the next year I left Junior School to begin at the new Comprehensive.

From that point on, my life took a different turn, for the transition was not a successful one, as we will see. But these precious four years of relative peace gave me the time I needed to scratch the surface of a hidden history – a history which I instinctively knew lay behind the strange atmosphere of the area.

Long, long ago, beyond the mists of fourteen hundred years, there lived a powerful chieftain called Cynddylan of Pengwern, a faithful ally of Penda, the notorious pagan king of the Mercians. Penda's personality still casts a long shadow in these parts, as will be shown. The celebrated historian Sir Frank Stenton points out in his *Anglo-Saxon England* (1943) that the Mercians, meaning 'borderers', did not take their name from the Welsh border we are now familiar with, roughly coterminous with Offa's Dyke, but from an earlier border. This older boundary between Teuton and Celt was actually much further east, 'the belt of high land between Cannock Chase and the Forest of Arden'.

We know this from place-names celebrating *Woden*, the chief pagan god of the Mercians, such as Wednesbury ('Woden's fortress') and Wednesfield ('Woden's plain'). The high ground was not only easily defensible, but also marked a crucial watershed. Borders were often associated with watercourses and rivers, and still are today. The River Tame flows east into the Trent, which drains into the Humber and the North Sea – the 'German Ocean', as the Romans knew it. The River Stour, by contrast, flows west into the Severn (or Hafren in Wales), which drains into the Bristol Channel (the *Mor Hafren* in Welsh).

Thus the region marked out the sphere of influence of the respective peoples. Everywhere east of what is now the Black Country and Birmingham was 'English', everywhere to the west, Welsh or British. Thus, this area was once a war zone, as I had always instinctively known since boyhood, and the final act of this conflict was so desolating that the echo of the tragedy still resonates in the landscape to this day, for those attuned to hear the piercing scream of 'the grey-beaked eagle of Pengwern'.

In subsequent tales, we will examine the 'fraternity' of writers mentioned in the introduction. But this first story is an exception, for the person who composed a valediction for her slain brothers and sisters, the obliteration of the ancient Brythonic culture by the *Saes* or Saxons – was a woman, Heledd of Pengwern. Heledd was no ordinary woman. She was a 'living goddess', for the Celts never abandoned the 'Sovereignty goddesses' of the type we examined earlier.

The chief of these was the Morrigan of ancient Irish myth, known in Wales as Modron or Matrona. No Celtic king ruled in his own right, but by virtue of his relationship with the goddess. In effect, he was a consort of the queen-goddess, and if he displeased her, failed to satisfy her sexually, or became disfigured in some way, he would be discarded, and another consort selected in his place. Any injury to, or failing in, the king, would automatically be transferred as a malediction to the land, and without *Gwlad* – the land – all was lost. Not for nothing is the Welsh National Anthem called 'Old *Land* of my Fathers', *Hen Wlad Fy Nhadau*.

The character of Morgan Le Fay, Arthur's wicked half-sister (and alleged lover), is based on this ancient archetypal goddess-figure. Cartimandua, a queen of what is now northern England, set aside her consort Venutius, and took his armour-bearer Vellocatus as her new husband in his place. Another example is Boudica, queen of the Iceni of East Anglia. Boudica was literally worshipped as an incarnation of the goddess of victory, Andrasta. Her husband, Prasutagus, whose attempt to mollify the Emperor Nero by gifting him half his kingdom in his will, was assumed by the patriarchal Romans to be the sole legitimate authority in the area, they knew nothing of gender-equality in Celtic society, and were contemptuous of women. The Roman procurator, Catus Decianus, whose 'rapacity' was responsible for the following uprising, was ignorant of local customs and cared less. It was a catastrophic mistake, for the avenging goddess, in the shape of Boudica, very nearly wiped out the Roman colony, in revenge for flogging her and publicly raping her sexually immature daughters after her husband's death.

But what was to become of the goddess when the land was lost? Boudica probably took her own life when her insurrection failed, but when the Celts were finally expelled from the lowlands, the final lamentation for the bitter loss of their ancient lands issued from the mouth of Heledd, in a song of keening or mourning called the *Canu Heledd*.

On November 15th 655 A.D., Penda was slain by King Oswy of Northumbria at *Winwaed* somewhere near Leeds. Cadfael, the regent of Gwynedd and hitherto a staunch ally of the Mercian king, abandoned him to his fate when he sneaked away with his army on the night before the battle. It is probable that Cynddylan's war-band left with him, but now that the old pagan was dead, he knew that the two Celtic statelets east of the Severn, Luitcoit and Pengwern, would be Oswy's next target.

Bede (872-735), the Northumbrian historian, says that 'after cutting off the wicked king's head' (Penda), Oswy 'converted the Mercians *and the adjacent provinces* (author's italics) to the grace of the Christian faith'. These 'adjacent provinces' were the Celtic, or at least Anglo-British, allies of the Mercians. To forestall any Northumbrian threat, Cynddylan struck first. Peada, Penda's eldest son, who had already converted to Christianity, was set up by King Oswy, his father-in-law, as a puppet-ruler of Middle-Anglia.

At Easter 656, Peada's wife, acting as an assassin for her father, poisoned him. Pressure on Caer Luitcoit, now the village of Wall-by-Lichfield, grew. The reference to bishops in the following passage must refer to some sort of attempt by Oswy to establish a new diocese, Luitcoit was the forerunner of Lichfield. To relieve this, the last free Britons in the lowlands mounted a cavalry raid in the style of the bard Aneirin's *Y Gododdin*. In Aneirin's poem, all the Celtic warriors are slain but one – the poet himself, but on this occasion Cynddylan was victorious. Heledd tells us of her glorious brothers' exploits:

My heart is aflame like a firebrand!
Brothers I had, better it was when they were alive,
The whelps of Arthur our mighty fortress,
Outside Caer Luitcoit they were victorious;
Blood was strewn for the ravens as they fiercely attacked;
Lime-shields were shattered by the sons of Cyndrwyn,
Glory was theirs, battle-plunder from Caer Luitcoit
Morfael took it.
Fifteen hundred head of cattle and five stewards,
Four-score horses and splendid armour,
Each bishop rushed to the four corners,
The monks hugged their books close,
But they could not save them ...

This blow to Oswy's expansionism was carefully calculated. A tiny kingdom like Pengwern would not have dared to take the offensive unless he was already pre-occupied elsewhere. In all probability, Oswy's attention was now focused on containing the threat to his northern border with the Picts, under their king, Talorgan. Penda's two surviving sons, Wulfhere and Aethelred, were still at large, and it is quite possible that Cynddylan was either offering them sanctuary or assisting them distally.

Oswy had mounted a long-distance raid into Shropshire before, in 643 or 644, when he sent a raiding party to recover his brother Oswald's mutilated remains from Maserfield (probably Oswestry), where Penda had had his dismembered corpse hung in a tree as an offering to Woden. This had been successfully achieved, and so now, in a desperate bid to eliminate the tiny kingdom, Oswy decided to make a surprise attack by night on Cynddylan's royal hall of Llys Pengwern, outside Shrewsbury.

The whole community were gathered for a royal feast and the entire aristocracy of the small principality were in attendance when Oswy's men suddenly burst in upon them. Just as only one survivor lives to tell the tale in Aneirin's poem, so Heledd alone is spared to relate the heartbreaking scene, the end of a civilisation which had endured for time beyond memory:

> The hall of Cynddylan is dark tonight
> Without fire, without light,
> And Oh! What a silence surrounds it!
> The hall of Cynddylan is dark-panelled,
> It shares no laughing company now.
> Woe to him who knows such a sad end!
>
> The hall of Cynddylan has lost its splendour
> Now that he lies beneath his shield in his grave,
> Its roof was not always open to the sky ...
> The hall of Cynddylan is dark tonight,
> Without fire, without song,
> The tears furrow my cheeks ...
>
> The hall of Cynddylan is dark-ceilinged
> now that the English have slain Cynddylan
> and Elvan of Powys ...
> The eagle of Eli screams loud.
> He is wet from gorging on the blood of men,
> the heart's blood of Cynddylan the fair.
>
> The eagle of Eli guards the seas, fish no longer brave the currents.
> He howls to see the blood of men.
> The eagle of Eli wanders in the forest
> At first light he feeds from the victims of his tricks.

The grey-beaked eagle of Pengwern cries most piercingly,
Greedy for the flesh of him I loved.

The eagle of Pengwern called afar tonight.
He can be seen gorging the blood of men.
Tren is too well-named 'the deserted city'.
The churches of Basa are in mourning tonight
as they hold the remains of the pillar of battle,
of the heart of the men of Argoed ...

The churches of Basa are in flames tonight,
very little remains of them ...
The churches of Basa are silent tonight, I too am sad ...
My tears are red my grief is so great ...
Alas Ffreuer, how sad is this night, the loss of loved ones,
Woe is me that they were slain...

As the historian John Morris observed in his *The Age of Arthur* (1973), this coup marked the end of Celtic resistance in the lowlands. Heledd was the last royal survivor, but any remaining British nobility, the Breton scholar Jean Markale tells us, migrated to Cornwall and the Quimper region of Brittany, where there was a long-established British colony still named after them. As Markale postulates in his *The Celts* (1976), the influx of refugees into Wales was probably so great that they were only allowed passage through the country to the coast and a ship overseas. The poorer folk, however, had nowhere to go except the meres, forests and caves.

Penda's second son, Wulfhere, succeeded to the throne of Mercia in 658. He immediately annexed the area and fixed a new boundary with the 'Welsh' at 'Wulfhere's Ford' near Melverley, fifteen miles west of the Wrekin. At Kinver, he raised a great new church, which still stands today, St Peter's. The Celtic forest-folk who remained now had new overlords – the Mercians.

2

Edric and the Lost Bride

As adults, we have forgotten most of our childhood, not only its contents but its flavour; as men of the world, we hardly know of the existence of the inner world: we barely remember our dreams, and make little sense of them when we do ... our capacity to think ... our capacity even to see, hear, touch, taste and smell is so shrouded in veils of mystification that an intensive discipline of un-learning is necessary for anyone before one can begin to to experience the world afresh, with innocence, truth and love.

R. D. Laing[4]

My boyhood fascination with the outlaw hero Robin Hood led me early on to ponder a particular question. Was Robin a real historical character, or merely fictional, or a mixture of history and myth, like Arthur? Was he a resistance fighter against the Norman regime, a '*silvaticus*'? Was he a personification of a pagan deity, *Herne* or 'the Green Man'? Although straightforward socio-political and military history interested me, what really fascinated me were these semi-legendary or mythological characters. Why were some people in history so difficult to pin down? What was the reason for it? Was there some hidden meaning behind it?

Fortunately, we had our own local equivalent of Robin Hood in our region, Edric 'the Wild'. Not only is his genuine history well-documented and attested, for he was a 'real' person – but his legendary history, which still persists even in our desiccated times, shows how the ancient connections between the folk-chieftain and the sovereignty-goddess of the land survived, concealed in fairy-tales and folk-lore.

When a people are finally overwhelmed or superseded, these stories told to children are often the only means of preserving the most elemental aspects of their culture, a covert form of resistance. In fact, solving the mystery behind these matters became a lifelong quest, one in which I am still embroiled today.

The toponymist Margaret Gelling established that there are more survivals of Celtic place-names in Staffordshire than in Shropshire much further west. At first glance this doesn't seem to make sense – at least not if the Anglo-Saxon encroachment was a gradual one. But it was not. As we have seen, the obliteration of Pengwern was sudden, violent and tragic. The emigration of the surviving nobles and landlords of Pengwern abroad meant that lands which had been cultivated for centuries, requiring no arduous work to clear woodlands or drain swamps, were suddenly available for distribution to Wulfhere's warriors as reward for their loyalty to him during the brief Northumbrian intrusion. As John Morris observed, the Anglo-Saxons found it was 'easier to cut down men than trees'.

The Celtic Saint Beuno, who had retired to a hermitage on the west bank of the Severn was walking by the river one day when he saw a man calling to his dogs on the opposite bank. He shouted a greeting to him but the man replied in a language he could not understand, English. Beuno died on 21 April 640, so we know that Mercian pioneers had already penetrated as far as the borders of Powys before then, if this anecdote is true. My friend Robert Bevan-Jones, author of *The Ancient Yew* (2002), who grew up in and around Shrewsbury, told me that in his opinion Gelling's observation was correct. Shropshire was swiftly anglicised, and people who live up against the eastern side of Offa's Dyke are still militantly English. They at least pretend to despise Wales, even though they can spit into it; indeed, some of their own relatives might be Welsh.

This sudden deployment forward to the Severn in the 660s meant that the meres and forests of south-west Staffordshire were bypassed, so a residue of Celtic-speaking folk survived in small settlements remote from authority. These people called themselves 'Cumbrians' or 'Combrians'. The incoming Mercians tolerated them, on the whole, and over a few generations the two peoples inter-married and the offspring were bi-lingual, with English the preferred tongue. The *Waelisc* or 'Welsh' were, however, considered inferior, and this came as a terrible shock to them. Hitherto, under the pagan king of Mercia, they had been faithful allies, on equal terms. But now that Wulfhere had converted to the Roman Catholic faith, they were demonised as virtual heretics, and their ancient folk-practices interpreted as diabolism. Penda himself had a Celtic name and was in all likelihood of Anglo-British stock. This was probably the reason for his success in cultivating alliances with the Welsh kingdoms, such as Gwynedd, Powys and Pengwern.

A 'Welshman' or *Walh* did not imply so much a foreigner, as most people think, as a 'stranger'. This 'strangeness' about the Celts was what astonished the Germanic peoples when they first encountered the *Volcae*, a Celtic tribe from which the word *Walh*, my own surname – derives. Edward Chitham, in his *The Black Country* (1972) compared the Mercians to the early pioneers of the 'Wild West' frontier of the US.

If the analogy holds true, which I think it does, then the Celts were very much in the same situation as the Native Americans later on. They spoke a different language to the invaders and worshipped different gods and goddesses. They were intermeshed with their respective tribal territories and ultimately saw themselves as spiritually at one with the island of Britain itself. They were physically of a different type, too, shorter, stockier, swarthier, with darker eyes and hair. They could cast curses and work magic called *drycraeft*. Moreover, they were stubborn, fierce military opponents, who would contest every acre of their precious *gwlad* or 'land' inch by inch for many centuries to come, not least because the spirits of their ancestors still resided therein.

They were poor and by no means numerous, but they still dreamed of the days when they had been part of the glorious, wealthy Roman scheme. Most baffling of all, they would not accept defeat, like anyone reasonable, but persisted in the crazy belief that 'Arthur', a mythical king, would one day return from the dead and, like Christ, liberate and redeem his oppressed people – the 'Combrogi' or 'fellow-countrymen'.

On the whole this coexistence was peaceful. The peoples lived hard-by each other, used the same markets and worshipped in the same churches. But the Welsh folk lived separately, as we know from place-names such as Walsall ('Welshman's vale'), Walton Hill, Wall Town, and Wall Heath in Staffordshire. In Kinver, Comber Ridge, and places such as Comberton, are records of survival of the aboriginal population, whose descendants are still living today.

Aristotle tells us that nature abhors a vacuum. The annexation of the Lost Lands by Wulfhere and his heirs had driven all but a meagre remnant of the Celtic population out of their ancient tribal heartland, meaning that there was a drastic decline in population. But although most of the ancient people had gone into the west, the spirits of their ancestors remained, rooted in the soil itself. Celtic Animism – the dominant religion of the Celts before the Christian conversion – saw every feature of the landscape, every hill or tor, every tree, every stream and river – as being *inspirited*.

One of the central themes of these stories is that this animism survived locally, and that pre-Christian cults, especially of goddesses, were still active among the vestigial Celtic population well into the Christian era, possibly even into our own time. The natural refuge for such cults was the forest. The whole area was then covered with dense woodland: oak, ash, hazel and birch. Conventional history gives us only a vague account of all this and is shot through with assumptions.

For instance, conventional history would have it that the incoming Mercians were erstwhile pagans, newly converted (by royal command) to Christianity, and that the 'Welsh' were Celtic Christians, but things may not have been so simple. Celtic Animism fused with Celtic Christianity to form a hybrid faith. The central tenets of Christianity were accepted of course, and the Celtic Church was part of the worldwide communion. But the concept of an immaterial spirit-world, and veneration of holy wells and springs, deposition of ritual objects in rivers, and *direct* communication with ancestor-spirits, animal-spirits, water-sprites – but above all the *living goddess* of the land herself – were never expurgated.

The Mercian settlers arrived in a region almost devoid of people – but infested with the spirits of the long-dead. They feared the woods and meres, where the 'strangers' or *Waelisc* lived apart, whose spells and curses were called *geas*. Although they could no longer resist militarily, they could blight crops, cause epidemics in herds, invoke storms and floods and generally make a nuisance of themselves, if provoked. The Anglo-Saxons naturally feared the night, when 'imps' (meaning 'offspring' of the Devil) and goblins emerged, but the 'Welsh' were nocturnally active, implying that they were in league with the infernal powers.

They were shape-shifters and could assume the forms of birds or animals such as hares, whose orgiastic behaviour in the spring, weird piercing cries and malicious damage to crops were assumed to be the work of the wicked sorcerer who had possessed them. They could transform or 'go into' a crow and flutter outside the homestead. If they croaked three times, it was a sure omen of death. If the crow actually entered the house, a family member would soon pass. They could cast the 'evil-eye' or cause insanity with a 'madman's wisp'. They could charm snakes. Their wizards were accomplished poisoners, experts in the preparation of toxic plants like henbane, yew-berries, hemlock and monkshood. They were therefore not exactly shunned, but they were left very much to their own devices.

The Mercian settlers were not very numerous, the *Tribal Hidage*, a Mercian tribute-list, says that there were 30,000 hides of land in the kingdom. Since each hide of land corresponded to the area required to sustain an extended family group, we can extrapolate that the national population was in the region of 150,000 people. Of these, perhaps half settled in the western Midlands. Of necessity, therefore, such a small population could not entirely insulate itself against occasional intimate contact with the 'strangers'. Interpreters were required, those of mixed blood called *Walhstods*.

Whatever the language barrier, women will soon overcome it. Children, especially if they are forbidden to contact other children, will naturally seek each other out. A young man will notice the maiden gathering firewood, and her smile will bewitch him whatever language she may speak. Secret trysts result in unplanned pregnancies. The families are forced to negotiate. The Mercians had more in common spiritually, therefore, with their 'strange' neighbours than with a remote, demanding and alien church. This resulted in a conversion which was partial, contingent, always nostalgic for the 'elder-gods'.

They gradually found that their lives were really not so different – that the 'others' were actually just like themselves. Over time, they began tentatively to converse, to lend tools, share hard times together, became friends. On a feast-day they found that they shared more or less the same folk-religion, and (secretly) honoured the same living goddess. In this way, perhaps, a primordial religion was preserved, which was more or less tolerated by the Church for many centuries. The unique local circumstances meant that the Roman Catholic Church was an imposition on both populations. The Celtic Christians had always denied the supreme authority of the pope, and 'the bald man' as they called St Augustine of Canterbury, his representative. This was because of the *corona* or Roman tonsure he wore, which he demanded the Celtic Church should also adopt.

At two meetings near Great Witley in Worcestershire in 602 and 604, he tried desperately to convince the seven British bishops to relent, and to adopt the Roman style of tonsure themselves. This they strongly objected to, for it was explicitly forbidden in scripture. The Britons preferred the style of their Druidic predecessors. This was, however, the prelude to an even more extraordinary demand. He asked the Britons to help him to convert their pagan enemies, the Anglo-Saxons, with whom they had been at war for over 150 years; a very tall order.

The British bishops had consulted a holy man, who had forewarned them of Augustine's agenda. He told them that if, when they approached him, he rose from his chair to greet them in Christian brotherhood – then they should submit to his legitimate authority. If not, they were to walk away from the negotiations.

But Augustine, having travelled so far to meet them (from Canterbury), could not bring himself to resile his dignity and submit to this humble gesture. The seven bishops rebuffed his project and returned to their homelands in the west. Augustine was furious. As they departed, he cursed them, shouting that 'the vengeance of God' would be visited upon them for their pride in refusing to convert their 'brethren', the Anglo-Saxons.

The Celts are natural rebels. We have only to examine the long list of their heroes and heroines; Caratacus, Boudica, William Wallace, Owain Glyndwr – even Ernesto 'Che' Guevara had Irish ancestry. For reasons which we will shortly delve into more deeply, they were easily receptive to the Christian faith, but *not* a religion which seemed an analogue of Roman imperial authority, requiring their submission. Nor did they easily accept theological developments, particularly the doctrines of St Augustine of Hippo.

A British monk called Morgan, Pelagius as the Romans knew him, undermined the whole teaching of the Catholic faith by denying the concept of original sin. This 'heresy' was naturally most pernicious in the islands of Britain, and a former Roman general, Germanus, was sent there to stamp it out. Even St Patrick himself, who converted the Irish almost single-handedly, went there originally with a brief to prevent the spread of the 'Pelagian Heresy'.

So, even for those among the residual Celts who were Christian or semi-Christian, Roman Christianity was resented, but for those who had reverted to semi-paganism these matters were irrelevant. Their Anglo-Saxon neighbours were in a different position. They had been staunchly pagan until only a few years before, and their knowledge of the new faith was very basic. They complied with the king's command to seek baptism, met under great trees to worship, or attended such churches as then existed – in Mercia they were scarce at first, Kinver being an exception. A strange tale is told hereabouts concerning its foundation. I first heard it when I was about 6 years old, from the former landlord of the Anchor Inn at Penn-Hole, where I learned to ride my first bicycle.

I still remember him very plainly, which is extraordinary in its own way. My memory of him means that an obscure tale, lacking any foundation in historical 'fact' has been retained by means of oral transmission at least from the 19th century until the 21st. A group of local friends, among them the archaeologist Edmund Simons, are attempting to unravel this mystery, but there is little I can offer them except a fleeting reference in the *Seisdon District Council Guide* (1966), which describes how King Wulfhere built the parish church of St Peter's 'On the Rock' as it is known, as an expiation for the crime of having slain his two sons, Wulphad and Ruffius, for their conversion to the Christian faith without his permission. We were issued with the booklet when we took up our new tenancy in 1967. I still have it now, for my father always said I would have need of it some day.

I hope that I have impressed upon the reader in these early foothills that this will be an odd book, certainly not to be taken too seriously in academic terms. The strange obsession with the history of the obscure village where I live is part of my own quirky anecdotal history. I feel some explanation of this individualistic approach is called for. As I began to write, the world was in global 'lock-down' (April 2020) because of the Covid-19 pandemic. I am most fortunate to be able to take my daily exercise in the glorious south Staffordshire countryside, and to sit and contemplate in the places where I played as a boy so long ago. William Cobbett, just before he died, encountered a young boy who seemed vaguely familiar as he took his evening constitutional. It was only a few minutes later that he realised that the boy was actually *himself*. Every time I go for my evening walk, I am on the lookout for a similar herald. In one sense, it is a kind of life-review process. My health is quite fragile, and I have learned that every day is a bonus. For all of us, it is later than we think.

Soon all our spirits must fly west, to 'the Land of Eternal Youth'. I have the feeling of being a pupa, and that all the events of my life thus far are dissolving into psychic fuel to be burned, propelling me into a potentially new spiritual form, beyond the gross material confines of this world. In a sense then, I am bidding farewell not just to my old familiar landscape – but also taking leave of my 'self'. As the psychologist C.G. Jung surmised from his own

'Shadow-work', the inner mindscape of the imagination cannot be accessed according to the rules of the outer world. It is amenable only by a recourse to the kind of symbolic language which we encounter in our dreams, or in myths or childhood fairy tales. The poet and philosopher Samuel Taylor Coleridge anticipated this crucial spiritual truth many years before Jung, while he was only a small boy.

I have now come to realise, as Coleridge did, that this symbolic language acquired in my infancy has to a very large extent dominated all my subsequent actions, for good or ill. Despite my many gross personal failings, a devotion to deciphering this mystery is a task I have always dutifully continued. Many people nowadays are obsessively interested in the history of their ancestors, 'family' history. My own father was very absorbed in these matters, and I definitely inherited his enthusiasm. I have a notion that this ruminative obsession with the past may be a kind of displaced ancestor-worship. 'Local' history, the history of places, also obsessed me from my earliest years, and it was just this interest in the history of the local that inspired me to find out how it related to national and international affairs. But the materialist or 'scientific' approach to history current in the twentieth century, often excluded a more imaginative, personal approach.

Old folk-stories and myths, even the valuable evidence of 'ghost stories' were looked down upon. The 'scientific' professional historians seemed to me to be missing an analeptic link, a living umbilical cord to the meaning of time itself, as if they were determined to invert the purpose of their own discipline. Like my father and great-uncle Victor before me, I was simply insufficiently resourced to complete a degree in the subject which was so dear to my heart. Instead, I tried to expiate this need via the medium of novels and stories. Eventually, I was accepted onto a Diploma in History course but neither my health nor my wealth were sufficient to the task, and I was forced to withdraw. I freely admit that the underpinning values of the course were too rigid and prescriptive for a mind like mine. But a valuable lesson had been learned.

The way I saw history was different, and although it was subjective, it was nevertheless *meaningful*. In my original application to the university, I made just this point – that on a country walk for a mile or so in any direction I encountered sites which were of major historical importance, now overlooked by passing motorists, oblivious of their significance. Almost anyone in any British town or village could do the same, for beneath a thin integument, layer upon layer of meaning lies concealed – not just archaeological strata, but 'spiritual sediments' too – if we could just break the stranglehold of a mechano-morphic culture. The biologist, philosopher and author Rupert Sheldrake has written extensively about his concept of 'Morphic Resonance', a theory of mysterious telepathic interconnections between organisms, mediated by a collective unconscious whose field of influence extends beyond the confines of the individual human body – and crucially, across time. This accounts for the well-attested but controversial experiences such as prescience of future events, for example. If his theory is correct, as I suspect, history is something more than an academic discipline – rather, it is in some sense a spiritual pilgrimage.

My father had a knack of finding 'extraordinary people'. Mr Bill, 'Cecil', was one such, the former landlord of arguably the oldest inn in Kinver, then in his seventies. The Anchor Inn was 15th century, possibly older than that, and stood on a trackway to Stourbridge from the Severn at Bewdley. Wine and fancy goods were carried by beasts of burden inbound, and finished metal-goods, increasingly nails, were taken on the return journey to the waiting Severn trows for carriage both domestically and abroad. Mr Bill had been the landlord in the inter-war years, I think, but was always ensconced in the ancient bar. He was a fount of fascinating stories, and especially ghost stories.

My parents were convinced of the reality of the supernatural realms, not because of any morbid fascination but through direct experience. When he visited us Mr Bill related that one evening, as he was shutting the bar, a latecomer arrived, just after the usual throng had departed. Mr Bill asked the man, 'Don't you know what time it is?' He was taking the cash upstairs and was wary of the man at such a late hour. In the dim light he looked dirty, unkempt and rather poor. Cecil thought he must be either someone coming off shift from the iron-works in the next village, or a 'navigator' off the canal barges that had given the pub its name, the anchor was their badge. Irishmen and others seeking work sometimes stayed in boarding-houses in the neighbourhood for a while until they got more permanent lodgings.

Assuming that this fellow was one such, Mr Bill served him a mug of beer on the house. He didn't want to bother about change, but asked him to drink his ale outside quickly, and to leave the mug outside for him to wash up the next morning. He then locked up, but in the morning he discovered the empty mug on the bar, inside the pub. He said that an ancient coin was placed beside it, which he claimed to be a medieval 'groat'. He promised to show it me one day. He also swore to have seen the Virgin Mary appear in a small grotto in a cavern behind the inn, in the morning, before he had touched a drop. To this day, I genuflect when I pass by the place.

Mr Bill usually wore a heavy black greatcoat, a cloth-cap and scarf and would sit beside our hearth with a pot of beer or cider and some cheese on toast without removing these, whatever the temperature. It was he who told us the tale of the murder of the boys, Wulphad and Ruffius, by their angry father, Wulfhere, a tale so moving that I felt compelled to record it in a novel called *In the Wake of the Comet Star.*

This legend is not 'history', it is 'just a story'. But it is very old. Even if it was invented by Mr Cecil Gilpin Bill, which I very much doubt, the fraud has endured over two centuries. If it is a genuine folk tale, 1,400 years old, the kernel of this event, which occurred right on the cusp of the sudden re-transition to Christianity, may be another of the local epiphanies which comprise waystations for the reader of these stories.

Whether the tale of his having murdered his sons, enraged at them for abandoning the elder-gods, is true or not, by the time Wulfhere died in either 674 or 675 his Mercian kingdom had expanded considerably into the south and west. Luitcoit and Pengwern, the old British kingdoms, had been swallowed-up, as we have seen, but two Anglo-British kingdoms, the Hwicce and Magonsaetan, were also absorbed. Worcestershire, Gloucestershire and Herefordshire all fell under centralised Mercian control from their capital at Tamworth in Staffordshire.

Originally, these regions had their own *reges* or kings, but these were replaced by viceroys, *reguli* and ultimately by *ealdormen* of the Mercian king, dependent for their continuing authority on him. Mercia was then a confederation of many small clans or tribes which had gradually been forcibly incorporated. This meant that the smaller groups, the *Pencersaetan,* of mid-Staffordshire, the *Weogoran* around Worcester, or the *Husmere* of north Worcestershire could rely on mutual aid in times of military emergency. The border with the surviving Welsh kingdoms was always volatile, with constant cattle-raiding until Offa's Dyke eliminated the threat, but the border with Wessex also needed a firm military presence, backed up with the threat of devastating retaliation.

Although they were latecomers to the faith, the Mercian kings were keen to establish their respectable Christian credentials by founding monasteries at many places in the newly acquired territories: Bath, Much Wenlock, and Ismere near Kidderminster, for instance. New sees were established at Lichfield, Hereford and Worcester, all with attached monastic communities. Although the hoary old pagan, Penda, fought till the death rather than dishonour the gods of his forefathers, his descendants became exemplary Christians. Indeed one, St Rumbold, became the youngest ever saint. Penda's third son Aethelred even abdicated the throne and retired to a monastery. Merewalh, another of Penda's sons who ruled over the *Magonsaetan* of Herefordshire, converted in 660. Merewalh's daughter, Mildburg, granddaughter of Penda, became abbess of the monastic community at Wenlock in Shropshire, and ultimately a saint. But this holiness may well have derived from a more ancient source than Christianity, for her grandmother is claimed to have been Heledd, who composed the lament for Cynddylan. She was by inheritance, therefore, the personification of the 'sovereignty-goddess'.

A holy spring named after her still exists nearby. Only a few years ago, an electrical-cable worker seriously injured his hand. He rushed to the spring, knowing nothing of its history, to wash the wound, which was quite a severe gash. The blood-flow was immediately staunched. Within days the wound began to heal without any sign of infection, and there was no corresponding pain.

Not far away, traditional gypsies claimed they were entertained by 'fairy-music' while encamped outside Ditton Priors within living memory. Wenlock means 'white enclosure', which may refer either to the limestone escarpment of Wenlock Edge itself, or to the lime-washed walls of the original priory buildings. The wild, bleak Catherton Common nearby is still half-enchanted, and this whole area has a slightly fantastical feel about it to this day, an atmosphere all of its own.

It was in this remote priory of Wenlock that a newcomer to the community experienced a 'divine vision' in 715. His experience was well-recorded at the time and inspired one of the earliest and most remarkable examples of regional literature in England.

In that same year, King Ceolred of Mercia, Penda's grandson, fought the West Saxon king, Ine, at a place called 'Woden's Barrow', possibly Adam's Grave in Wiltshire. His father, Aethelred, had abdicated the throne to become a monk – but Ceolred had no such inclinations. He seems to have inherited his grandfather's disdain for Christianity and treated the Church with barely concealed contempt. Mercia was primarily a military power. It became the pre-eminent kingdom of the Anglo-Saxon heptarchy by dint of raiding and intimidating its neighbours, and exacting heavy tribute from them. This caused resentment, which still festers to this day.

When Mercian power eventually declined, the status of the region and its people also went into a decline from which it has never really recovered. Today, it has been demonstrated that employers consistently discriminate against candidates with a West Midlands accent at job interviews, for example. Our national institutions – the elite universities, the legal and judicial system, government institutions, high-ranking military posts, the civil service, the Church or the national broadcast media – rarely include people with a Black Country or Birmingham accent in their ranks. There are some regional celebrities, of course, but they will usually be sports personalities, comedians, popular musicians, industrialists, authors and the like – successful and wealthy, perhaps, but rarely any threat to the established power structure. We will return to these matters in their place, but one of the most astonishing things is that the local population has never capitulated to the tyranny of 'received pronunciation' (and I trust, never will). They stubbornly persist in retaining their 'peculiar' dialect, despite the economic and social penalties. For the Mercians are both deeply tribal, and deeply proud. To them the manners of the 'southerners' seem effete, pretentious and pompous.

In 714, the year before the Wenlock monk had his vision, Guthlac, son of the Mercian nobleman, Penwalh, died. He had served as a soldier in the Welsh wars and was sorely troubled by all he had seen in these savage, unrelenting campaigns. When the 'Mercian incendiaries' as Welsh monks called them, rode into a village, everything was immolated. Every man, even if it 'were an old man pissing up a wall' was put to death.

Male children would be taken as slaves into Mercia and castrated to prevent consanguineous pollution. Girls would be taken as slaves, too, and disfigured by having an ear cropped or a nose slit. Maidens were raped, old women burned. These are scenes no ordinary man can continually relive without submission to the infinite mercy of God, for whom 'the sins of a man are no more than a burning coal, extinguished in the sea,' as Langland put it. Like so many other ex-soldiers, Guthlac could not adjust himself to civilian life and instead sought the sanctuary of the monastery of Repton, a 'double-house' – that is, a community of both monks and nuns – where he intended to become a *frater*; but this was not to be.

Guthlac's irascible temperament did not incline him to success in community life. Instead, he retired to the fenlands at Crowland in Lincolnshire, then called Lindsey. Here, he lived frugally as a hermit in the stinking marshes. Initially, he was sorely troubled by 'demons' (in fact, the deceased spirits of the former occupants, as we discussed earlier on), whose sibilant conversations about him were conducted in the old Celtic language, which they assumed he would not understand. But Guthlac had lived in exile in Wales, and had learned the British language, enabling him to anticipate the impish tricks of his otherworldly tormentors. Many Mercian soldiers must have followed Guthlac's example, and perhaps it was he who inspired our anonymous monk.

He too, had known a violent past before entering a religious community, for in his vision of the afterlife, he was accused by a man he had injured in a fight in his secular days. If he sought to expiate such sins, and to gain ultimate spiritual knowledge within the cloister, his wishes were soon to be granted, by virtue of undergoing a spiritual experience of an almost ineffable nature, a tour of the primordial contents of the human soul, of regions beyond this material world.

> I know a man in Christ who fourteen years ago, was caught up to the third heaven, whether in the body or out of the body, I do not know – God knows.

Here, our 'man in Christ' was taught secrets which must never be revealed, heard words which must never be uttered. But such an experience is not the privilege of saints. In all ages, and in all cultures, people have been 'caught up' through the grace of God, epileptic seizures, trance-states, extreme sickness and fever, but most common of all – a near-death experience, or 'NDE'. The recent worldwide pestilence trenchantly reminds us of how thin the veil was between life and death in former times.

How, we do not know, but our monk suddenly became ill. His brothers and sisters of the cloister gathered around his deathbed and performed the last rites, and at 'first cockcrow' he died. But to the astonishment of all, some time afterwards his soul suddenly returned into his body, much to his dismay and disgust. He pleaded with his shocked brothers and sisters to leave his poor miserable body be – for it was a wretched thing of no value. For some days he raved in his blindness, his eyes were wild and bloodshot. His wits were impaired for a while and he could not remember who he was. But as the intense experiences of his *ekstasis* subsided, the Wenlock brother recounted his journeying beyond this mortal coil. The blessed angels had empowered him with a commission. He was permitted to discuss all he had seen with honourable and religiously inclined men and women – but was to have no truck with infidels, cynics or mockers. He sought out a named priest (Begga) whom the angels had revealed to him and humbly confessed all his sins. Following the confession, the monk told the priest that the angels had revealed to him that – in secret – Begga had worn an iron-girdle around his loins as self-punishment for sinful thoughts these many long years. This turned out to be accurate. The monk also sought out a woman who 'dwelt in a far distant region' whom he had never met. He sat with the incredulous woman and recounted every one of her many sins in order to her, and in sordid detail, as a sign that nothing on this earth remained hidden from the host of Heaven.

These miraculous insights were accompanied by a vaticination which had more serious political consequences for Mercia, and his own monastery. For, while out of his body, the monk had seen a vision of King Ceolred of Mercia, who was yet living, and the benefactor of Wenlock, being judged by angels, found wanting – and cast down into hell. There is a thin line between prophesy and sedition, and as we have seen, Ceolred was a wicked and malicious man who would have had no qualms about revenging himself.

As a child I developed a severe lung infection from which I never fully recovered. Having dodged extinction during the Cuban Missile Crisis just after I was born, a few months later, in 1963, the most severe winter since the 'great frost' of 1709, combined with a lethal 'flu epidemic to almost extinguish my fragile young life again. My breathing became very shallow before I began to turn blue. There was no way out of Himley Plantation through the frozen snowdrifts, and we had no telephone. At the last gasp, literally, my mother remembered that once before they had revived a cat with 'flu by giving it a saucer of warm milk with sherry mixed into it. The same remedy was applied in my case, and my lungs suddenly cleared so that I survived the night. In the morning my father called the surgery from a neighbour's house. I cannot recall this incident myself, but it was by no means exceptional in my early years, indeed it became the norm. A recrudescence of the disease was inevitable. Our cottage was officially condemned as unhealthy, but because of my grandmother's feud with my father he refused to relinquish any of his property rights or to move to healthier accommodation. This only intensified my grandmother's efforts to drive us out, and in this campaign she was encouraged by my aunt.

She would dress up for her weekly opera-singing rehearsals with my grandmother, who accompanied her on the piano. If I happened to be nearby, my grandmother would hush me and send me to hide beneath the stairs. But I would soon be discovered by my deranged aunt, whose respectable operatic demeanour would immediately be replaced by uncouth screams of, 'Get that *boy* out of *here*! Get that *brat* out of *here now*!' I learned to despise her, and the gentleman she eventually married rather late in life. Despite that, she bore him two children, and as a result I was cast adrift, and my parents with me. I bear no malice to my estranged cousins for any of this, by the way, and wish them all good fortune, wherever they may be.

The upshot of all this, was that I developed an intense dualism at a very early age, which it was impossible to reconcile. The constant fear of imminent death at night meant that I would insist that a naked electric lightbulb (shades were excluded, for I felt that spirit-forms lurked within them) remained on, and I would always become exceptionally agitated if this were denied. I felt spiritual presences, often malignant, around me in the darkness, and my thoughts were certainly not those of any normal toddler. They consisted, in the main, of speculations about the dreamscape which manifested in my unconscious state, of what could lie beyond infinity, and the survival of the personality beyond death. Because of my physical infirmity, I was a slow to walk but made up for this by my precocious ability to converse easily with (usually amused) adults. I could order all my mother's grocery list at Mrs Hall's village shop when I was 2 years old. My parents encouraged this, and I related all of my nocturnal and spiritual adventures to them without fear of any reprimand.

I remember that the most sensitive problem of all, was my own awareness of how at risk I actually was – that it was only a matter of time before we must be parted. This was distressing, of course, but I was not to be comforted with any soothing platitudes. Instead, I was reassured that *for us* there could be no absolute death – nor any parting.

The 'Friend of God' Henry Suso (1295-1366) tells us in his *Horologium Sapientiae*:

Thou shalt understand that it is a science most profitable, and passing all other sciences, to learn to die. For a man to know that he shall die, that is common to all men; as much as there is no man that may ever live or he hath hope or trust thereof; but thou shalt find full few that have this cunning to learn to die ... I shall give thee the mystery of this doctrine; the which shall profit thee greatly to the beginning of ghostly health, and to a stable fundament of all virtues.

Perhaps it was out of some deep need to soothe my fears of imminent demise that my parents reassured me that, even if that did come to pass, this was not the end. My spirit would be simply liberated from the body, until it reincarnated elsewhere. This strict adherence to the ancient Celtic (and indeed, Teutonic) doctrine of reincarnation of the soul was, at bottom, responsible for our rift with conventional Christianity. That spiritual phenomena existed was a plain fact, which, living in a haunted house, we accepted as a given.

Although these events took place in the early 1960s, I should emphasise that the backdrop of the cultural and psychedelic revolution played no part whatsoever. My parents treated 'hippies' with the same sort of disdain as they did conventional Christians and despised all modern innovations and fashions. The one exception was a small black and white television set.

The disturbances in the house seemed to coalesce around me, and I was told they intensified just after I was born. My grandmother was well aware of the history of the place but pretended that nothing was amiss – in much the same way she was content to let the property go to hell. She was rarely at home during the day, she was a private music teacher, and in the evenings she would be at choir practice or involved in some other church activity – she was the organist there.

My grandfather was a hard-bitten veteran of the Great War who had witnessed many horrific conflicts, but even he was afraid to venture to the outside toilets we all shared after dark, preferring to use a chamber-pot. In the next cottage my great-uncle Victor was particularly troubled by the haunting. It was I who discovered him in a state of catatonic shock one morning, and it is still my belief that he was frightened to death. He never recovered from a brain haemorrhage and died a few days later. His neighbour, Annie, was equally convinced that my uncle had been terrified, and he had seemed unusually perplexed about something on the previous evening.

It is not my purpose here to explicate the phenomenon of spiritual apparitions or related disturbances, except insofar as it explains the strange private philosophy which my parents inculcated in me. For they believed as an article of faith that the spirits were in a state of anxiety, confusion and ultimately ignorance of the fact that they were dead. It was a duty on us, therefore, to attempt to communicate with these spirits, and to liberate them from their tormented state. It is my belief now that these early childhood traumas set a pattern, of crisis and recovery in my life – crucially punctuated by intense and disturbing psychical and spiritual phenomena. This homespun spiritualism, however, was not so unsophisticated as it might sound, for C.G. Jung, one of the most eminent psychologists and philosophers of the 20th century concurred:

> It is a primordial, universal idea that the dead simply continue their earthly existence and do not know that they are disembodied spirits – an archetypal idea which enters into immediate physical manifestation whenever anyone sees a ghost. It is significant too, that ghosts all over the world have certain features in common ... I must content myself with the hypothesis of an omnipresent, but differentiated, psychic structure which is inherited and which necessarily gives a certain form and direction to all experience. For, just as the organs of the body are not mere lumps of indifferent, passive matter, but are dynamic functional complexes which assert themselves with imperious energy, so also the archetypes, as organs of the psyche, are dynamic instinctual complexes which determine life to an extraordinary degree. That is why I call them dominants of the unconscious. The layer of unconscious psyche which is made up of these universal dynamic forms I have termed the collective unconscious.[5]

So, the experience of the Wenlock visionary was not unique, and was especially apposite in a society completely dominated by spiritual realities, some derived from Christian religion, others from more ancient belief-systems and folk-practices. What made his testimony remarkable, however, was that in AD 716 King Ceolred died 'gibbering with demons and cursing the priests of God', just as had been foretold.

Saint Boniface, an Englishman from Crediton in Devonshire, originally named Wynfrith, thought the monk's after-death vision was a sure sign from God of Ceolred's turpitude and forthcoming damnation. Boniface spent most of his adult life converting the pagan German tribes, but he still took a keen interest in the political affairs of his homeland. It may be true that as a West

Saxon, Boniface was bound to take a hostile view of the Mercian king, but it was Ceolred's contempt towards the Church which really rankled. Boniface was sufficiently intrigued by the prophesy that he undertook to investigate the monk's tale for himself.

Many years after these events, Boniface remained so convinced that the Wenlock monk had experienced a truly divine revelation that he wrote to King Aethelbald, Ceolred's successor and a notorious libertine, to take warning from the fate of his wicked predecessor, who had plainly been seduced by a demonic entity:

> Ceolred, your venerable Highness's predecessor, feasting in splendour amid his companions was – as those who were present have testified – suddenly in his sin sent mad by a malign spirit, who had enticed him by his persuasion to the audacity of breaking the law of God; so that without repentance and confession, raging and distracted, conversing with devils and cursing the priests of God, he departed this light without a doubt to the torments of hell.

This warning was read out to the king (even royalty were still illiterate) by a priest called Herefrith, who had been entrusted with the dangerous mission on Boniface's behalf. As Professor Sims-Williams comments in his *Religion and Literature in Western England 600-800* (1990) – an ominous obituary exists for a 'man of God' bearing the same name at exactly the right time. Aethelbald spent his entire reign of over forty years debauching himself with nuns and his courtiers' female relatives, until his own guards suffocated him while he was sleeping at Seckington outside Tamworth in 757.

We will never know the identity of the anonymous monk, but thanks to Boniface we at least know something of the 'contemporary conceptions, hopes and fears about death, judgement and the hereafter, and about the omnipresent world of angels, demons and departed souls ... a view of the world in which spirits were often down-to-earth, the unseen was sometimes visible, and the ineffable could be expressed in language.'

In this crucial century between 660 and 760 Mercia had transformed itself from a pagan backwater with a wild western frontier into the pre-eminent military and economic power in the island. These hardy and uncouth pioneers had temporised about accepting Christianity, it is true, and this damned them in the eyes of monkish chroniclers from neighbouring kingdoms, such as Bede, who castigated them for their heathenish proclivities.

Once West-Saxon political dominance had been achieved following the Battle of Ellandun in 825, it became possible to portray the Mercians as backward, uncivilised simpletons, brutish and gauche, a national cultural stereotype which still lingers on: a 'Birmingham Screwdriver' for instance, is a hammer. In truth, there is something to this hostile caricature as there always is – but it is an unfair portrayal, because I believe it is a learned-behaviour of the local population to act out the received archetype, which has been culturally imposed on them by distal forces. This is one reason, for instance, why the Black-Country dialect, notoriously impenetrable to outsiders, and the closest thing we now have to Anglo-Saxon speech, remains resilient – even in an age of mass-media saturation, ethnic diversity and mass immigration. These folk despise anyone 'posh', educated or 'brainy', and suspect refined manners and 'fancy' language.

This maudlin tendency, the wilful ignorance of the 'new', and an intrinsic, even instinctual impulse to denigrate anything elegant or sophisticated, can seem exasperating to outsiders. But I believe it may partially derive from their obdurate resistance to the Norman regime and the imposition of its language, Norman French. The West Mercians had managed to resist occupation by the Danes thanks to their national heroine (and goddess archetype), Aethelflaed, the 'Lady of the Mercians', and so at least had remained independently 'English', retaining their ancient customs and language. Thanks to their vital contribution, the long dreamed-of unified nation of England became a reality.

In 1066, after the Battle of Hastings and then the rapid Norman Conquest, all this was dramatically changed. The conquered folk were reduced to serfdom, and their hounds 'lawed' by having a front-paw mutilated to prevent the chase. A poorly organised rising in 1069 failed, and William 'the Conqueror' 'harried the North' so mercilessly that over 100,000 people perished in a virtual genocide. The 'standard of living' of the English race was now slavery in all but name (the Normans nominally abolished slavery, but imposed a simulacrum in practice), as they tried desperately to subsist on land which no longer belonged to them – but there was still one way they could resist.

They could stick-together and continue to speak the language of their illustrious forefathers. Their descendants are almost morbidly attached to all things old, and dismissive of change, contemptuous of 'progress' (the motto of the Wolverhampton & Dudley Brewery used to be 'Unspoilt by Progress').

For 39 years, King Offa of Mercia ruled over the mightiest nation in England, and even thought himself an equal of Charlemagne (the emperor himself was rather piqued by the comparison), but this energetic country was soon to fall from power following his death on 29 July 796. Yet, very profound spiritual forces were at work in the region, and an almost unremarked attempt to 'express the ineffable in language' had been made. It was not to be the last.

In previous books, I have examined the rise and fall of Mercia in some detail, so I direct readers interested in the process of the decline of Mercian power to those earlier volumes. For my purposes here, however, a brief account of the final years of Mercian hegemony, then its incorporation into a new unified state of England – and finally the eclipse of Anglo-Saxon culture by the Norman invaders – will suffice.

For like their Brythonic predecessors, the Anglo-Saxon, Anglo-British and Anglo-Danish peoples of the island were ultimately doomed, not so much to obliteration or genocide (their descendants and glorious language are still living today), but to subordination, servitude, or exile, traumatic experiences which were to leave an indelible mark on the character of the land and its folk.

In 829, King Wiglaf of Mercia was driven into exile by Egbert, king of Wessex. By 867, the effete Burgred, king of Mercia, was forced to call for aid from King Aethelred of Wessex and his brother, Alfred, to eject the 'Great Heathen Army' of the invading Vikings from Nottingham, which they had fortified. This amply demonstrates the relegation of Mercia as the foremost English nation. King Burgred was forced into exile in Rome.

The eastern half of Mercia fell to the invading Danes, but West Mercia was never conquered. A viceroy, Lord Aethelred, ruled over the region as a client-king of King Alfred of Wessex. To cement the alliance between the two English realms, Alfred arranged the marriage of his daughter, Aethelflaed, his eldest child, to Aethelred.

In August 910 an invading Danish army was annihilated by an army commanded by either King Edward 'the Elder' of Wessex, or Aethelred, or both men, at Wednesfield Heath in Wolverhampton (known to history as the Battle of Tettenhall). We know something about this great English victory thanks to the efforts of Aethelweard, a member of the West-Saxon royal family who retired to the banks of the River Severn at Bridgnorth in a rock-hewn hermitage where he translated the *Anglo-Saxon Chronicle* into Latin.

Within six months of the battle Lord Aethelred died, and the Mercian nobility took the unprecedented step of choosing his widow, Aethelflaed, as their new ruler, the 'Lady of the Mercians'. In a series of campaigns this indomitable woman recovered the East Midlands, but just as the Danish nobles of York were about to capitulate to her, she suddenly died at Tamworth on 12 June 918.

The Mercians chose her young and inexperienced daughter, Aelfwynn, as her replacement, but her uncle, King Edward the Elder, deposed her and had her immured in a monastery at Shaftesbury in Dorset. She was never heard of again. West Mercia ceased to exist as an independent state. Instead, it became one of the gigantic earldoms of the unified English nation and during the reign of the notorious King Ethelred 'the Unready' this vast earldom was given to a Shropshire man, Edric 'Streona' ('the grasper', because of his acquisitiveness).

Streona was one of the worst villains in English history, and it was through his treachery and intrigue that Cnut of Denmark became king of England. Edmund 'Ironside', the rightful English king, was almost certainly assassinated by Streona's agents, who lurked beneath his privy 'with a very sharp knife' – though some say the wicked deed was done with a spear, or even an arrow.

Streona's fate was a grim one, for Cnut would prove to be a remarkably astute and reasonably civilised king. He had Streona garrotted, flayed, beheaded, and his body parts thrown to the stray dogs of London. Cnut had once sworn to 'raise him (Streona) higher than any man in England'. True to his word, he had Edric's head set-up on a spike on top of the gatehouse of London Bridge. But this despicable man left a namesake behind in Shropshire, a nephew, who was to become a legend of quite a different sort – Edric 'the Wild'.

The chronicler Florence of Worcester introduces our hero thus:

> There lived in these times a very powerful thegn, Edric, called 'the Forester', the son of Aelfric brother of Edric Streona. Because he scorned to submit to the king [William I], his lands were frequently ravaged by the [Norman] garrison of Hereford and by Richard Fitz-Scrob: but whenever they invaded into his territories, they lost many of their knights and men-at-arms. Therefore, having summoned to his aid the princes of the Welsh, namely Bleddyn and Rhiwallon, this same Edric, about the feast of the Assumption of St Mary [15 August 1067], devastated Herefordshire as far as the bridge over the River Lugg and carried away much plunder.[6]

Although the Norman occupation of England was rapid and ruthless, in these early days, less than a year since Hastings, the outcome was by no means assured. William's army was tiny, no more than 12,000 men, and heavy losses at Hastings and an outbreak of severe dysentery had taken a toll on this meagre number.

To add to his problems many of his men were mercenaries who left his service once they had done their job. Many other knights returned to their estates in Normandy and Brittany, and William joined them in the spring of 1067 to comfort his wife Matilda, who would be crowned as England's queen at Easter 1068. Therefore, although his army was highly professional and effective, it was insufficient in number to hold down the whole country without the cooperation of the English local authorities and a compliant Church. Edric's domains were exactly the sort of territory where the limits of the Norman authority could be tested.

The wild frontier with Wales was of considerable concern to William's able and ruthless lieutenant, William Fitz-Osbern, 'foremost of the persecutors of the English people', according to the Shropshire chronicler Ordericus Vitalis. To subdue Edric and his Welsh allies Fitz-Osbern gathered a large force which concentrated at a new castle built on Edric's former lands at Wigmore in Herefordshire. This timber-built motte-and-bailey castle was eventually to become the seat of the mighty Mortimer family, 'Lords of March', for 500 years. But initially, it was an isolated outpost in very 'debatable land', for it overlooked wild Edric's own stronghold of Lydbury North, just over the county border in Shropshire.

King William returned to England from Normandy in December 1067 and immediately took the pacification of the English in hand personally. Hereward 'the Exile' (or 'the Wake') was at large in the fenlands around Ely with a renegade force. King Harold Godwinson's surviving sons returned from exile in Ireland with a fleet and raided the coast of Devonshire, while his elderly mother, Gytha, incited a rebellion in Exeter.

But in the autumn of 1069, a much more serious threat emerged. Viking freebooters under King Sweyn Estrithson of Denmark, as well as Letts, Poles and pagan Lithuanians, landed in the Humber estuary with 300 ships. William's army was simply not strong enough to eject them, and so instead he paid them a large sum to leave his realm, which after plundering the region mercilessly, they did.

Stiperstones.

Winter's Gibbet.

William's revenge on the local rebels who had enticed them to invade was savage, leaving all of Yorkshire and Durham a desolate wasteland for more than a century. So harsh was his vengeance and the famine which ensued in a bitterly cold winter, that people resorted to selling themselves into slavery in Scotland, and some starvelings even consumed the bodies of their dead children. Once this genocide had been completed, William marched south-west, to deal with 'wild Edric'.

As soon as he knew William was pre-occupied in the North, Edric and his Welsh allies combined with insurgents in Cheshire to besiege Shrewsbury Castle. The town was taken but the castle held out long enough for William to march to its relief. Another uprising had taken place at Stafford, and it was hoped that Edric's forces would combine there to confront William's extremely depleted and starving force and defeat him. At the head of a skeleton army, William was still the most skilled soldier of his age. Nearby where Stafford Castle ruins now stand, the English and their Welsh allies were easily put to flight by the professional Norman army.

Edric fled across the border into Wales, burning Shrewsbury town on the way. William Fitz-Osbern rebuilt the castle there and ordered the rebuilding of castles at Chester and Stafford before the king's army moved on to deal with any further threats in the south. By Easter of 1070 the English realised that the uprisings had failed in their objective of dislodging the Normans. Even the 'wild man' gave up the struggle in the summer of that year, and despite being 'the most vigorous of men ... was reconciled to King William'.

This meant that for some time thereafter, Edric was constantly under the Conqueror's eye, and was enlisted into William's personal retinue for campaigns in Scotland and to put down rebellion in Maine, on the borders of Normandy itself. If this account of Edric's activities is true – and we have only a brief entry by Florence of Worcester for the year 1072 to guide us – then our hero's fate was an ignominious one. Even he, among the 'last Englishmen', had been vanquished – and his *Sylvatici* or guerrilla fighters were all killed, exiled or dispersed.

A fleet of over 300 ships left England at this time, bound for the Crimea, where the Byzantine emperor allowed the refugees to settle in colonies named 'New York' and 'New London'. Not long afterwards, Hereward 'the Wake' accepted a similar fate to Edric, only to be slain by his new-found Norman comrades-in-arms. But if legend is true, Edric's adventures had only just begun – for in this book, as in life, legend is always *more* than the truth.

Like the British before them, the Mercians over many generations had become emotionally and psychologically interwoven with the land. When the Danish threat came, the West Mercians had valiantly defended themselves, preserving their ancient language and culture. When the Normans arrived, they saw them as merely a fresh wave of Vikings, who could be worn down and ultimately appeased in their turn. They were wrong. Hastings was the death-knell of their centuries-old culture, and there could be no going back.

Edric had no choice *but* to go back to his old domains in Shropshire – no longer a valiant outlaw, beloved of his folk but reviled as a collaborator, a traitor, an outcast in his own land. In his *De Nugis Curialum*, a twelfth-century scandal sheet for the royal court, the Herefordshire writer Walter Map (1140-1210) who described himself as a *marchio sum Walensibus* or 'man of the Welsh Marches', describes Edric's fate in some detail, proving that the 'wild man' was still a living memory over a century after his 'de-manifestation'.

Edric was never to taste death itself. Walter Map was, as I am, a Briton of Welsh descent living in the debatable 'Lost Lands'. With such a pedigree, and a mind alive to ancient traditions, both Welsh and Anglo-Saxon, he could read across elemental mythological motifs from both cultures, encapsulating the obliteration of a civilisation so much more pithily than any conventional history ever could:

> This is the story of Edric the Wild, that is, the Forester, so-called because of the nimbleness of his body and his merry words and deeds: a man of great prowess, Lord of Lydbury North ... accompanied by a single page, he was returning one night from hunting in the woods when he lost his way ... he came upon a large building which the old-English called a 'Guesten House' or tavern ... the English have one such in every parish, low drinking-dens all.

This proves to be no ordinary forest-hostelry, but a place of enchantment – an interface between this world, so rapidly vanishing, and the ethereal fairy realm beyond. Edric sees light and fire within the inn, and peers inside, to be greeted by scenes from a bawdy house – young maidens disporting themselves in a frenzied dance, nine in all, but among these – one not like the rest.

More beautiful certainly, peerless among all women, 'more desirable than the mistress of any king', Map informs us. But this 'glamour' (the word means literally 'sexual magic') differentiated the girl from her 'sisters' in a subtler way – her extraordinary magical influence over him – enchantment.

At the first glance, Edric was 'wounded to the heart', stricken with an obsession so profound that no power on earth could resist it. He would have this woman, come what may:

> He had heard tales of wood-nymphs and night-demons, and of how they took their revenge on the unwary ... yet Cupid, rightly painted as blind, made him forget all this. Creeping around the tavern, he suddenly burst in through the back-door ... and seized the one he adored ... her crazed sisters fell-upon him and his page, and tore them with their nails and gashed them with their teeth ... but Edric escaped with his prize ... little good it did him, for though he had his way with her for three days and nights, she uttered not a word or sound, even during the passion of their lovemaking ...but on the fourth day, she relented, and spake these words: 'Hail to you my sweetest dearest lover, and hale shall you always remain, but on this condition; you must never taunt me about my sisters and how you seized me, or ever speak the name or reveal the location of the sacred grove where you abducted me ... or ever reveal anything to do with it. If you do this I will be a good wife and mother to your child ... but on that day when you break this oath, all happiness will desert you, and I will leave you never to return, and you will ceaselessly mourn for me throughout all the ages, until, unable to endure your grief, you will hasten your own end.

Edric vowed that he would honour the maiden's wishes, and soon afterwards he was married to Lady Godda, his fairy-bride. But although Edric kept to his pledge, it was impossible to conceal the strangeness his wife wore about her like a garment. Her beauty was legendary, and all who bore witness to it remarked upon it, so that eventually stories of this paragon reached the ears of King William himself.

Summoned to London by royal command, Edric and his bride were received at court by the king, whose amazement 'gave proof of her fairy origin'. As another ancient culture was eclipsed by a new, the 'living goddess' was present for the denouement – for 'Godda' was indeed a 'special person', the local *Matribus et Genioloci* of Shropshire.

Originally, Shropshire, meaning 'the bush' or 'the outback', was named after this local goddess – Goddeu – and the Lady Godiva of legend is probably derived from her, too. Edric became more and more besotted with her as each day passed; but on one fateful evening:

> It happened that when Edric had returned from hunting he sought his wife and could not find her ... when summoned she was slow to come and he gave her an angry look, 'I suppose it was your sisters kept you away so long?' The rest of his sarcastic reproach was spoken to empty air, for as soon as the word 'sisters' was spoken she instantly vanished. Then he bitterly regretted his foolish ill-tempered outburst, and immediately rode to the place where he had first seized her, but neither his tears nor appeals could bring her back. Day and night he cried out for her, but all in vain, until he pined away for continual sorrow.

Such is the fate of those who mate with 'demons, and succubi and incubi', for Edric's lost bride was a 'Melusine', a sacred spirit of the springs and rivers. She was a fairy-spirit, what the Irish call the *Sidhe* – the root word is related to our English 'Seat'. The 'hollow-hills' where the ancient ones lay buried in their mounds, were considered gateways to Tartarus, the underworld.

The tombs were, literally, the places where the remains of the noble dead 'sat', for all eternity. Legend says that Godda bore him a magical son, called Aelnoth who became a holy man. But for Edric there could be no end to his searching, for by his sacrilege against the goddess he had lost the sovereignty of the land. Finally, in his anguish he searched the lead mines beneath the Stiperstones for his lady, and he remains down there to this day.

The miners often heard Edric groaning, and bitterly regretting his surrender to William the 'Cong Kerry' as the Shropshire folk say. Often they would hear Edric 'knocking' to indicate where the best lead-ore seams were to be found. Here in the Shropshire Hills, the long and glorious Anglo-Saxon story finally ended – except in very exceptional circumstances, when Edric and his lost bride are reunited, to ride out over the bleak Shropshire hills on crazed steeds, pursued by huge, white, red-eared dogs with blazing fiery eyes – the hounds of hell, baying behind the 'Wild Hunt'.

The 'Wild Hunt' or 'Wild Ride' is an ancient theme in Germanic mythology. The Germanic version of Godda is Gode or 'Lady Gauden', and it is fitting that in all the reports we have of the spectral chase, Godda is well to the fore, riding beside Edric, who takes the place of the Germanic god Woden. When the hunters appear, Edric sounds warning to clear the way on his hunting-horn. As the unearthly din comes nearer, it is wise to cover one's eyes, or better, to throw oneself on the ground prone – for to look into the eyes of the Lord and Lady spells death for the unwary. In Wales, the equivalent hunt is led by Gwyn ap Nudd, Lord of Annwn, the Celtic underworld. The hunt was part of local folk-culture long before the coming of the English. It is said that in Edric's case, he rides out with his bride, companions and hell-hounds 'whenever war is going to break out ... they ride across the hills in the direction of the enemy country, and if they appear, it is a warning that the war will be serious.'

The Shropshire folklore expert Charlotte Sophia Burne (1850-1923) interviewed an old lady who, as a young girl, had been out walking with her father one night near Minsterley, in the heart of the hill-country, just before the outbreak of the Crimean War. Suddenly, the hunt appeared, riding to the north. The father had seen the hunt riding south in Napoleon's time and cried out to his daughter to cover her face, and 'on no account to speak, lest she be driven mad'.

But the girl could not resist a peek at the handsome spectacle as it thundered by, and saw Edric dressed in the fairy colours, green and white, beside his beautiful lady, her long golden hair flowing down to her waist. Edric wore his dark hair short. He carried a short-sword at his belt, wore gaiters and boots and blew a gigantic hunting-horn. The lady wore a hunting-dagger at her waist, she noticed, before the crazy scene vanished as suddenly as it first appeared. They were seen again, before the Boer War, then again in 1914, but there was curiously no report in 1939 – perhaps the fairy-folk considered that conflict a continuation of the 1914-1918 war – which it was.

Or perhaps the estranged couple have found one another again, and are reconciled at last? Could Edric's cruel punishment and penance for betraying his land, folk and bride, be finally at an end? Sadly not, I fear, for the prophesy is that Edric can never die 'until all wrong has been made right', not, I think, a condition we are likely to attain anytime soon. So, in these unstable times – let walkers beware the Stiperstones by night, lest England's enemies are stirring – and the manic entourage rides by once more.

3

The Wylde Wood

I readily believe that there are more invisible beings in the universe than visible. But who will declare to us the nature of all these, the rank, relationships, distinguishing characteristics and qualities of each? What is it that they do? Where is it they dwell? Always the human intellect circles around the knowledge of these mysteries, never touching the centre.

Thomas Burnet[7]

May 11, 2020 – an accidental pilgrimage into the past. It may not be apparent to the reader yet, but there is a plan of sorts to this book. In this plan, this chapter, or essay, or story, was to consist of a confluence between the history of the western forests of 'the vert' as it was known, and my own formative years in the Forest of Kinver, specifically Gibbet Wood between Kinver and Stourbridge. I felt somehow apprehensive about recounting this quite crucial part of my story because I knew that at some point it must entail visiting the site of my boyhood home there, long since demolished.

The last time I saw the house was in 2004, when I had taken a detour through the wood to see it for one last time. A friend had tipped me off that it was soon to be knocked down as part of the landscape remodelling to restore the old sand-quarry to its former condition. My parents had moved out eight years previously, but it was still my family home, and always will be.

After visiting my dog's grave beneath the apple tree in the garden, I discovered the back door open. My father's bean-canes still stood propped up against the water butt. I climbed the stairs to my old room and discovered one of my toy soldiers there. The mural of three flying mallards was still there in the bathroom, but the sink and lavatory had been smashed to deter itinerants or squatters. I took one final glimpse of the hearth before leaving – remembering vividly the time when I had first knelt in front of it on that freezing spring day in 1972. In the last few years, as I have been mulling over this story in my mind, I have resolved many times to make one last journey there, maybe even to take some photographs. The wood is blockaded with obstacles and fenced-off now, just as the past is beyond the pale. An array of signs from Group 4 Security, Staffordshire Police, and various other agencies warn intruders off. I knew I had to see the place before embarking on this tale, but always contrived to abort the mission at the last moment due to some emotional block.

Fortunately, the matter was taken out of my hands by chance. The bus service where I live is a national scandal in normal times, but during the 2020 pandemic even that had been reduced to a derisory schedule which as often as not breaks down en route. As we approached the site of the former Stewponey pub, now a block of flats, the gallant, long-suffering and charming bus driver announced that the last bus was about to break down for the third time on his shift – an apt symbol for my godforsaken country. He was forced to pull-up in a small lay-by near the little lane which led up to our old cottage. Since we were advised the mechanic would be some time coming and were obliged to maintain social distancing, I decided to walk a little way up the lane, on the pretext of answering a 'call of nature', and so it was to prove in its way.

Once I had climbed the steep hill a little way, I could not stop myself continuing for about half a mile further to where my only real home had been, right at the heart of the wood. I was suddenly disoriented, for nature changes things a great deal in twenty-five years. I was forced to navigate by finding old trees I remembered, and wondered somewhat whimsically, if they could remember me. A plantation of conifers which stood no more than 3 feet tall when we moved out, now towered over me, some 30 feet high.

When we first moved there, it looked more like Utah than Staffordshire, with a huge sand-quarry for building sand concealed behind the trees. Mr Edward Marsh, the landowner, and Mr Samuel Element, a local haulage contractor, saw the financial potential in the fine building sand that lay just beneath the topsoil, as the housing-boom was gathering-steam in the early 1970s. The weighbridge-complex where my father and I sometimes worked was gone, overgrown by gorse and shrubs. Quite soon, I saw the old tree which stood at the end of our garden, and I stood before a mass of gorse and bluebells where the two cottages once stood.

I took my shopping with me from the bus and walked the few miles home, past Stourton Castle and through Hyde Meadow, now a purple haze of bluebells. I made a posy of other wildflowers picked from our old garden to lay before my parents' photograph at home. Had it not been for this 'accident', I doubt I could have told this tale – at least not as it should be told.

There were many things to learn about my new woodland home. The first thing was, how much *wilder* everything was. It was, in one sense, an immersion in nature, but right at its heart, this gaping hole, this noise, this oil and machinery, these greasy men in overalls, drinking their wives' soup out of thermos flasks in bulldozers during their isolated lunch-breaks. The daylight hours (and indeed, in the winter the darkness before dawn) were announced by the *beep, beep, beep* of the huge earth-moving machines, gigantic wheeled yellow dinosaurs they seemed to me as a young boy, then obsessed with those ancient creatures. Surely this sandstone must be triassic, 250 million years old. Convinced of this, I took to looking for fossils from the age of gigantic beasts. Not a sausage.

But things were very different on the ornithological front, my other hobby. The huge sandstone cliffs, up to 100 feet high, were the ideal habitat for sand martins, and year after year they swarmed in from the African *Sahel*, their shrill tweeting overpowering the industrial roar. There were other rare birds. In the fields adjoining Barratt's Coppice, lapwings wavered and tottered over the ploughland, drawing predators away from their cunningly concealed nests, with their mottled, pebble-shaped plover eggs. Their cries of *peewit, peewit,* were a sure sign of spring in those days, just as the swifts nesting under our eaves announced summer's coming.

Small areas of primordial marshland which had escaped drainage, and never been disturbed by a plough, sheltered nesting coots and mallards. But one bird, not a native species, dominated the fringes of the woodland, the pheasant. Our landlord Mr Marsh was a keen patron of shooting and fox hunting. A series of gamekeepers patrolled the wood, and they treated us as intruders there. They constantly spied on us and intimidated me and my pals whenever we were caught in prohibited areas. Just so that we would remember where these were located, the occasional pot-shot would be taken at us.

They were in a direct line from the Norman 'foresters', 'verderers', 'regarders', 'rangers' and other 'woodwards' – guardians of the 'venison and vert', and we were cast in the role of feudal peasants, tolerated only on account of our utility. The local pub is still called The Foresters Arms. Despite being under covert surveillance I would sometimes discover a pile of iridescent golden pheasant-eggs on the ground and take a few home for breakfast. We had no need to poach in any case, for my mother worked for the Marsh family and was always supplied with pheasants, partridges, rabbits and hares; we never wanted for game.

The hunt, however, was a different matter. We all despised the vile business, and I recall that on one occasion my father let the quivering quarry into our outhouse where it remained hidden until the hounds had gone past. If this had been known at the time we should certainly have been evicted and my mother dismissed from her employment, so the stakes were high. My father was not a sentimentalist, and if we had kept chickens, for instance, he would have had no qualms about shooting a predatory fox. It was the cowardliness and cruelty which he despised, and the symbolism of the hunt, the ritual celebration of subordination and control, with its Norman-French hunting cries of *yoicks* and *tally-ho*. Even in the 20th century, it seemed an anachronism, and I was very anti-hunting; but strangely, I actually miss the colourful spectacle now that it is seen less frequently.

I miss the birds too, the sand martins and plovers gone forever, their habitat effaced within a single generation. I count myself fortunate now to have such memories, to pass on to those whose only experience of nature (if any) will be a 'virtual' one. For with regard to exposure to nature, at least, my boyhood was as unconstrained, idyllic and lazy as that of Huckleberry Finn. Yet the process which ended in the hole-in-the-air where my home once stood, had already begun. Time was already marching, dereliction, decay and extinction, ineluctably advancing.

The word 'forest' did not refer originally to dense trackless woodlands, as it does today, but to specific reservations or preserves which were designated as hunting territories for the elite Norman aristocracy. The original word *foris* meant 'outside' of normal law. There were only a tiny number of Norman settlers in England, a mere 8,000, but of these, only the great *donjons*, or keepers of castles, and the Forest Wardens and their officials (verderers, foresters, regarders etc.) were allowed free access to these demesnes. These were held from the king himself, on payment of fees to the Crown.

The Anglo-Saxon kings too, were fond of the hunt, but pursued the activity in natural wildernesses, which, being unsuitable for agriculture and settlement, afforded ample opportunities for good sport. But the new Norman Royal Forests were something entirely different, completely under the personal control of the king, and exempt from common law. Human beings in the reservations were considered a pest. The whole object of the Forest Laws was to protect 'venison', which meant not just deer, but wild boars, wolves, foxes, hares, coneys (rabbits), pheasants and partridges – from hunting, poaching, and other human encroachment on 'the vert' or greenwood.

These wild animals were the personal property of the king. An Anglo-Saxon chronicler said that William 'loved the deer as if he were their father'. Poachers were on occasion blinded by rubbing salt and vinegar into their eyes. It was also a crime to disturb the mating grounds of the wild creatures of the woods, or to collect timber unless a special licence had first been obtained from the royal officials of the 'Kingswood'. Those who were unlucky enough to be caught might lose a hand for their trouble. Dogs could be kept by freemen within the forest providing they had first been 'lawed' by the forest regarders by having their front paws cropped. All weapons, especially bows and hunting-knives, were prohibited. Within the forests, the inhabitants had been literally segregated from their natural environment, and their status relegated to being of less value than that of wild beasts.

Elsewhere in the country, these forests consisted of woodlands, moors, marshes, fens and other deserted places but in the Midlands the heavy clay soils of the Severn and Trent valleys were exactly like the forests we imagine when we think of Robin Hood and his outlaw band. Sherwood, that is, the 'Shire-wood' of Nottinghamshire, Derbyshire and South Yorkshire, really was a natural prehistoric forest, containing gigantic ancient oaks. The Royal Forest of Kinver, though not as extensive, was just as dense and impenetrable, and merged into other vast Royal Forests, Morfe, Wyre, Feckenham, Dean, Needwood and Arden in a great swathe which covered the entire western Midlands.

The King's Foresters had an evil reputation. Alan de Neville ('the Devil'), Chief Forester to King Henry II, was rumoured to be a Satanist, and in their secretive and exclusive rituals many cruel abominations were perpetrated. These allegations were partly due to de Neville's support for King Henry in the controversy following the murder of St Thomas Becket. Inevitably, the officials were resented and hated, and so were forced to socialise among their own kind.

This militia was a law unto itself, and it is quite possible that ancient pagan cult practices survived among them. This extraordinary change in the way people related to the land did not arise out of mere perversity. For the Normans, hunting and hawking was not mere exercise or sport, but a preparation for warfare – mounted warfare. The hunt was, in essence, military manoeuvres for a class of hereditary military professionals, and the key to their iron grip on the country was their skill in horsemanship and their cunningly designed and virtually invulnerable castles.

On payment of fees, those residing within the reservations could feed their swine on beech nuts and acorns in areas set aside for the purpose called 'pannage'. They could also collect firewood ('estover'), graze sheep and cattle ('agistment'), take fish from ponds ('pescary') and cut peat or turf for the hearth ('turbary'). The reason for the complex structure of the various levels of officialdom was that collusion between the more local verderers and the population was common.

The regarders were really inspectors of the constables, rather than exercising a direct judicial function. It may strike the modern mind as strange that the ravenous and dangerous wolf should have been protected as a species. Wolves were quite common until they became extinct in England in the fifteenth century. But the wolf-hunt was especially prized by the foresters, so that they could exercise their gigantic hunting hounds, which could keep pace with a horse and easily tear a man to pieces.

The Forester's Lodge for the Forest Warden of Kinver was Stourton Castle, and the Stewponey Inn, mentioned earlier, began life as the jailhouse for any forest trespassers or other malefactors. This nearly 1,000-year-old legacy of Norman jurisprudence was still vaguely present as I grew up in the shadow of the castle and jail. It is small wonder that my mother, whose clan name was 'Forest', ensured that the first book I ever read was *The Adventures of Robin Hood*.

In our time, on every workday evening, the Stourbridge to Bridgnorth road at Stourton is a two-mile traffic-jam, as commuters dash for the release of the countryside. But for many hundreds of years this same intermediate zone signified just the opposite of liberty, a place where every man bird and beast, every tree and bush, was strictly accounted for, regulated and controlled.

The process began with William the Conqueror's son, also called William II, 'Rufus', because of his red hair and ruddy complexion, who had a hunting lodge constructed on the west bank of the River Stour. His love of the hunt precipitated his eventual demise when he was killed by an arrow that pierced his lung while hunting in the New Forest, in Hampshire. This forest had been created at the expense of hundreds of English settlements, which were cleared to make way for the hunt. The word 'lodge' sounds quaint, but a royal hunting-party would have consisted of potentially hundreds of people in the king's entourage, all of whom would have required provisioning on a lavish scale. The Reverend Sabine Baring-Gould thought that the word 'Stewponey' derived from Estepona in Spain. The landlord of the pub had allegedly married a Spanish lady and named the pub in honour of her birthplace, according to this account. In fact, the place-name derives from the Anglo-Saxon *Stewen ponden* 'storage ponds'. As residents of the new housing complex have discovered, the area floods swiftly and often: 'Stour' is related to the word 'storm', indicating the power pent up in the river. Ponds were created for carp, pike, eels and other edible coarse fish. At the lavish feasting at the lodge, high-protein foodstuffs such as meat and fish were consumed in vast quantities.

King Richard I, the 'Lion Heart', made a grant of just under £25 in order to expand the hunting-lodge into a defended castle. His brother John became a regular visitor when he succeeded Richard in 1199. His vast cavalcade made at least eight visits during his turbulent reign, and John was very fond of Kinver, for he was a keen huntsman.

Another famous former resident of the castle had been Cardinal Reginald Pole (1500-1558), papal legate to England, who was born there. In 1549, a conclave came within fifteen minutes of declaring him pope. He had to rest content with becoming the archbishop of Canterbury during the reign of 'Bloody Mary', though he inclined to leniency towards so-called heretics himself.

During the English Civil War there was a cavalry skirmish on Whittington Heath and the castle briefly came under siege. So, this was the liminal cultural inheritance into which I had been rather suddenly thrust. It was all my mother's doing. But there was another, grim, historical legacy, for the place was not called 'Gibbet Wood' for nothing.

In his romantic novel *Bladys of the Stewponey* (1897), Sabine Baring-Gould makes the Stewponey pub a nexus for a fraternity of highwaymen and desperadoes. The reality of highway robbery was more prosaic. In December 1812, just before Christmas, a notorious murder took place in the vicinity and, just as in 1978, during the furore following the murder of the local newsboy Carl Bridgewater, this tiny hamlet – unremarkable save for a few local landmarks – became the centre of a national hue-and-cry.

When the culprit William Howe's body was conveyed to the murder scene from Stafford jail where he had previously been executed by hanging – to be suspended on a gibbet over a style as a grim warning to other footpads – over 40,000 onlookers came to gawp as the last major gibbeting in England took place. For months afterwards sightseers returned each week as Howe's body decomposed, and local evangelists declaimed from the scriptures beneath the mouldering corpse. A year afterwards, some medical students stealthily removed the skeleton for practical use – but that was not the end of the story.

Even as Howe's rotting corpse swung on the gallows, some lads had gathered one night to mock the cadaver. 'How bist thee tonight Will Howe?' asked one of the boys, only to be answered by a ghastly groan: 'I am cold … and clammy!' The gallant crew ran back all the way to Stourbridge in terror.

In the 1940s, during the blackout, a lady was forced to walk along Gibbet Lane to summon help when her car had broken down. She became aware of a man following her and began warily glancing behind her as she increased her pace. To her horror, she noticed that the man's neck was stretched, and that his head hung at an angle – as if his neck had been broken – before the spectre suddenly disappeared into the trees. A century before, a man had been rapidly pursued and allegedly attacked by a similar ghostly figure. All these tales, and many more besides, were eagerly devoured by my parents, and from the beginning we knew that we had chosen to live in a notoriously 'evil' place, despite its natural beauty.

As soon as darkness fell, the atmosphere in the wood became very different, and as a 10-year-old I felt the change all the more deeply. In all ancient cultures, there are tales of the 'Lord of the Forest', a shape-shifting demon of the woods. A dark, dense wood at night is a familiar motif in nightmares, the fear of being lost in the unknown in dark places where malicious spirits lurk. But as autumn came on, I had no choice but to learn to make my way home from school up the lonely track in the dark. My parents insisted that I confront my fears, and they encouraged self-reliance in spiritual matters. For all that, I was only a young boy, and soon became aware that there *was* something evil in the wood, specifically concentrated near the spot where Squire Benjamin Robins had been fatally wounded and the gibbet once stood. By spiritual intuition, we soon identified the actual place – which has only been verified to me as historically correct a few years ago. How on earth did we come to live in such an odd place?

In 1969, my paternal grandfather died. He had been the last obstacle to my grandmother's plan to completely disinherit my father and bequeath her estate in its entirety to her newly married daughter, my aunt. The blow was not merely financial, but emotional, and my father became increasingly embittered, angry, and in ill-humour at all times.

My mother worked at an Italian restaurant attached to the Dick Whittington Inn, a fourteenth-century manor house once owned by the famous Dick's grandfather. I was always rather glad to accompany my mother to work, where we could be out of my father's hair for a few hours. I have always been fascinated by the inn and had very jolly times there. The owner of the restaurant was a Sicilian who had been a prisoner-of-war in England. He had married an English woman who had capital, and so their large family travelled in from Worcestershire to run the restaurant business. Their grown-up children all had Italian names but spoke with a broad Worcestershire burr. One of my father's many irritated complaints was that I had begun to pick up their accent, which I was required to rectify.

The inn was notoriously haunted, most notably by the spirit of Lady Jane Grey (1536-1553), 'the Grey Lady', who often appeared on the stairway. A plot was hatched by her young husband, Guildford Dudley, and his father John Dudley, Duke of Northumberland, to influence the dying King Edward VI to disinherit his sisters, Mary and Elizabeth, in favour of the 16-year-old Jane. The object was to prevent Mary's accession, because of her devout Roman Catholicism. Jane was an equally devout Protestant. Jane was kept largely in the dark about the details until she was suddenly proclaimed queen in July 1553. Mary immediately gathered an army and the coup failed. Jane's reign famously lasted only nine days.

Mary soon established that the girl had been duped. She was, after all, her cousin, and a great-granddaughter of King Henry VII, and her instincts were to execute John and Guildford Dudley but to spare the hapless Jane the block. But the act of colluding with them had been treason, it was decided, and poor Jane would suffer the same fate as the men. As a little girl, she had laughed and played in the grounds of Whittington Manor, so perhaps her spirit was drawn back there, to happier carefree times, before love and state politics supervened.

There were several odd incidents I can still recall. On one evening slates were hurled down from the roof, and the guard dog started barking at someone moving around up there. The police were called, and they went out onto the roof assuming a burglar was lurking there, but they found no-one. One of the waiters was in the stores one night when he swore he saw the shape of a woman glide past and walk straight through the wall in front of him. He was a devout Catholic, took no drink and was ultra-conscientious, honest and hard-working. He was also notoriously tight-fisted. He saved every penny for a house he was having built in Sicily, and had his young son working alongside him every weekend to save his pay. But he was adamant that neither he nor his boy would enter the stores again, he was so frightened.

Giuseppe, the owner of the restaurant, was in despair, because the place was packed on most evenings and he couldn't let service standards slip. All the young members of the family adored my mother and asked her to help reassure the waiter by performing a kind of spiritual exorcism. She had a reputation as a sort of spiritual medium, and in the late 1960s youngsters were fascinated by all things mystical and occult.

My mother insisted that if she were to do this, any silliness or flippancy must be set aside. We all crowded around the entrance as they went in with candles. When they emerged the waiter seemed happier, but he was always a little anxious. By contrast I would always cheerfully go in there, and I earned a bit of pocket money by bottling-up.

But all this was no more than a distraction from the fact that my parents were both very unhappy and that the marriage was in jeopardy. My mother's health was always extremely delicate and she could not keep up with the shifts at the restaurant any longer. On several occasions my mother took me to stay at my maternal grandmother's house. Usually, after a few days my contrite father would come to get us, but it was clear that a split was imminent.

One morning after my father had gone to work my mother explained to me that things could not go on like this. She was going to *turn* things, by which she meant, a focusing of the will in a certain direction, with the objective of extricating ourselves from our present misery. I tried to imitate her as best I could. She grabbed her coat and scarf and I carried the umbrella as we set out on a mission to remodel our world.

The first stop was Jennings's newsagents shop in the village High Street. There was an advertisement in the window for an assistant to the housekeeper at Dunsley Hall, once home of the murder victim of 1812, Squire Benjamin Robins. The hall was now the residence of the Marsh family of *Marsh & Baxter* fame. The family had made a large fortune out of making sausages and other pork products. A telephone number was provided, to arrange an interview with Mrs Thomas, the housekeeper. Despite it being a bitterly cold and damp day in March my mother and I set off immediately to the hall over a mile away without calling ahead. We walked into the yard and my mother confidently enquired if Mrs Thomas might be available. After a few minutes, this lady emerged, clad in an apron and hat, dusting flour from her hands. She sat us down in the kitchen and made us a pot of tea, and a tray of freshly baked scones. My mother immediately impressed her, and they had quite a long chat. She happened to mention that there was a vacant cottage nearby, at a peppercorn rent. She said that providing Mr Marsh was agreeable, my mother could give notice to her former employers and commence work at the beginning of next month. On the way out, we stopped by at the estate manager's office. He gave us directions to the cottage in the wood, and a key, and so on we trudged.

By the time we got to the Stewponey it was sleeting and so we sheltered awhile in the village shop – the same place where I was to have the consultation with a Spiritualist medium mentioned earlier.

There were two cottages, built during the 1930s for the workers at the nearby piggery which kept the Marsh & Baxter factory fed with meat. They were well-built, and the cottages, though somewhat antiquated were in good order with spacious gardens front and rear. One was occupied by Mr & Mrs Cunningham, then quite elderly and infirm. This was one reason why the estate wanted someone to move in, so that they would not be so isolated in their retirement, and it made sense to have someone on hand in case of intruders. The earth-moving machines were a particular target for criminal gangs at the time. I sacrificed some pages from the *Radio Times* I had bought in Jennings's. Onto this I placed some sticks and pieces of timber I found in the coalhouse. Kneeling before the grate, I puffed and blew until a welcome blaze lit up the gloom. From that moment on, I knew we were on the move. We went home. By the time my father arrived home later that evening, he was presented with a *fait accompli*. My mother was very enthusiastic, and once she had made up her mind to something he knew as well as I that the thing was settled. Thankfully, my father grudgingly concurred with the adventure.

When my cousins drove us up there on weekends as the spring came on, the verdant canopy echoing to birdsong, baby rabbits darting across the paths, there was no hint of the menace to come, or the time of trial ahead. But even at this early stage, we talked about the infamous murder, which still cast its eerie shadow.

On one of the last of these trips before we moved in, we all foolishly walked into the wood itself one Sunday. There were six of us, four adults and two children. Suddenly, a very tall man appeared in camouflage gear carrying a loaded shotgun. He rudely challenged us and demanded we leave immediately. This was one of the gamekeepers, and not a man to mess with. My father explained that we were to move in soon and were merely trying to find our feet, but the keeper was having none of it. Whether we moved in or not was none of his concern, these woodland tracks were strictly off limits. He said that only a week before some saddles had been stolen at the hall, at which my father asked if he was implying we were thieves. The intimidating fellow gestured with his gun for us to be on our way – a charming introduction to our new home, and as it turned out, a sign.

As soon as we moved in, I began to explore. The wood was then quite extensive, and there was only one legitimate track to the cottages, not a road, but a service-way for the lorries which came to pick-up the sand. In winter the bulldozers and lorries churned it into a quagmire, but in summer the sand blew in whirls like the deserts of the Sahara, fine dust settled everywhere. Although I was then still at school in Kinver, my pals lived nearer to Stourbridge, so I resented putting an extra mile or more on my walk home and sought out farm tracks or snickets between the houses on the main road. In all, there were seven different ways of getting to the cottages. All these were on private land and there were occasional run-ins with householders, but for the most part, providing no damage was done to fencing, I was able to utilise these short-cuts.

But the difficulty came when I had to return over Whittington Heath or off Gibbet Lane through the wood. It was clear that I had to either take my chances with the gamekeepers or learn to outwit them. There were just two ways back to the cottages through the wood. One, and the one I used most frequently, was a side road behind the Round Hill sewage-treatment works. The other way in, and one I avoided at all costs, was to walk on to the brow of the hill where Robins had been shot, to climb over the gate where the gibbet once stood, and thence through the wood. In daylight I soon ran into our gamekeeper friend. On one occasion he made me turn and walk round all the way to the main entrance at gunpoint. He said that he knew everywhere we went, all our routines, and that although we could not see him, he had his eye on us at all times.

He had dens and hides all over the wood and was a master of camouflage. One day he had deliberately disguised himself as a tree, on a path he knew I walked along. Had it not been for his green Wellington boots I would never have noticed him – he even wore camouflage paint. I pretended that I hadn't seen him and went on my way. He was quite mad. So, apart from evil spiritual presences, it was obvious we had a malign human threat to deal with. The crunch came in the autumn, with the dark nights.

One Sunday, I had just gone to bed when right below my bedroom window there was a furious pounding on the back door. I froze, for it was genuinely scary. My parents were still up reading, and my father came rushing into the room. Opening the window, he shouted threats and profanities at whoever was out there. We all got dressed and went out looking for the intruder, but they were nowhere to be seen.

It is an acquired skill to move around silently in woodland at night. Any false move instantly gives one's position away. The only escape route which made sense was into the quarry itself – but there were no tracks, and against the backdrop of the cliffs anyone would easily have given themselves away. Had I been lurking out there, I would have been in fear for my life, because my father had armed himself with a golf club and wouldn't have had any qualms about using it for non-sporting purposes. From that night on, these disturbances became regular for about a year. Mr and Mrs Cunningham were not targeted and said they had never known anything like it up there before.

What was worse, was that more often than not, the incidents took place when my father was away with his work, so my mother and I spent anxious evenings waiting for the door to be pounded. We waited at the ready, my mother with the golf club, and I with a cricket bat – and as soon as the door-knocker went or the back-door was pounded, we would leap up and open the door ready for whatever came – but nothing. It seemed to us impossible that anyone could possibly run clear of the front or back garden into the dark without being seen. It became so uncanny, that one evening we had a family conference, and it was decided that whoever or whatever was disturbing our peace was going to meet with misfortune from now on.

Just in case Howe or similar spiritual entities *were* indeed responsible for the disturbances, we invoked our own ancestor-spirits to watch over us and protect us. By candlelight (it must have been during the power-cuts of the early 1970s) I wrote a warning to the intruder in red ink, advising them that ill-fortune would follow sevenfold if they did not immediately desist. This was pinned to both the front and back doors at night, signed by me. One morning, the warning had been taken by someone, leaving just the pin. These protective measures duly taken, we awaited developments.

We took other more normal precautions. My father's insurance-round was a huge area of North Worcestershire, South Staffordshire, and the Black-Country. One evening he went to settle a claim out on a farm in the Clent Hills. The farmer explained that his son had decided to emigrate to Australia on the assisted passage scheme. He couldn't carry on without him – and what was worse, he had to go out and shoot his son's dog that evening. He couldn't keep him any longer. My father immediately said we had need of a good guard-dog. So one evening, to our great surprise, my father arrived home with Tommy, our faithful canine companion for many long and happy years to come. But there was a problem. Tommy was still pining for his master, and would not eat, drink, or crucially, bark. After a few days, my father said it was no good. Tommy would have to go, a mute dog was no good to us. I can rarely recall being so miserable. I silently prayed that Tommy would find his bark. On a Tuesday morning, the bin-men came, and suddenly there was a clatter as they dropped the bins in alarm. My prayer had been answered, Tommy was snarling, barking and howling! Soon he wolfed down his food. When I say 'wolfed down' the simile is accurate because he closely resembled an actual wolf. He was wild and strong, always snapping his lead and disappearing into the wood after rabbits. He would sometimes be gone for days before returning completely exhausted.

One evening my mother and I took him out after dark with a torch into the lane. He began to growl and snarl, pulling at his chain, before erupting into savage barking. My mother called out to whoever was there that she was going to loose the dog, to flush them out. Whoever it was, they managed to escape silently somehow. I have a hunch it must have been the keeper but have no proof. Soon afterwards the incidents ceased. The gamekeeper left his employment, I heard he had tried to intimidate someone once too often and was dismissed. Others followed, but none quite so strange as him. But that wasn't the end of our dramas, for in early 1975 the area was terrorised by a more evil presence – Donald Neilson, the 'Black Panther'.

There was a link between Neilson and Howe: both acted on inside information. In 1812 Howe managed to infiltrate himself, first as a groom, then as an occasional footman, at Ombersley Court in Worcestershire, seat of the Lords Sandys. The after-dinner conversation turned to the new banknotes, redeemable for gold, which were making it so much more convenient for the gentry to settle accounts. Howe learned that Squire Robins was to withdraw a large sum in banknotes, as well as personal valuables, from the new bank in Stourbridge on 18 December, so as to settle various debts before Christmas. Howe arranged to be in Stourbridge on that day and had laid a cunning trap in advance.

As soon as he observed Robins coming out of the bank from a nearby pub, Howe left town and quickly walked the two-and-a half miles to Fir Tree Lane, as it was known then, where he lurked with a pistol, about a quarter-of-a-mile from the Wolverhampton-Kidderminster road at Dunsley, the modern A449. The trees were quite bare of leaves, and a sudden snowstorm had begun to drift as Robins breasted the hill through the trees about half-a-mile from home. He saw a man there hailing him in the white haze, who asked him directions to the Kidderminster road. Robins was immediately alerted. This man could not have walked ahead of him unseen from Stourbridge, and so must, he reasoned, have walked off the Kidderminster road in the first place. The squire motioned ahead, but instead of falling-in alongside him to walk towards the road, Howe suddenly dropped back behind Robins, discharged his pistol into his back at point-blank range, rifled his belongings, and made off into the dark, leaving the hapless squire for dead.

Howe made his way back to Stourbridge, to the Angel Inn, where he had lodged the night before. Soon, news of the attack on Robins spread around the town. The squire was not dead, he had staggered back to Dunsley Hall and alerted the authorities. Howe decided that it would be prudent to switch his lodgings to the Duke William pub in Coventry Street. Early the next morning he walked towards Bromsgrove via the Hagley Road, hiding his pistol in a hayrick before he left town. He drifted around between Bromsgrove, Droitwich, Birmingham, and Ombersley for a few days. He sold Robins' watch in Birmingham for £2, a foolish mistake. Eventually he made his way to London, having sent his belongings on ahead under a false name.

Robins had staggered the half-a-mile to Dunsley Hall with a pistol-ball lodged in his spine. As a boy, I was shown the spot, covered up by a rug, where he had crawled in through the door. The bloodstains were so heavy that they could never be entirely removed. Robins lived for ten days, and was lucid enough to give a detailed description of all the day's events, of the robber, and precisely where the attack had taken place. This was one reason for the gibbeting later – the tradition was that the murderer must hang at the place where the crime had been committed.

After the hanging a murderer's body was usually sent to the 'Barber Surgeons' for dissection. Any remains were ground down into powder to be scattered to the winds – ensuring that no bodily resurrection was possible. But because of the local furore, and in the midst of the national crisis of the Napoleonic Wars, Howe became the last major example to all 'ramps-men', footpads and highwaymen in England and dangled from the 'gibbet-tree'. Howe was arrested in a lodging-house in London. From there he was taken to Stourbridge, and then on to Stafford jail, where he was tried, hanged, and his corpse conveyed to be gibbeted at the murder scene.

Donald Neilson was a notorious burglar and armed robber, originally from Yorkshire, who in 1974 'upgraded' by becoming a murderer. In his many armed robberies on small sub-post-offices he killed three and wounded and terrorised many more. Because of his dark clothing he became known in the media as the 'Black Panther'.

For some years he had been following press-reports in the region, which reported an ongoing legal wrangle about the estate of George Whittle, the owner of the local bus company in the Wyre Forest and Shropshire. Neilson knew that a large fortune had been settled on George's young daughter Lesley Whittle, then only 17 years old. Neilson broke into the Whittle family home at the village of Highley in Shropshire on 14 January 1975. He abducted Lesley from her bedroom and left a ransom demand for £50,000 with well worked-out instructions. A telephone number was provided to a callbox in nearby Kidderminster, but there was no reply.

The police planned to observe cash transfers, which were to take place in remote places pre-arranged by the 'Panther' with Lesley's brother. But Neilson soon realised his plan was compromised, and that he needed to get out of the area with his abductee, who was by now very frightened and ill.

He evaded the police, and hid his victim, still alive, tethered to a wire in a drain at Kidsgrove, where she was eventually discovered dead. Then he drove to Dudley, where he shot a security guard six times before abandoning his vehicle. In the car, a cassette-tape was discovered, with a recording of Lesley's voice on it, and a further ransom demand.

For seven weeks, the entire nation was focused on our region, in the desperate hope that the girl might be rescued. One evening, my father was returning from work when he saw a man in what looked like military fatigues dart across the quarry, scale the cliffs into the wood, and disappear. In the atmosphere at the time he felt he had no choice but to report this to the police.

We little knew it then, but the fiend was only a few miles away with his captive, and a few weeks later poor Lesley was discovered hanging by the neck dead, in the drain in Kidsgrove. Such tragedies leave their mark on the local psychic landscape. Only three years later, another such catastrophe occurred a mile away, when a young newsboy, Carl Bridgewater, was shot dead in 1978. In a tiny hamlet, in a relatively short space of time, evil had made its mark on several grim occasions. There is nowhere to hide from it, seemingly, especially not in the 'wylde-wood'; nor should we seek to – at least that was what I was taught.

We must rather face it, come to terms with it, understand it, put it in its proper perspective. I grew up in a rural idyll, wild, beautiful, timeless, but yes – there were dark places, and a dark legacy. Thinking of these early experiences, I have come to believe that certain places are designated as 'special' in some way – because of generations of psychic investment, an aspect perhaps, of what Sheldrake calls 'morphic resonance'. In the same way a 'sacred' place is holy, having absorbed countless and continuous offerings of prayer and sacrifice – so a place may also become desecrated and defiled, where damned souls lurk by night. Sometimes, they show their hand. As I grew older and increasingly drunken in the evenings, I became the scariest thing stumbling through the wood on most nights, but even then, there was a *presence* one always felt, an inchoate terror on eldritch nights which one always felt must manifest eventually.

Last Christmas, I happened to be in a local pub when I overheard William Howe's name mentioned. I said that I had been brought up in the wood. One of the group explained how he had been walking his dog at exactly the place where the gibbet once stood. His dog suddenly began whimpering and lay down. Immediately the man sensed a sharp drop in temperature, and was seized with terror, this in broad daylight. Ahead of him, he saw a dark cloud, about the size of a man, which hung for a while in the air and then slowly floated into the trees. The temperature and atmosphere lifted and returned to normal as soon as the apparition vanished. As he related the tale to me, I could see how anxious and horrified he still was. He asked if I had ever had any similar experiences myself. Well, just a few.

There were always strange things happening around the place. The gamekeepers had gradually become redundant as Mr Marsh and his circle grew older, so the shooting and hunting eventually ceased. But in their way, they were at least some sort of security, and once they were gone, trouble soon followed. One of the bulldozer drivers reported to me, white-faced and in all sincerity, that one morning he had seen a 'witch' on one of the woodland tracks who had stared at him menacingly before vanishing into the woods. I asked, jokingly, if she wore a pointed hat. 'Yes!' he replied, 'she was a *witch*!' He was quite serious.

Not long afterwards another grim discovery was made by the quarry-men one morning. Dead, eviscerated rats had been laid out in an inverted pentagram in the sand-hole. Candle-stubs and other paraphernalia were lying there, and a 'spell' (what kind of serious witch would leave *that* lying around, I thought) of some sort. These people were potentially dangerous. For the only time I remember, my father kept a loaded shotgun in the house, borrowed from a friend. I came across such people every so often, sometimes 'sky-clad' around a fire. I remember once wishing them good evening as I weaved my way home from the pub. As time went on, there were professional criminal raids on the bulldozers, which were driven off straight through the wood at night.

Over the years, we almost became a part of the wood itself. Perhaps that was intended. The ancient Druids practised a kind of 'tree-shamanism'. It held no terrors for us and was probably a lot safer than a lot of other places nearby. There was always though, a hint of menace there. At certain places in the wood, the birdsong ceased, the sunlight never quite penetrated the understorey, and a strange corpse stench hung about the place. The gamekeeper used to hang up dead weasels, rats, magpies and crows to rot, to keep their living kindred at bay – but this was something *other*: a dankness.

One night I had the shock of my life when a young girl, about 18, came screaming out of the wood. Seconds later, another screaming hysterical girl the same age, and then two young lads who literally vaulted the gate to run to their car nearby. The girl was quivering in fear and said that they had just seen a 'demon' in the woods, which had chased them. Since I shortly had to walk through that very part of the wood to get home, I had a keen interest in what they had seen, and where.

The girls were desperate to get out of there, but the upshot was, that they had gone to some rhododendron thickets in the wood to do what courting couples do when suddenly they heard the sound of heavy footsteps approaching. Then, the bushes were held aside, and a gigantic being, with a shaggy outline – 'like a fur-coat', they said – had peered in at them. The girls had taken fright and ran down the path to the gate, followed by the boys, who swore they saw the entity loping off into the woods towards the quarry. They drove off at speed down the bumpy lane. I refrained from walking that way home on that particular night.

In early 1980, I got a job for 6 months at Stourbridge Art College in Oldswinford. I used to cycle in down Gibbet Lane, and one morning I got a puncture on the rough track. I decided to hide the bicycle in the wood and collect it on the way home. I hoisted it over the gate on Gibbet Hill, the exact spot where Robins was shot.

In the wood a little way on, one of the gardeners from the estate had planted a jungle of rhododendron bushes he had acquired from his counterpart at Alton Towers. Untended, these had now overgrown a large tract of woodland. This was the perfect place to conceal my bike, but as I approached, I saw a kind of fuzzy dark mist rising, which glided off down the path ahead. The thing seemed to resolve into a bipedal entity of some sort, before it went through a hedgerow and away into a ploughed field before vanishing. There was a penetrating cold; after my exertions I was actually quite hot and sweaty but the temperature change was extremely abnormal. I was over an hour late into work and received an appropriate dressing-down. I decided to leave the bike where it was that evening. The most terrifying experience of all was yet to come.

One evening, I met up with a pal to go drinking in Stourbridge, sometime in the early 1980s. We had both just split up with our respective girlfriends and so it was a 'heavy session' – I can't claim sobriety, unfortunately. The time came for us to be thrown out, and so I staggered home down Gibbet Lane. I went through my usual short-cut, at the back of the sewage-works, clambered over the barbed-wire fence, and onto the woodland path. As I was walking into the darkest part of the wood, less than a mile from home, from about 100 yards to my left there was the most piercing shriek, no mere scream, but the veritable 'cry of the banshee'.

I froze on the spot. I knew it was no vixen. Then I went berserk. I uprooted a fence-post from the ground and tore it from the rusty wire. Brandishing this I shouted out a challenge in the foulest language I knew. I even frightened myself, truth to be told. I could hear my heart pounding in my chest – the only sound. I stood completely rooted, motionless, and soundless.

Sooner or later one of us had to move, to make a noise, and as soon as he or it did – I would be on him. Five minutes went by. Nothing. Eventually, I marched on, at a pace few light-infantrymen could have equalled, still brandishing my improvised club, until I reached home, and a welcome dram of whisky. Whatever it was that night, it was not human, or of this world, that much I do know.

I was astonished when, one day in 1995, I telephoned my mother (they had finally agreed to have it installed) to be informed that the estate wished my parents to relocate to a more appropriate dwelling suitable for their years. It seemed unthinkable that we should ever live anywhere else. I was stunned, but in the end it all turned out for the best. Our life in the wildwood was over. Yet, in another sense, it was not. If Howe's unclean spirit can wander the wood for all time as a penance for one act of evil, then surely ours may, who made a place of good cheer in the wilderness for thousands of days and nights.

If some future traveller should wander up Sandy Lane at Christmas, my mother's birthday, he may see a light enticing him to some hidden cottages he had never noticed before; and from the chimney-pot, the smoke rising from the Yule-log now lit in the hearth, from the kitchen the smell of roasting pheasants in the Dutch-oven as the Christmas festivities commence. We will be there eternally.

4

Layamon

In Worcestershire are names of three hermitages, and all are at-'stone' places on a trackway. Blackstone and Redstone are at ferries over the Severn, and the hermit dwelt in a cave in the cliff; it was from the last place that Layamon came. The third Worcester hermitage was a cave in a curious isolated rock called Southstone near Stanford in the Teme valley ... now there is every indication that the hermits were not only stationed on trackways, but that they performed occasional duties to those who used the tracks.

Alfred Watkins[8]

J.R.R. Tolkien compared the English poet Layamon with his Icelandic equivalent Snorri Sturluson (1179-1241), with whom he was roughly contemporary. Coming from a literary scholar of Tolkien's eminence this is high praise indeed, but whereas every Icelandic school-pupil will be aware of the cultural importance of the *Eddas* and Sturluson's contribution to their national culture, the same could not be said, I think, of Layamon and his *Brut*, a vast poem, a saga of sorts, of over 16,000 lines, for the vast majority of the peoples of Britain. Scholars in the most prestigious universities are aware of its significance for English literature, and some historians and historiographers perhaps, but outside these circles he is little known.

This obscurity is both perplexing and fascinating. Layamon called his *Brut* a *Chronicle of Britain*. There is something interesting here in the way this history was transmitted, for this was not Anglo-Saxon history in the tradition of the *Anglo-Saxon Chronicle* or Aethelweard's *Chronicon*. Layamon derived his poem in large part from the Norman poet Robert Wace, whose *Roman de Brut* had been written in 1155. This, in turn, was material translated from Latin into Norman-French from Geoffrey of Monmouth's *Historia Regum Britanniae* written about 1136. Geoffrey's book was a conflation of his own ideas, legends and records adduced by the historian William of Malmesbury, but most crucially, excerpts from a book in either Welsh or Breton which had been loaned to him by an archdeacon of Oxford, called Walter.

No-one knows exactly what this book was, but it seems probable that it was derived from the *Historia Brittonum* written by Nennius, a Welsh monk of Bangor in the eighth century. So, Layamon was clearly aware that he was a link in a chain of literary forebears which stretched far back, whose subject matter, though consisting largely of history, was not confined to just that. It was also poetry, designed to be sung, and experienced in the heart as well as the head. Each 'link' in the literary chain would make his own, personal contribution, for his own time, and Layamon certainly did that. He took the brave decision to write his epic in his own, then rather despised native language, English. His *Brut* is one of the foundation stones of our national literature. Having taken this decision, Layamon did something even more surprising. The great hero of his poem is not an Englishman, like himself, but a Romano-Briton, King Arthur, the arch-enemy of his forefathers. Arthur's reign dominates Layamon's history, and the poet introduces new tales about him, famously the 'Round Table' motif, and Arthur's being conveyed into Avalon by elfin women.

If he had been a Welshman, a Cornishman or a Breton, we might easily account for these new stories, but Layamon was of Anglo-Saxon descent, far from places where he could have picked up these tales – though I think I have a simple explanation for that. But as to *why* this 'simple-hearted Saxon priest' made it his life's work to sit beside the wide River Severn writing down the entire history of the island – that may be a rather more complex puzzle to solve. Was it just a hyper-graphical amusement for a clever clerk in hard times, a mere pastime – or was it a 'spell' or a prophesy, something deeper than our modern consciousness can comprehend?

Cador proceeded over wealds, and over wilderness, over dales and over downs, and over deep waters. Cador knew the way that towards his country lay, by the nearest he proceeded full surely right towards Totnes.

This Cador, or Cadorius, is one of the characters in Layamon's work, a kinsman of King Arthur and Duke of Cornwall. He is fated to die in the 'last dim weird battle in the west' – Camlann, where Arthur's enchanted reign finally unravels, and his realm is engulfed by the darkness.

The reason I insert the quote here is that this little passage was previously quoted by Alfred Watkins in his classic *The Old Straight Track*, a book which has fascinated me from boyhood onwards. If I were ignorant of anything referred to in a text, my father encouraged me to go immediately and rectify this from encyclopaedias rather than pestering him. There were plenty lying around, for he had once been an encyclopaedia salesman, among many other occupations.

I began to notice more than a scattering of references to Layamon and his *Brut* throughout the book, and even then it occurred to me that Watkins was trying to drop some oblique hint that there was more to this hermit-poet than a cursory glance would reveal. He was inferring that Layamon, and others like him, were members of a caste of anchorites, exercising religious functions and performing votive rites at key nodal points in the landscape, such as river-crossings. These individuals, known as *gutuaters* or 'prayer fathers', preceded Christianity, and their antecedents inhabited the sacred landscape power-centres long before any organised priesthood. When Christianity arrived, they simply infiltrated the church institutions, notably as clerks; Layamon was a clerk.

Although clerks were miserably poor, they were quite well-educated, and so could scrape a living on the basis of their peripheral relation to the Catholic Church. One in twenty men at the time was a clerk of some kind. But during the papal interdict from 1206-1213, Pope Innocent III ordered the suspension of all church rites and the closure of churches in King John's domains as punishment for his legendary blasphemy, turpitude and deceit. All baptisms, weddings, funerals, holy communion and church ales abruptly ceased, a religious 'lock-down' at a time when the population were deeply religious and superstitious, which lasted for over six years. John volunteered to convert England to Islam in exchange for a large sum of cash; the Caliph of Morocco assumed he was jesting – but he was in deadly earnest.

Many of the Aragonese and Brabancon mercenaries he hired to eliminate his English enemies, so-called *routiers*, were, in a crude sense, pagan, and notoriously anti-Christian, but even these cut-throats were astonished at John's excesses: arson, blinding and mutilation, starvation in dungeons, mass-hangings, and roasting people alive on grid-irons, among them. In his psychotic drunken rages, which on one terrible occasion culminated in child-murder, John was demonic. All 'normal' civilised human intercourse subsisted under this sick regime. In these times uniquely hostile to Christianity, Layamon became a lonely outpost of spirituality amidst a sea of wickedness and evil.

John was a regular visitor to Kinver Forest, which then merged with the Wyre Forest where Layamon lived, and was buried in Worcester Cathedral when he died (probably by poison) in 1216. The malignant king was therefore a real presence in the neighbourhood, a centre of moral pestilence. I began to postulate that the covert motive for Layamon's poem, and the reason for it being composed in English, rather than French or Latin – was because it was a thinly veiled attack on John's regime, using the Arthurian myths as an analogy to his own times, for his own oppressed folk, an example of 'cultural resistance' of a piece with the other examples we have seen before.

There came a time when Arley Redstone, outside Stourport-on-Severn in Worcestershire, was on my patch as a field social worker, so for the first time, I was able to investigate the area personally. The problem was, I couldn't find the hermitage. I noted a long road on a housing estate there called 'Layamon Walk'. At least there *was* some faint memory. I occasionally asked locals if they knew anything, but always drew a blank. But I was quite sure that there was some strange destiny in it all, and that Layamon's presence was very near.

As a boy, my parents barely scraped a living, but were both always employed in some way or other. On the day when my father had to bank his cash, present his accounts and receive his weekly schedules at the Dudley offices of the United Friendly insurance company, my mother would work a double-shift at the Himley House Hotel. My father always took this as an opportunity to treat me to new, extraordinary experiences. There was the joy of my first encounter with exotic beasts at Dudley Castle Zoological Gardens – a Norman castle, with a Zoo containing lions, tigers, gorillas, giraffes, huge serpents, and at one point a killer-whale called 'Cuddles'. There was also the Dudley Borough Museum, the first I ever visited, wherein the infamous 'Dudley Bugs' were displayed – fossilised remains of prehistoric trilobites, sea-creatures whose weird remains were found in the limestone caves beneath the 'Wren's Nest' rock-outcrop in Dudley.

We visited Holbeache House where the Gunpowder Plotters of 1605 had been run-to-ground, I even held Robert Catesby's abandoned cap in my little hand. We toured Moseley Old Hall, home of our ancestor Colonel John Lane, and refuge of Charles Stuart during his flight from Worcester in 1651. On one day, my father said that we needed to get clear of the smuts and smog of the town – up to Turner's Hill, nearly 900 feet high.

On three days a year, it was possible to see the shimmering haze from the Bristol Channel, eighty miles away – the open sea. I just couldn't see it, though my father kept pointing to a slender silver sliver. 'Look, *look* ...' he urged, and then, for a few brief seconds, something really did glitter in my vision, and I instantly knew the power of gazing from hill to hill. It was my first introduction to what the archaeologist Christopher Tilley calls the 'Phenomenology of Landscape'. What he was suggesting in his *A Phenomenology of Landscape: Places, Paths and Monuments* (1994) is that ancient tribal societies were literally enmeshed with the landscape, not so much 'on it' but 'of it'. Watkins had always advocated what he called 'foot archaeology' as a means of breaking through abstract, academic conceptualisations of history – to reveal the hidden 'meaning' which bonded humans to the land, and to one another, in tight-knit kinship groups.

The ancient megalithic monuments were, he thought, a sort of camera obscura, devices for focusing or projecting what it *meant* to be a part of this clan and its land – the power of the king's reach – the word *Rex* derives from the same root as 'reach'. It was also vitally important to know the limits within which the king's protection operated. At such and such a range of hills, or at river boundaries, other tribes lived, potentially dangerous enemies, 'outlanders'.

In fact, like all really good ideas, I had already divined all this before I read it, but the most telling confirmation came at Arbor Low Henge one summer morning. The farmer on whose land the impressive monument stands – it is known-as the 'Stonehenge of the North' – spoke with me at some length about his own interpretation. I doubt he had ever read Christopher Tilley's work, but in essence, he was saying the same thing, and there can be few better places to test out the theory in practice.

Now, for the best part of a century, much ink has been spilt and much nonsense talked about ley lines, particularly in the counter-cultural context of the 1960s, but the frustrating thing is that this has diminished the important insights Alfred Watkins originally contributed. I have always been entirely convinced that the original concept, of a network of pre-surveyed trackways, burial-mounds, and megalithic monuments *did* exist in Neolithic Britain, and that at junctions of these tracks huge passage-tombs and megalithic stone circles were constructed according to a master-plan. The guardians of the ways were a caste or class set apart, who surveyed and superintended the construction and maintenance of the trackways and monuments.

No 'mystical' or supernatural gloss is necessary in order to mark Watkins's theory out as an innovative contribution to antiquarian debate. I *knew* this to be true as a small boy atop Turner's Hill, just as I still know it when I gaze out from the Worcestershire Beacon or Titterstone Clee. Cynics may scoff, and that is their right, but for me this revelation is, without doubt, a sort of religious faith, what the poet Malcolm Guite calls a 'sense of sublimity, suggestion and transfiguration, the sense of an outward expression in landscape of the inner glories of the soul'.

The mediation of the 'meaning', the psychical umbilical cord between the tribe and the motherland, was provided by a cult of ancestor-worship and communication with the dead, particularly the deceased souls of mighty rulers from the dreaming-time. As the farmer at Arbor Low observed, the monument stands in the middle of a great flat circle, and on surrounding prominences, burial mounds were placed atop these at equidistant points.

The tombs rooted the spirits of the noble men of olden times, and amplified their greatness, but also focused upon the tribal temple, where it could be reborn anew each year with the mid-winter solstice. Some such idea is still faintly echoed in the tombs and monuments of Westminster Abbey today. Pre- and post-Covid at the Summer Solstice neo-Druids, pagans, mystical Christians and other visitors gather at Stonehenge for the sunrise, but during the 1980s, Wiltshire constabulary deployed thousands of riot-police to enforce an 'exclusion-zone' to prevent any such gatherings. On 21 June 1900 the Chief Druid was physically manhandled by the police who threw him off the site as he pronounced a *geas* or curse on Sir Edward Antrobus who then owned the land on which the monument stood. He had the temerity to charge a small admission fee to raise funds for restoration. Stonehenge has become iconic for the neo-pagans, neo-Druids, 'hippies', ley-hunters and others, symbolic of a need to recover meaning in the modern world. We feel some collective need to convene with the spirits of the ancient ancestors buried in this national necropolis, which is why the violation of the Chief Druid in 1900 and the persecution of the 'New-Age travellers' in the 1980s were both, in their way, such petty acts. But I don't object to making a voluntary contribution for the upkeep of monuments on private land. As we have seen, many landowners are a living link to the ancestors, and know more about their own turf than occasional visitors with romanticised expectations, who as often as not leave detritus in their wake.

All over the region, tumuli from the Neolithic era stand out in the landscape, crude structures of timber and roughly hewn stone covered over with earth, in which they placed the bones of their dead. The practice continued into the Bronze Age, when new round barrows were constructed; over 20,000 remain in Britain today but there must once have been many more which have been gradually ploughed-out throughout the intervening centuries.

When Watkins plotted his leys he began to notice a peculiar phenomenon. The line almost invariably never went through the dead-centre of the structures. Rather it passed just to the side of them, suggesting to him that the barrows were constructed so as to be just off the actual trackway itself. Therefore, the tracks preceded the tombs, suggesting that to be buried on 'the way' implied holiness, a sacred route for the soul now that the bodily journeying was completed. To have been invested with such a hallowed status the tracks must have been very ancient even in Neolithic times. All along the sacred ways, mark-stones were erected – Watkins thought the word 'market' was derived from places where travelling pedlars set out their wares along the tracks.

Some of these became regular, and community festivals took place on ritual occasions. Other stones began to be added, so that stone circles proliferated. The mighty passage-tombs like Knowth, Newgrange and Dowth in Ireland were truly awe-inspiring – places reserved for the semi-legendary ancestor-spirits. Many of these sites seem to have once been ditched and moated, water deliberately channelled there to serve as a reflector for the sun and moon.

These 'Lows' as they are known, are so-called from the Anglo-Saxon *hlaew* from which we derive the word 'halo'. At night, beacons were lit so that travellers could find their way across the landscape in the darkness. Fords were supremely important junctions, as were crossroads, emblematic of the liminal and transitional, places of passage between psychical and spiritual, as well as terrestrial space.

Death of the Whiteleaved Oak.

Reflections at sunrise, River Severn.

Over a period of many thousands of years, some of these places became so important and significant in their own-right that massive hill-forts, temples, and other high-status buildings were built on them. Controversially, Watkins thought that churches, too, were important indicators of ley lines. Although they came much later on in chronological terms, they were often themselves built on pre-existing pagan holy places. Pope Gregory the Great explicitly instructed St Augustine of Canterbury to make his task easier by integrating the ancient places into the new faith. Not every church is so ancient, of course, but in the Herefordshire countryside where Watkins was doing his initial research, many are.

Now, it may have been no accident that Watkins's controversial revelation, often cruelly mocked by conventional archaeologists, came to him precisely in the place it did, because the western Midlands was of particular significance for the ancient surveyors, or 'dodmen' as Watkins called them. Graham Robb points out that Whitchurch in Shropshire lies at the exact mid-point on a line drawn across the main island, and very close to the crucial 52nd degree of latitude.[9] A similar mid-point existed in ancient Gaul called *Mediolanum,* and this was also the name of ancient Whitchurch.

The region contained the centre of the 'perpetual choirs' of Britain, at Whiteleaved Oak in the Malvern Hills, which range is also on a substantial ley line, and also almost exactly on the 52nd degree of latitude. (This ancient oak, itself taken from a cutting from a previous much more ancient tree, was tragically destroyed by fire days after I wrote this.) It has been surmised that the 'nodal' or nexus points along the leys corresponded to 'notes' sounded on a vast, intelligent musical sounding board – the living earth itself.

In other words, Watkins was promulgating his concept of 'psycho-archaeology' in an area where the faint pulse of the ancient system was still detectable, for those with the necessary 'antennae', and in a region where the extraordinary telluric energy had once flowed most forcefully.

I have come to believe that Watkins was onto something, and Graham Robb has done excellent work to confirm me in this view. Sceptics will still demur, and demand that more scientific evidence is adduced before they will accept such a proposition. This is, of course, fair enough, because if I am right our ancestors were not painted savages living in unsophisticated ignorance – they were veritable god-men. But were there really 'giants on the earth' in those days?

Now, the word 'lay' denotes a short poem designed to be sung, and also means someone who is not ordained into the clergy, whereas the word 'ley' in Watkins' proposed system derives from the Anglo-Saxon word for a clearing for pasture in the woodlands (he began to notice the preponderance of 'ley' place-name endings along the tracks). There is, of course, no conventional connection between the two, but Watkins, whose mind was curiously alert to reading-across place-names and etymology, may have noticed that a clue to Layamon's motivations could be cryptically concealed in his name. He was a lay preacher, writing verse in a traditional form designed to be sung, living in a clearing in the forest at a well-known and long-established cave hermitage.

This brings us back to the concept of 'perpetual choirs'. Edward Williams (1747-1826), known by his adopted name Iolo Morganwg ('Iolo of Glamorgan') was a stonemason by trade, but he soon established himself as the leading figure in the revival of Druidism. He claimed descent from a line of authentic Welsh bards who had transmitted the oral lore of the ancient orders.

There may be some truth in this, because Ben Mc Brady, an Irishman, claimed to be the last in such a line of Irish Druids in the late 20th century. The mainstream view has been that Morganwg interpolated some of the material from his own imagination, a kind of Druidic pseudoepigrapha. Iolo spent much of his life wandering through his native land collecting these traditions before the anticipated extinction of the Welsh language. Thanks to him, this process was arrested, and there are now over a million Welsh speakers, of *Iaith y Nefoedd* or 'the Language of Heaven', as it is called.

In his *Triads of Britain* Iolo says that 'In each of these three choirs there were 24,000 saints; that is, there were a hundred for every hour of the day and night in rotation, perpetuating the praise and service of God without rest or intermission.' Robin Heath and John Michell explain that:

> The function of these choirs was to maintain the enchantment of Britain – by chanting. Their song was a constant religious chant, varying with the cycles and seasons and, like time itself, never ending. It was reflected in the popular mode by the music that was heard at festivals around the country. In that way, everyone was held under the same musical spell that maintained harmony in their relationships and surroundings.[10]

The legendary white-leaved oak (the most venerable of the Druidic order wore white garments, and the oak was their most sacred tree) had been burned to a cinder in July 2020 – an extremely ill omen for the land and its people in the midst of a global crisis unequalled for generations. The tree marked the exact centre of a colossal decagon, and at ten termini along the axial leys ten *bangors* or Druidic colleges, each with its perpetual choir, were established. These were Glastonbury, Stonehenge, Goring, Stony Stratford, Croft Hill, Uttoxeter, Ellesmere, Carno, Llandovery, and Llantwit Major.

Such a feat of geodesy, and the sheer imaginative scale of a project to terraform the whole island – and then to sonically energise it with everlasting song – is, admittedly, mind-boggling to most. But if we could just lay aside our rigid cultural preconceptions, we may find, as Watkins did, that we hear very faint echoes of a long-vanished spiritual 'praise-matrix'. Originally, it was not just Wales which was 'the Land of Song' – but the entire island of Albion, under the governance of a faith not pietistic or doctrinal, but natural.

We are stricken, in this island. The blasted oak is an emblem for a culture which is truly 'lost'. Now, the whole island is a 'Lost Land'. We are all grieving, divided, counting the costs. In the black Easter of 2020, all was quiet, save for the ambulances in the early hours. For some, dawn came as they struggled for breath in such a vehicle, their final journey. The whole world, of course, is counting the cost, but somehow this fissiparous pathogen was foreshadowed here by the petty squabbling over Brexit, the evident socio-economic divide between the generations and the separate nations and regions, the upsurge of race-hate and fascism. The arsonist who destroyed our sacred tree was a mere accomplice to our national and global catastrophe.

Yet the seeming evil-doer was only the handmaiden of nature. In his *Aurora* (1612) Jacob Boehme, the 'Teutonic Theosopher', says that the tree in which 'the sap no longer riseth ... must be cast into the fire'. The old oak was already dead, possibly from the continuous attentions of visitors 'decorating' it with dainty offerings over the centuries, perhaps from disease. But from small acorns, great oaks may grow, if we tend to them awhile.

It may not be too late to restore our proud inheritance, to re-enchant the land. Indeed, the final prophesy of King Edward the Confessor on his deathbed in January 1066, was that England would fall to the 'agents of the Devil' within the year. Asked if there were any hope of redemption for his doomed people, Edward replied that this would only come when; 'A green tree, stricken in twain by lightning, shall be restored, and put forth fresh leaves.'

The Old English word *Treow* meant 'truth', in the sense of remaining true to an oath, but it also meant 'tree'. At quinquennial festivals these oaths were taken by eager young warriors in oak-groves, sacrifices supervised by the Druids – Druid means 'oak-knower'. Julius Caesar reported that the Druidic religion had originated in Britain, and that for those who wished to study their perennial philosophy seriously it was necessary to journey by sea there, to receive a course of tuition which took as long as twenty years to complete. It is curious, but Caesar happens to be one of our most reliable sources about the Druids. He actually knew a Druid, named Diviciacus, the only Druid whose name is historically recorded. But despite this explicit statement of his, modern historians, especially since the 18th century, have sought to depict the religion as being generic among all the Celtic tribes.

According to this theory, three main 'waves' of Celts invaded Britain over a period lasting about 800 years, and it was these peoples who introduced the Druidic faith to Britain. My contention is that Caesar (and Diviciacus, who ought to have known) – was correct, and that Druidism was actually a pre-Celtic philosophy which was introduced to the Continent from Britain. For many centuries, these 'Isles of the Blessed' were a semi-legendary sanctuary, a land of giants, magicians, wizards and seers – those who conversed with the gods and goddesses themselves.

If the Druidic antecedents were indeed those who raised the megalithic structures and surveyed the ley lines, and were of British origin, as postulated by the Oxford historian Sir Barry Cunliffe – then the history we have been taught for generations will be turned on its head. The conventional model of 'waves' of settlement, called for the sake of convenience 'Celtic', was pioneered by the historian and antiquary Edward Lhuyd in the early eighteenth century. But modern DNA research proves that there were no 'waves'. The base population of the islands was established long before the Celts, in the pre-Neolithic immigration (actually re-immigration) from the Basque region of northern Iberia. The percentage of ancient DNA increases the further west one travels – in England 68%, Wales 81%, and in Ireland an incredible 88%.

Cunliffe has adduced evidence that these people actually spoke some sort of proto-Celtic language 3,000 years ago. He thinks that the philosophy, culture and language of the Continent was shaped by a mighty ancient culture, a sea-going empire whose original base was the Atlantic littoral. The great power-centres of this trading culture, Newgrange, Knowth and Dowth, Carnac, Callanish, even Stonehenge and Avebury, are all within easy access from the sea.

In this 'golden age' the so-called 'Celtic Fringe' was a powerhouse of science, philosophy and art – as it was to become again for a brief period in the 'Dark Ages'. So, the crazy story my father told me, that our most ancient ancestors came by sea from the *west* not the east, is perhaps becoming 'fact'.

Not that there ever are any 'facts' of course. Robin Heath and John Michell criticise the 'evolutionary' approach to history as being in effect, racist:

> Britain is the most archaeologized country in the world. Yet after centuries of digging and research, the nature of prehistoric culture is still a mystery. Ancient artefacts say nothing for themselves, so their interpretation depends on whatever myths and theories of prehistory happen to prevail. These in modern times have been conditioned by scientific materialism and rooted in the 'rise of man' overview of Darwinism ... even when the evidence is considered, the conditioned view is that ancient science was a primitive affair. The tribal folk who practised it were stumbling from primal ignorance, taking first steps towards the light of modern understanding.

The authors ask the question: 'if the established overview on ancient Britain is totally wrong, what sort of picture should replace it?' Heath and Michell were in no doubt about that. In the summation of their epic labour their call for a return to the mythic times is as resonant today as the visions of William Blake in his:

> It was a spell-bound society, held under a priestly enchantment, highly ritualised and never changing from one generation to another ... the sites of Stonehenge and Avebury were known and sanctified long before the Bronze age came to Wessex ... the Bronze age people it now seems, repaired and made permanent a system which, even in their time was archaic and venerable ... there is no reconciling this with the current evolutionary view of prehistoric life and culture ... A possible view, requiring nothing new in the way of faith or fantasy, is the traditional one, that our ancient ancestors were like the mythical giants and heroes, nearer to the gods than we are, and capable of such great achievements

in science and ritual magic that we are only just beginning to recognise them.

Watkins was thoroughly convinced that this sacred quality of the ley lines was indicated in place-names, such as 'Tot', 'Toot', or in Wales, where the word probably originated, 'Twt'. A Celtic god-form called Tout, Romanized as Toutates, was a variant of the Roman Mercury, the guardian of pathways and travellers. The original such god was the Egyptian deity Thoth, but when Alexander the Great took control there Thoth became the Greek god Hermes, the guardian of wayfarers on unknown paths. Watkins postulated that 'hermits' such as Layamon were originally devotees of Hermes, the deity whose task it was to lead 'departed souls over unknown trackways into the nether world'. At crossroads, mark-stones called *Herma* were placed, and offerings to the god laid there.

All over the country, mounds are still called 'Toot', and there is a heavy concentration in London – Tottenham, Tooting, Tot-hill in Westminster, and Totteridge. Now, London is sited where it is precisely because it was a convenient crossing-point over the Thames. In Hampshire no fewer than 8 ferries and fords supported a hermit whose duty was to 'help the traveller on his way'. It is by no means impossible that Layamon was among the last of these guardians, and that keenly aware of that fact, he decided to record as much of the island's mythical history in writing as he could before the last relics of the system were finally obliterated.

Significantly, he began his poem with the landing of Brutus the Trojan at Totnes (another 'Tot' name) in Devonshire, in about 1185 BC. A mark-stone, called the 'Brutus Stone' still stands there. This account is always dismissed as legendary, but the so-called 'Bronze-Age collapse', which destroyed Ancient Mycenae, Egypt, Cyprus, and the Assyrian and Hittite empires, really was attributed in large part to a mysterious proliferation of bellicose 'sea-peoples' who appeared from nowhere, like the later Vikings. It is a fact that the long-established settlements on Dartmoor nearby were mysteriously abandoned at just this time. Were they the first victims of the new immigrants?

Layamon's *Brut* may be considered not just as the foundation on which all later English literature rests, but also as a link to an almost impossibly ancient religious lore, exemplified by the Druids. Sir Norman Lockyer claimed that: 'The Druids of Caesar's time were undoubtedly the descendants of the astronomer-priests, some of whose daily work has now perhaps at last been revealed.' But by a strange irony, it was the Christian Church which preserved the decaying and senescent system. Steeples became the new beacons in the landscape, as often as not standing on the site of the ancient mark-stones.

If Watkins, and later Heath and Michell are correct, it was not just churches which were superimposed on the ancient system. The famously straight Roman road system in Britain was 'more or less planted on the old British tracks'. The Romans wiped out the upper echelons of the Druidic religion but, Watkins observes, 'the bard, the magician, the hermit and the pilgrim ... survived, the implement of their work and authority – the sighting staff – survived in the rod or sceptre of power, the wand of office, the pilgrim's staff and the magician's wand.'

About eight years ago, some friends and I went out to search for Layamon's obscure hermitage. We walked through a beautiful nature-reserve at Arley Kings beside the Severn, until we reached the housing estate with the road named 'Layamon Walk'. A lady there told us that she had always assumed Layamon to be a French name but knew nothing of his history. She did know, however, that some old caves were located behind a private caravan park about half-a-mile further on. We enquired with the park warden if it might be possible to take a look at the cave – a sensible precaution, as the place was patrolled by a fierce-looking guard dog.

Then, at long last, there it was – the cave where, by the light of tallow-candles, one of the greatest epics of world literature was completed, the labour of a lifetime. In Layamon's day, the soft sandstone had been carved into effigies of the saints, but these had now long since crumbled away. Here, Welsh drovers bound for London with their herds and flocks halted to seek blessing from the holy one, as their forefathers had done for generations. This was no mere ritual, but a joyous social occasion, for the 'prayer-father' was not a remote cleric, he was a friendly man who joined the evening throng around the campfire, sharing food and drink – and tales.

Tales of Arthur, that mighty king, stories which were translated into English for Layamon by the head-men, some of them hitherto unknown outside the Celtic lands. I am convinced, in fact, that Layamon would have done all he could to elicit these stories, so as to embellish his own poem. It will be objected that all of this is mere conjecture, that Watkins, Heath and Michell, and the present author, are merely projecting our own interpretation onto the landscape, and by so doing deluding the public with a phoney philosophy generated by our fevered imaginations. But standing reverently outside the 'cave of making', where a man laboured year after year to write down obscure tales of a forgotten race and its hero-king, in the despised language of another conquered folk – we all three felt deeply touched and proud – honoured to share this space for a few precious moments, where history had been made, and the world changed – by a 'simple-hearted Saxon priest'. I intuited something else as well. I began to feel that the responsibility to continue the great labour of the ages, the sacred record of 'the Matter of Britain', had somehow, in some vanishingly small way, fallen on me.

5

'A Wanderer in Albion'

Fame is the spur that the clear spirit doth raise
(That last infirmity of noble mind)
To spurn delights, and live laborious days.

John Milton

According to some philosophers, such as Rudolf Steiner and Owen Barfield for example, humankind has entered upon a new and transformative age of the 'Conscious Soul' or 'Consciousness Soul'. This development, which will unfold over a period of over two millennia is characterized, according to Barfield, by an attitude of 'I only know, because I have experienced.' The old comforts of tradition, family, work, community and faith are gradually evaporating and losing their relevance, as humans become increasingly isolated and cut-off from one another. This egoic individuation, and the resort to a 'mechano-morphic' relationship to our world, so that, as Herbert Marcuse postulated in his *One Dimensional Man (1964)* we have become a functionality, or an extension of – even an organic 'battery' for – the machines, has now reached a point where, from being holy creatures of God we are being reduced to a role as powerless avatars in a computer-generated 'game'.

This process, alleged to have commenced in AD 1413, has been gathering pace ever since, and spiritual developments on other planes are reflected in our own material one, in the isolation, paralysis, alienation and despair so evident in our culture today. The epicentre for the entelechy of the Consciousness Soul, for reasons we will examine later, was Britain, specifically England.

But this 'flight from nature' as Steiner called it, is not without purpose, or meaningless. For, only by evolving (as a species) a new state of consciousness, called by the Ancient Greeks *Metanoia* or 'new Mind', can we hope to achieve *conscious* freedom. Such a process, Barfield called 'Final Participation'. Now, I am not an expert on these ideas by any means, but they were so similar to those with which I had been inculcated in childhood that when I discovered them, they immediately struck a chord. In our traditions too, the 'soul' was a thing one 'made', through one's life-experience, not a subcutaneous phantom, coterminous with the physical body which one was born with. This consciousness, I knew experientially, was not limited to or confined by the 'individual', but was 'co-extensive', to some degree.

As a youth I was fascinated by novels such as *More than Human* by Theodore Sturgeon (1953), and *The Inner Wheel* by Keith Douglas (1970), in which a *gestalt* or 'group-mind' was developing among a new generation possessed of extraordinary psychic powers. Lacking any institutional support, my only guides were my parents, and once I had reached a certain age, about 14, I think, they gradually left me to my own devices. My intuition, that it was now my own responsibility to explore the world, and derive my beliefs from experience, has resolved itself into a weird philosophy peculiar to myself. The reader may be intrigued by how I came to it, and so I feel an attempt must be made to explain.

As a child, I was a precocious reader, but even before I discovered books I had another obsession – maps. My first purchase at a toy shop was a world globe, and my dearest possession in my dotage is my parents' seventeenth-century map of Worcestershire by the famous cartographer Robert Morden. One of my first hobbies was to go to various places at random to check that they were, in fact, present as depicted on the map. This grew into something rather more serious as time went on. Pinned up on my bedroom wall was a large map of Great Britain and Ireland. From careful study I knew all the major route-ways, and approximate distances between the major towns and cities from an early age.

From the age of 13, I attended a school in neighbouring Worcestershire about 5 miles from my home. A friend's father picked me up by car in the mornings but could not hang around if I was late. A five-mile walk was quite a fag on such mornings, and since the school was a disciplinarian pseudo-prep school a stern telling-off and a detention usually followed. One such morning, tramping south along the A449, I saw the driver of one of the sand-lorries from the quarry recognize me. He pulled over to offer me a lift. I quickly jumped into the cab, and was soon walking up the drive into school, only slightly late.

The idea dawned on me that these sand-wagons travelled in every direction, all across the country. This was a time quite different, by the way, to the paranoic nightmare of the 21st century. Hitch-hiking has become all but impossible in England, at least. Ireland is a different matter. Suffice to say, taking advantage of the strategic crossroads next to the Stewponey, I soon ventured in all directions exploring the island. By the time I left school I might disappear for days, sometimes weeks on these missions, usually alone, sometimes with a friend.

My father and I were supporters of Wolverhampton Wanderers F.C., and he would quip that I had become 'a Wanderer in Albion' (West Bromwich Albion F.C., 'the Baggies' are our bitterest local rivals). My parents were amused by my peregrinations and adventures, whereas most modern parents would probably be worried. We could always communicate on a kind of 'telepathic' level, and instantly knew if any of us were ill or in trouble – without the need for telephones etc. The same was true in the case of our pets.

The initial focus for my explorations was the putative ley-line system, megalithic monuments, battlefields, air-crash sites, and in the early days, Offa's Dyke. I attempted to walk the 149-mile length of the dyke but gave-up about two-thirds of the way along. But there was something more to these excursions than youthful adventure. I found the process of moving through the landscape and watching it unfold before me oddly therapeutic. At some remote places I had a strong sense that my arrival was somehow 'expected'.

But more practical concerns now supervened. I had, much to my teachers' surprise, acquitted myself quite well in my final school examinations, but despite this, none of the local colleges ran a history A-level course. This meant that with only one A-level, in English, I was insufficiently qualified to enrol for a degree course. For a brief but extraordinary interlude in 1979, I worked as stage-crew for the legendary Led Zeppelin at the Knebworth concerts, and I could have continued in similar employment.

Instead, I went to work as a driller in a factory in Cradley Heath – an absolute purgatory from which I was soon mercifully released by the blessed Mrs Margaret Thatcher. Within a year of her coming to power in 1979, the industrial Black Country (along with similar industrial conurbations in the Midlands, North, Scotland and Wales) were more thoroughly devastated than anything the Luftwaffe had managed to achieve, a third of all industrial capacity was simply wiped out. Even had I wished to remain in industry, that option was now a non-starter. It soon became perfectly clear that my generation had been written off.

By the time of Thatcher's re-election in 1983 following the Falklands War, I had already begun my steady descent into the new 'underclass'. I was not alone. As I traversed the length and breadth of the country, I encountered many other 'refuseniks' from Thatcherism, travellers and 'hippies' mainly, and would often stay among them in their temporary communities and encampments. Even at the time, I realised that I was witnessing an historical transition, and that like those who had preceded me, the culture of my forefathers was being ruthlessly ripped apart yet again, this time by a faceless transnational capitalism, with a globalising free-market liberal ideology. But for many of us, this enemy did have a human face, in the shape of Margaret Thatcher, whom we loathed and despised.

Not that this was the majority view, however, as her political hegemony for more than a decade attests. In fact, the Black Country and the western Midlands were grudgingly supportive of the Thatcher project. As a callow youth, I could not understand this. We will return to the cultural reasons for this seeming paradox later on, but one rather helpful consequence of her tenure was that the antiquated British road system was massively modernized and expanded, so that my wayfaring became quicker and easier than ever before.

Gradually, and especially during the Miners' strike of 1984-85, I became uncomfortable with the political complexion of my home region. My partner was a north-country girl, and I moved north to stay with her. I came to especially love the bleak Staffordshire Moorlands, the Peak District, the Pennines and North Yorkshire Moors. A collection of poems by Ted Hughes, illustrated with superb photographs by Fay Godwin called *Remains of Elmet* (1979) had drawn me to these wild, unforgiving places. The breathtaking beauty of these hills and dales liberated me from thoughts of the industrial decline I had left behind. But as the relationship disintegrated, my alcoholism and drug abuse grew more dangerous – I was always only one step away from the complete mental health breakdown which eventually overwhelmed me.

I reverted to the lifestyle of a wayfaring itinerant or 'industrial gypsy', until I at last came to rest in Nottingham, where we began this book. There, the industrial decline was less pronounced than in the formerly heavily industrialised areas, but the poverty and deprivation were more deeply entrenched and endemic. The 'Red Light' district there was medieval.

Culturally, however, Nottingham, the 'Queen of the Midlands', was in every way superior to Birmingham and the Black Country, with a rich history and, as I have mentioned, a strong literary tradition. Although some of the suburbs were supportive of Thatcher (including, perversely, the deprived 'ghetto' areas, represented by Martin Brandon-Bravo M.P, an arch-Thatcherite), the city was a radical hotbed with an active counter-cultural focus based around Canning Circus, where I lived. Everywhere else I had lived before, I felt like a misfit, but there, at last, I felt 'at home'. To be a misfit in Canning Circus was almost *de rigueur*.

Comforting as it was to have finally found some kind of human solidarity, life in inner-city Nottingham was unrelentingly tough. My post-code 'NG7', became a cypher for rioting, prostitution, alcohol and drug abuse, social exclusion, poverty, and violent crime. And yet, the multi-ethnic community was very resilient and strong, despite all this. It was virtually impossible to apply for work, study, or any other form of social advancement with my post-code. Sometimes, it was necessary to work away from the area in the south, usually the south-east, as a factotum in the regionally tiered economy of those bitterly divided times. I would sub-let my flat to a close friend on these occasions, and we would alternate our working seasons, rather as people had to do in South Africa under apartheid.

On one such occasion, I was away working in London for 6 months. I would alternate monthly visits between Nottingham and my parents' house in Gibbet Wood. After a substantial Sunday dinner at my mum's I could not resist a visit to my favourite pub, a few miles away. There I remained until closing-time, but I was so confident in my hitch-hiking skills that I imagined an early start would soon see me back in the 'Great Wen' – or 'New Jerusalem' according to one's taste, on the following day. It was February, and despite an early start, I was hung-over and poorly. I got as far as Pershore in Worcestershire, hoping to push on to Oxford over the Cotswolds and then onto the A40 to London, but as I was dropped-off in Moreton-in-Marsh, the snow started to drift heavily. All routes out were blocked, but I heard that one last train to London, via Oxford and Reading was expected.

I waited patiently in the dark on the freezing platform until the train mercifully arrived. These were the days of the old compartmentalised carriages, and I quickly had one of these to myself. At last, I was out of the bitter winds and driving blizzards, so I craftily lit-up a pipe full of very smelly hash. The train arrived at Oxford. A distinguished elderly gentleman pulled the sliding-door aside, and asked if it would be OK to join me? He was bald on top, with long flowing locks to the rear, wore round-spectacles and carried a large brown briefcase. I indicated that I had no objections, and he sat down – but as soon as the train creaked-underway he exclaimed: 'I say, what a wonderful smell there is in here!'

I saw no point in obfuscating and explained my earlier activities. 'Oh, don't mind me, I'm from the '60s!', he joked. I asked where he was bound. 'Spitalfields,' he replied. I asked what he did for a living. 'An historian.' I think I really did gawp and said something inane like 'wow!' I explained that history, especially its 'meaning', was my favourite subject, almost an obsession. We alighted in London and continued our conversation for another hour in a pub, before at last we parted, but not before he had given me his contact details.

I had just met Raphael Samuel (1934-1996), one of the most eminent social historians of the 20th century. His parting advice was to follow through on my innate love for history, for the land and its folk. It was my duty, indeed, so to do! The elitists loved nothing more than to stifle the incipient talent of the free-thinkers, the 'outsiders'! Therefore, I was to contact him for any further information as may prove necessary. For some time, I dithered about this, but eventually I applied, and was accepted some years later – but not for a history diploma.

I decided instead to study Applied Social Sciences, with some notion of becoming a social worker in Nottingham, where the management of despair had become the only growth industry. Because of my (quite minor) offending history, absurd obstacles were put in my way with regards to obtaining the necessary professional qualifications. Eventually, I was awarded an MA, but as soon as I returned to Nottingham and my old address, the 'traditional' total employment exclusion became operative as before. Eventually, my benefits entitlement ran out, so that I faced imminent eviction.

The upshot of all this, was that for a period of about 20 years I really had become a 'Wanderer in Albion', and I began to feel that there was some strange destiny involved in this wanderlust. For, unless I had *experienced* the north, east and south – I would never have been able to contextualise my final journey into the west, and this book would have been neither possible or meaningful. My seemingly aimless wanderings had never really been anything of the kind – they were the necessary precondition for my later literary endeavours. Of course, I could have just remained at home and taken the map on my bedroom wall 'on trust', but in accord with the spirit of the age of the Consciousness Soul – I felt I could only 'know what I had experienced'. Thus, I approached my homecoming with the air of an anthropologist arriving in a strange land.

Of course, in a sense it was strange, while also being paradoxically familiar. Most of my old friends were still around then, my parents were still living, though in a different cottage nearer to civilisation – and the towns and villages of my youth were still reassuringly there just as indicated on the map. But the *culture* had changed, had been changed, by twenty years of Thatcherism – for Thatcherism did not end when the lady herself departed tearfully from Number 10 Downing Street in November 1990. By a stroke of good fortune, I was in London at the time and watched her political demise at close quarters, rather gleefully.

John Major, her replacement made a genuine effort to chart his own course, but the guilt among his party for their having dispatched the lady so mercilessly meant that his tenure was marked by continuous bickering and backstabbing. When John Smith, the Labour leader died suddenly on 12 May 1994, a right-wing Labour coup installed Tony Blair as his replacement. As Thatcher said herself, Blair was her 'greatest achievement', and when he took office in 1997, she was immediately invited to visit him at Number 10.

The Thatcherite revolution would continue, but this time under 'New Labour'. Such are the ways of the world's most sophisticated democracy. This book is intended in part as a contribution to cultural studies. Therefore, the preceding political-historical preamble will prove germane to what follows, for much had indeed changed in these crucial, brutal, two decades.

A book whose major themes are cultural loss, grieving and the inevitability of death, such as this one, is in danger of succumbing to a phoney nostalgia, romanticizing the past for its own sake. But technological and social change is gathering pace at such an exponential rate that entire cultures can be obliterated in the space of a few years. I certainly would not wish to romanticize the working-class culture of the industrial Black Country. My brief membership of it was, as I have said, a purgatory. In a later tale, any such tendency will be ruthlessly excised, but this chapter is unique in that it concerns one historical transition I personally witnessed, and the one which has marked my character and fate most indelibly. As Richard Hoggart remarked:

> ... this very emotional involvement presents considerable dangers. Thus it seems to me that the changes described in the second half of this book are, so far, tending to cause the working classes to lose, culturally, much that was valuable, and to gain less than their new situation should have allowed. To the extent to which I can judge the matter objectively, that is my belief ...[11]

An academic or social scientist such as Hoggart is obviously obliged to be as scrupulously objective and uncontentious as possible in their depiction of social transition and change. As a writer, I am not, and in fact any such an attempt at even-handedness would seriously undermine my attempt to find out what it is that he (the writer) truly has to say. I suppose it is unlikely he will ever quite succeed. But his reader is in a luckier position, like Marlow's listeners in Conrad's *Heart of Darkness*: 'Of course in this you fellows see more than I could see. You see me.'

As one who witnessed the culture war of the 1980s at first-hand, and was irreparably handicapped by it from the get-go, it would be disingenuous of me to detach myself from events and their consequences – indeed I cannot, for I was so emotionally damaged by the ongoing process. I have no 'political' axe to grind, but the devastation, desolation and contempt visited on my culture deserves to be mourned in just the same way Heledd Cyndrwyn, Walter Map, and Layamon lamented their own loss.

For, despite economic indicators to the contrary, and the illusion of 'prosperity', Hoggart was right. The working classes did lose much more culturally than they gained, and I would go further. In my opinion, the Thatcherite project so poisoned particularly English culture (the Celtic countries now have their fate in their own hands) – that only an equivalent counter-revolution or a complete systems collapse can rescue us from total Americanisation. The Brexit referendum of 2016, depicted as an attempt to restore British 'national' independence, has, in fact, delivered us into just such a backlash vassalage or reverse colonialism – at least for the time being.

Round Oak Steelworks, Brierley Hill.

Merry Hill Shopping Centre, Brierley Hill.

In the early 1990s David Smail, the eminent psychologist and writer, attempted a sort of 'case study' of the 1980s in the UK. Lest it be thought that this chapter is a mere polemic against Margaret Thatcher and her ideology, a ventilation of my youthful frustration and sense of victimhood – let me assure the reader this is far from being true. In fact, Smail's excellent book entitled *The Origins of Unhappiness* (1993) was one of the key texts which converted me from such a perspective.

For Smail, with his superb grasp of the way in which we are all (or practically all) victims of distal powers over which we have no control or influence, convinced me that Thatcher, so demonised by the left, should be exonerated of ultimate blame for the project which came to bear her name, and which is still the dominant political ideology here over 40 years after she came to office:

> Margaret Thatcher and her government were merely representatives of a culture which had been flourishing in the Western world long before it made its presence felt so forcibly in Britain ...Thatcher's downfall just after the close of the decade was not [caused by] her failure as a politician, but her failure as a manager. She was too much of an individualist and had become an obstacle rather than an enabler of those powers whose path up till then she had done so much to smooth. She was replaced by a man who was barely a politician at all [John Major] ... quintessentially General Manager UK.

I think it was Kenneth Clarke, Thatcher's sometime minister and later Chancellor of the Exchequer under Major, who coined the term 'UK PLC', as if the political union of four ancient and proud nations was a mere economic conglomerate. I often wondered when I would receive my dividend. But sad though it may be, Smail's central argument holds water; 'this land is leased out ... like to a tenement or pelting farm' as Shakespeare put it. The Black Country, England's equivalent of the German Ruhr, was bound to become the target for ruthless de-industrialisation, precisely because the kind of alienating and exploitative work, the heavy-industrial production which had underpinned its economy for 300 years, could now be exported overseas to places where 'labour can be bought more cheaply and conditions of production controlled less scrupulously'.

Instead of heavy-industrial production, the people of the Black Country and similar areas were redesignated as consumers. For many, such a transition was a liberation from the confines of a limiting and stifling culture where one could never 'get ahead' of one's neighbours. These upwardly mobile people aspired to go into business and own their own houses, and who can blame them for that? Many certainly succeeded in this and bless Mrs Thatcher's name to this day. Their redundancy packages from heavy industry often formed the down-payment on their first mortgages, and some were only too eager to take the money – there was little serious organised union resistance, as there was in the northern mining areas.

The Black Country coal mines were already long gone. My village pit was consigned to history not by Thatcher, but by a Labour government. For those who could not break free in this way, the poverty and social stigma of mass unemployment for a lifetime was probably little worse than the dreary, arduous, dangerous and poorly paid work they had previously performed.

With their native common sense, the Black Country folk realised they had been 'sold down the river', and most accepted, even welcomed, the new consumerist regime. As Smail says:

> To replace with the values of the market, within the space of a decade, the ideology of a social system which at least purported to be based on the values of truth, justice, and equality traceable back to the Enlightenment was no mean achievement.

The means by which this 'cultural revolution' of the right was achieved, was by the revival of Benthamite utilitarianism. Jeremy Bentham (1748-1832) envisaged what he called a 'panopticon' – a system of total surveillance and control of the populace, who would be regulated by a 'constitutional code' which would encompass the jurisprudence of all 'Liberal' democracies to enforce absolute control of all aspects of social, community and ultimately personal life, by the lawful authority.

Bentham was, like so many other philosophers who came after him, quite eccentric and detached from the realities of the chaotic industrial ant colonies which had sprung-up in the wake of the so-called 'Industrial Revolution' in England in the 17th and 18th centuries. His main concern was to prevent any violent revolution such as had occurred in France in 1789 from spreading to England and the rest of Great Britain and Ireland.

The ultimate expression of this revived 'panopticon' was the emergence of a cult of managerialism in Britain, mediated by a monstrous regiment of management consultants, in the 1980s. Smail describes these transformational times thus:

> Traditional methods of assessing vocational ability and professional competence were ... suddenly replaced by new definitions of competence, formal systems of appraisal, restrictions on information and communication, and authoritarian lines of accountability. These 'new' systems of discipline and surveillance, backed by the very real threat of unemployment, were usually introduced as the spin-off of reorganization and change ... virtually no place of work escaped the upheavals of reorganization: large public institutions in health and education, small family businesses, public and private companies of every size and description seemed to be overrun by management consultants ... The besuited managerial group having a 'time out' weekend at an expensive country club could equally well turn out to be the board of a large engineering firm, a group of NHS administrators, or the senior academic staff of a university department. Everyone who wasn't made redundant underwent a change of role or a change of rank ...

As one who underwent this venal and pretentious process myself, respectively in local government, the NHS, and the criminal justice system, it was accepted that an 'away day' would usually prefigure a round of redundancies, followed ultimately by the closure of entire swathes of public services. As the lady herself put it, 'There is no alternative.' No aspect of public or private life was unaffected, and the steady march towards the abandonment of all notions of justice, welfare or social responsibility was underway.

Forty years on, amidst the wreckage of what was once a great nation, we see the ultimate result. No nihilist or malicious anarchist could have devised a plan better suited to destroy a national culture than the management consultancy brigade achieved, by simply boring us to death in conference centres.

The supreme emblem of this remarkable cultural and economic transition of the Black Country from 'old' industrial production to 'new' retail-based consumption was the Merry Hill Shopping Centre at Brierley Hill, built on the site of the former Round Oak Steel Works, 'the Earl's' as it was known in Dudley, after Lord Ward, 1st Earl of Dudley. The shopping centre was opened in 1985 by Richardson Developments. Round Oak closed on 23 December 1982 after 125 years of production. By then, only

1,500 workers remained to collect their redundancy payouts, down from a peak of over 3,000. I remember many of them spending freely behind the bar of the Stewponey when I was a barman there in the run-up to the closure. They were all on double-time. There was a sense of grim fatalism about it all. One oddity was an SAS training exercise which took place among the virtually abandoned infrastructure. The whole area was closed off without warning as Chinook helicopters hovered over the site all night – a sign of things to come, perhaps.

Merry Hill was, of course, a great success – for Richardson Developments at least. For Dudley, Halesowen, Stourbridge and Brierley Hill retailers it was a disaster, and these once prosperous market towns soon became the shabby run-down shadows of themselves they now are. Since the 2008 economic collapse even Merry Hill itself struggles to attract adequate footfall, and like the disposable Hollywood movie-sets it so resembles, will soon enough be 'history' in its turn. Only an old rhyme recalls the spectacular scenes of the old puddling furnaces of 'the Earl's':

> When Satan stood on Brierley Hill
> and all around him gazed,
> he said, 'I never more shall be
> at hell's bright flames amazed.'

Although the vista is tawdrier today, the Adversary still finds more than enough mischief, vice, and crime in the Black Country to keep him and his minions more than happy.

Yet this so-called 'Black Country', an epithet popularised by a visiting American diplomat and author, Elihu Burritt (1810-1879) is actually very green in certain hidden places. Only a mile or so from Merry Hill the dense woodland of the Saltwells Nature Reserve is a tangle of willow, birch, brambles and wild flowers, teeming with birdlife. There were coal mines here in medieval times, which soon flooded with underground saline water alleged to have healing properties. A clay-pit and canal workings added to the weird terrain, and Lady Dudley began re-landscaping work which culminated in the opening of the urban nature reserve in 1981, just as the de-industrialisation process was in full swing.

There are many other such places dotted around the Black Country, such as Ham Dingle at Pedmore a few miles to the south-west. The 'learned' Dr Robert Plot (1640-1696), a famous naturalist, heard tales of miraculous healing cures at the Saltwells, and of fairies dancing in the dingles, but even in his day the area was undergoing rapid industrial transformation.

Amidst this contrasting jumble of urban decay, shopping-malls and surreal wilderness, an otiose, disenfranchised population has been forced to adapt itself to the changed economic and political conditions as best it can. Many of the more prosperous have taken flight for the nearby countryside, the 'green borderland' of the Black Country, leaving behind those less fortunate. Twentieth-century immigration means that the Black Country is almost as multi-cultural as nearby Birmingham, the 'second city' of Britain. The children of these immigrants often acquire the distinctive Black Country dialect. For the coming generation the only experience of that industrial legacy will be their pride in the new Black Country flag, perhaps (the design is thought controversial by some), or a visit to the Black Country Living Museum. The changed urban landscape, dominated by US franchises selling junk food, could be anywhere in America.

It is a culture whose meaning has slowly bled away. This is what accounts for the extraordinary nostalgia among the elderly population, and the resilient popularity of *The Black Country Bugle*, a local paper which stubbornly celebrates the glory days of industrial enterprise, skill and prosperity, alongside dark tales of poverty, exploitation and foul murders. It is really a kind of continuous grieving, for a time when the area was distinctive and proud, the world's workshop. The photographer John Myers, who lives in Stourbridge, took the trouble to record the decline of what he calls 'Middle England' in the 1980s, poignant images which have only recently been given the recognition they so richly deserve – the denouement of a unique culture and its people.

For my parents' generation, 'consumption' was a disease – tuberculosis. Many of my mother's siblings died of it, and she almost succumbed herself. Today's consumption is just as pernicious and deadly, not only for its mind-benumbed supplicants, but also for the biosphere. As Smail observes, the old working class has been replaced by a new 'consuming class':

> Consumption is of course, not restricted to any one social stratum, but then, neither was work. Just as the economy used not to be able to function without an industrial proletariat exploited for the means of production, so now, in countries such as Britain, it cannot function without a semi-employed proletariat

exploited for purposes of mass consumption. 'Enjoyment' thus becomes the social function of the mass of society on which the Business economy depends.

Instant gratification is encouraged through the intimidation of parents (themselves often little more than infants in terms of their cultural intelligence) by their 'kids' – so-called 'pester power', another generation whose only motivations are to have, want and get. Artificially stimulated excitement is mediated by a constant bombardment of the senses from advertising, so that people are continuously drenched with banal hyperbole. In the 1980s especially, the voice-overs for these commercials were often couched in the argot of the East End gangsters of the 1960s such as the Kray twins, almost as if there were an implied threat of violent retribution should the consumer prove reticent. Thatcher's revolution had a distinct cockney accent.

The other obvious cultural change was the elevation of finance to a form of Black Magic or pseudo-religion. Until the 1980s it was not thought necessary to broadcast infantilised 'news' programmes just after cock-crow, interspersed with regular updates on the progress of the FT Shares Index, Wall Street and the Dow Jones. Before that time most people would have been at work before 7.00 am, and only a few toffs owned shares or bothered to read the runes of the financial markets. By a strange irony, it was often the radicals of the 1960s counter-culture who formed the avant-garde of the transition to consumerism. Women's liberationists did briefly attempt to resist the mass-media fetishization and objectification of their gender, but in vain.

The object of the new regime was to by-pass subtler messages, using images which 'punched straight into the nervous system'. The products were linked to raw, primal, animalistic craving and desire – precluding the need for thought or discrimination, using, in particular, sexually provocative and explicit images and messages. Any who objected to this vulgarity were portrayed as prudish or hypocritical. Women, ironically, often portrayed their cultural prostitution in this way as their 'right to choose' (choice, of course, was a key mantra of the liberals). As Richard Hoggart predicted, not only has increased literacy been used, paradoxically, as a device to 'dumb-down' the culture – but 'addictification', using 'fast' food, explicit sexual images, drugs and especially pop music has enveloped the imagination of the mass-consumerist in a kind of noxious brain-fog.

All is well, however, so long as everyone is 'having a good time'. Even the iconic symbols of the counter-culture, indeed especially these, have become totally captive to the power of the Business media. The Glastonbury Festival, for instance, at its inception a celebration of peace, love, and musical free expression, now resembles more a vast Category C prison or a Nuremberg rally. So expensive and exclusive has the festival become now that most people watch it on the BBC – itself reduced to providing programming deliberately designed to be childish and immature.

In a later chapter we will examine the kind of culture this barbaric tedium replaced – the culture of industrial production whose inventiveness shocked the world. From the foregoing it will be quite obvious that I set my face against these changes early on, but I am not particularly nostalgic for what went before. The old Black Country was dirty, dangerous and brutal. George Orwell summed up the character of the old working class thus:

> ... in all societies the common people must live to some extent against the existing order. The genuinely popular culture is something that goes on beneath the surface, more or less frowned on by the authorities. One thing one notices if one looks directly at the common people, especially in the big towns, is that they are not puritanical. They are inveterate gamblers, drink as much beer as their wages will permit, are devoted to bawdy jokes, and use probably the foulest language in the world. They have to satisfy these tastes in the face of astonishing, hypocritical laws ... which are designed to interfere with everybody but which in practice allow everything to happen. Also, the common people are without definite religious belief, and have been for centuries. The Anglican Church never really had a hold on them, and the Nonconformist sects only influenced minorities. And yet they have retained a deep tinge of Christian feeling, while almost forgetting the name of Christ.[12]

By 1830, over 50% of the population of England were living in urban areas, an astonishing transition in itself, and one which was not paralleled worldwide until the beginning of the 21st century. As I will seek to show, the process first began in South Staffordshire and North Worcestershire 200 years before that, in about 1630. The term 'Black Country' is strangely apposite, because unlike neighbouring Birmingham the urban area is not a city, but a vast congeries of villages and towns which have merged, while retaining their cultural distinctiveness. This process of the conversion of rural countryside into urban industrial sprawl was by no means peculiar to the Black Country, it merely began there. Richard Hoggart describes how his own family were affected by the exodus:

My family came rather late to the process. My grandmother married a cousin and at that time her family were still rural, living in a village about a dozen miles from Leeds. Sometime in the seventies she and her young husband were drawn to that expanding city, into the steelworks on the south side. She set about raising a growing family – ten were born but some were 'lost' – in the vast new brick acres of Hunslet. All over the North and Midlands the same thing was happening, the villages losing their young people, the towns staining the countryside around with raw cheap housing. They were insufficiently provided with medical, educational, and other facilities: their streets, inadequately cleansed and lighted, were being packed with families whose pattern of life was still to a large extent rural ... TB took a heavy toll.

My 'family history', insofar as I can discern it, was so similar to this account as to be almost identical. But in the Black Country, the working class never quite converted themselves into an urbanised folk – they were particularly resistant to that process, in fact. The miners from Baggeridge colliery loved nothing more than their Sunday morning walk to a far-off country pub in the fresh air and sunshine. They were all skilled anglers and poachers, and all kept dogs. Even though their forefathers had been industrial workers for 300 years, they little knew it themselves. The process had so dehumanised them that Mrs Thatcher's grand project seemed little different to all the other exploitation that had gone before.

The canniest among them may have known the grim statistics – the times when the average male life-expectancy in Dudley, for instance, had been 16 years. Little wonder then, that they did not lament the smuts and smog by day and the red glare of the furnaces by night, when they were gone. For many, a brief interlude opened up, when they could escape to the places from which their wretched ancestors had once been expelled in the first place – the real 'country' just over in the west – and the old places, the ancient ways.

6

Bella

> I advise anybody who is tempted at any time to venture into Black Magic, witchcraft, shamanism – call it what you will – to remember Charles Walton and his death, which was clearly the ghastly climax of a pagan rite.
>
> Detective Superintendent Robert Fabian[13]

The harvest in the village of Lower Quinton, Warwickshire, in 1944 had been miserably poor. After years of total war every sinew was strained to produce home-grown foodstuffs so as to minimise food imports. The holds of the merchant ships were needed for armaments and men fighting Britain's enemies overseas. The nation was mobilised as never before or since to 'dig for victory'. A Women's Land Army had been recruited in 1939 to provide extra labour for the vital campaign, and schoolchildren in rural areas were often temporarily pressed into service to help bring the harvest home. There was an Italian prisoner-of-war camp at Long Marston nearby. These prisoners sometimes laboured on the land, but once Italy changed sides in October 1943, they were at liberty to roam unsupervised or travel to nearby Stratford to see Shakespeare's plays, or films at the cinema. When the harvest came late, and the yields were poor. Some muttered that a local man was to blame, by the name of Charles Walton.

It was whispered that Walton had caught a toad, attached a tiny miniature plough to its legs – and set the creature loose to run through the local fields, blighting the crops and bringing sickness to the beasts. Some said that Walton was a 'cunning-man' or warlock, descended from Ann Tennant, a woman who had been murdered by one James Hayward (he was later confined to Broadmoor), in

September 1875 at Long Compton, quite nearby. Hayward had accosted the 79-year-old woman and stabbed her to death with a pitchfork under the delusion that she was a witch. It was an ancient tradition, that a witch must be killed in this way. Despite Hayward's diagnosis of insanity, rumours persisted that Tennant had indeed bewitched the lad, and that his claims of an extensive witch-coven were true. Seventy years later, the same fate was to befall her alleged descendant, Charles Walton.

Walton was said to have a strange power over animals, especially horses and fierce dogs, but also birds, which flew straight into his outstretched hand. In 1945, the affair was extraordinary, so much so that the respected Detective Superintendent Robert Fabian 'of the Yard' was immediately assigned to the case, the so-called 'Witchcraft Murder'. Witchcraft was still illegal in 1945, the Fraudulent Mediums Act, the last of the laws prohibiting it was finally repealed in 1951. There is much greater tolerance of paganism in the UK today than there was during the mid-twentieth century, and many more practitioners, but in those days the idea of ritual murder in an English country hamlet seemed preposterous. Warwickshire, however, had long traditions of witchcraft. The Rollright Stones, a group of megalithic monuments some miles from Meon Hill where Walton's mutilated body was discovered on a farm called 'the Firs', where he had been cutting hedges – was said to have been created by a witch's curse in pre-Christian times.

Meon Hill itself was haunted by a strange 'Black Dog' which appeared from nowhere and had no obvious owner. Fabian encountered this mysterious dog near to the murder scene, before hearing the legends. He thought it must belong to a small boy who appeared soon afterwards – but as soon as Fabian mentioned the dog, the lad fled in terror. In 1885, another boy had seen the black dog on three consecutive nights before a death in his family; the dog was a sort of psycho-pomp. On the final occasion the dog was accompanied by the apparition of a headless woman. The boy's name was Charles Walton. Sometime after Walton's murder, the body of a black dog was found hanging in a tree nearby. It didn't need Scotland Yard to divine that something very queer was going on in Lower Quinton.

Almost certainly, Walton's death was a perfectly ordinary homicide, requiring no resort to theories about Black Magic, paganism or witchcraft. But the long-standing interest in the case, and the fact that no murderer was ever apprehended – added to the disquiet which has lingered about Meon Hill and Lower

Quinton ever since. This chapter seeks to analyse this gruesome case – and an equally grim unsolved murder in the neighbouring county of Worcestershire a few years before. It could well be that these murders foreshadowed an 'unsettledness' which has disturbed our culture in the post-war era – intimations of the resurgence of genuine spiritual forces of a quite disturbing nature.

It does seem remarkable that this infamous case remains unsolved to this day, because Walton's employer, Alfred Potter, displayed behaviour following the homicide which clearly indicated his culpability in the matter. Potter managed the Firs on behalf of his father's company. Labour was in short supply due to the exigencies of wartime, and Potter was in the habit of employing local casual labourers to keep the farm in order. Walton was always keen to perform such duties, for his retirement pension of only ten shillings a week was derisory, especially so as he lived with his adopted niece, Edith, and was responsible for the heating and shopping bills, as well as the rent on the house which they shared.

Potter later claimed to the police that he often paid Walton for hours which he had not worked. This was the first of many discrepancies in his account. In fact, Potter was paying Walton (and two other employees) less than he claimed back from his father's company, pocketing the difference. Robert Fabian was aware of this, and also knew that Potter had been late in paying several employees, including Charles Walton. Following the murder, both surviving employees left Potter's service, probably realising his guilt.

On 14 February, Ash Wednesday 1945, Edith returned home from work about 4pm and was surprised to find her uncle not at home. Walton's habits were regular as clockwork, and so after a while she asked her neighbour Harry Beasley to assist in searching for him. They immediately went to the Firs and Alfred Potter joined them as they walked to where Potter claimed to have last seen Walton cutting hedges sometime between 12.00 and 12.30 pm. He gave at least three separate times at which he claimed to have seen Walton, in 'shirtsleeves', working on the hedge-cutting as he walked home from the College Arms pub. Before long, they came upon the body of Charles Walton.

The old man had been brutally murdered. He had been beaten about the head and face with his own walking stick, and there were injuries to his hands and arms where he had tried to fend off these blows. Then his throat had been slashed open with his own slash-hook – the implement used for cutting the hedges – which had been buried in his throat with great force. Finally, a pitchfork had been thrust into his neck so powerfully that it completely pinned his body to the ground – so as to keep his spirit from arising from the earth, perhaps?

To pagans these were unmistakeable signs of the so-called 'triple-death', but to the shocked general public it seemed like the work of a maniac. His pocket-watch was missing, which was invariably about his person. Strangely, this watch was discovered at his former home 15 years later, despite an extensive search at the time. His trousers had been unfastened and his flies undone. His shirt too, had been unfastened, and many people have claimed subsequently that a cross had been cut into Walton's chest, perhaps the source of the witchcraft theory as a motive. Despite Potter's claims to have seen him with his shirt-sleeves rolled-up, Walton was wearing a short-sleeved shirt, and was found with his jacket on. Whoever did the deed was possessed of an unnatural strength and violence, at least in those terrible final moments of Walton's life.

There are strong indications that Potter was the culprit, and it is just possible that he had some notion that Walton *was* indeed a witch or warlock of some kind. It transpired that Potter claimed he was on his way to remove the body of a dead heifer from a ditch just before he allegedly saw Walton working on the hedges. If Potter believed Walton to be the cause of the heifer's death, by casting the 'evil eye' on the animal, perhaps in revenge for delayed payment of wages due to him – then the ferocious brutality may be explained.

There were other persons under suspicion, however. George Higgins, Walton's 72-year-old close friend, was working nearby. Close friendships can turn into bitter enmity. Fabian though, thought Higgins was too elderly and frail to have inflicted such terrible injuries. Edgar Goode was a steady boyfriend of Edith, Walton's niece. Now, intra-familial sexual abuse was not much spoken of in the 1940s. No evidence points to anything untoward about Walton's relationship with his niece, and she passionately defended him from any accusation of his alleged relationship with witchcraft or sorcery in a 1971 TV interview on February 14, St Valentine's Day. Edith had been looked after by Walton from the age of three.

There can be no question that Potter was the prime suspect at the time – despite his trying to shift the blame onto the 'Fascist' Italian prisoners-of-war nearby. Their involvement was soon discounted. Potter even admitted that he had handled the murder weapons at the murder scene when the body was discovered, presumably to give him an alibi in case fingerprint evidence were found. No such forensic evidence was found, but faint bloodstains were subsequently discovered on the trousers he had been wearing on that day – despite careful cleaning by his wife.

But no conclusive evidence was found to charge, prosecute and convict Potter, so Fabian returned to Scotland Yard. In subsequent accounts, Fabian sensationalised the 'mystery' and even went so far as to allege that Walton had been abducted by a coven, then taken 12 miles distant to the 'Whispering Knights' – one of the monuments which together comprise the Rollright Stones – and ritually sacrificed in a 'Druid' ceremony on the sacred day of Ash Wednesday, when a victim's blood was shed onto the soil to ensure a fruitful harvest. Either Fabian was himself guilty of wicked misrepresentation and sensationalism, or he really did suspect that *something* extraordinary was going on at Meon Hill. He claimed that the local community had greeted his enquiries with a 'wall of silence'.

He was not alone in this intuition of hidden depths to this case. His colleague, a detective named Alec Spooner, visited the site of the murder on the anniversary for many years, in hopes of discovering ritualistic practices. The famous anthropologist and Egyptologist Margaret Murray was so sure that the locals were covering-up occult activities that she disguised herself as a visiting artist and stayed in the village for a week. She, too, felt certain that Walton's murder was inextricably bound up with a surviving English witch-religion.[14]

These persistent speculations have, needless to say, become a considerable nuisance to the local populace – most of whom have no living connections to these weird and violent events so long ago. Fabian's later claims of organised paganism were so risible that the Wiccan author Gerald B. Gardner dismissed them as complete fantasy. Fabian was not averse to playing up the salacious aspects of his career, and indeed became something of a TV celebrity in the 1950s. In 1954, his *London after Dark,* was an exposé of the Soho vice trade, for instance.

Margaret Murray was obsessed with the idea of the persistence of paganism in a covert form in rural communities. It is true that especially when she was in her 80s when she visited the area, she was a busybody who saw what she wanted to see, a confirmation of her deepest intuitions on the matter. But although both she and Fabian projected their own experiences and prejudices onto the case, Murray's hypothesis had something to it, perhaps, for recent archaeological evidence seems to support the idea of a surviving witch-cult in the western Midlands – which had endured since pre-Roman times. A woman's intuition should not be lightly dismissed, especially a woman of Murray's calibre. In 1945 she was the first to make a connection to a previous and quite local case, which she thought also bore the hallmarks of a ritualised pagan murder.

On 18 April 1943, Rob Hart, Bob Farmer, Tom Willetts and Fred Payne – all then schoolboys – trespassed onto the private estate of Lord Cobham at Hagley Hall in the Clent Hills of Worcestershire. They were looking for bird's eggs, a common enough hobby in those days, though any edible types would have been a supplement to their meagre wartime rations. The four came to a large hollowed-out tree – a Wych-Elm. Bob Farmer climbed up and peered inside the hollow trunk. He saw what he took to be the skull of an animal inside and reached down to pluck it out. To his horror, he realised it was human, with hair still adhering to it, and rows of teeth in the jaws. 'It's a mon's skull!', he shouted to his companions, and showed it to them before replacing it. The shocked boys were in a quandary about what to do next. They were trespassing, and poaching was a serious offence. Rather than reporting the incident, they swore to keep it a secret among themselves.

But Tom Willetts, the youngest of the boys was so disturbed by the find that he told his parents. When the police examined the tree, they found the skeletal remains of a young woman wedged in so tightly that the tree had to be felled to remove them. Nearby, some distance from the tree, her left hand had been detached and buried separately. A piece of expensive taffeta cloth had been stuffed into her mouth, presumably to prevent her screams from being heard and to suffocate her. Forensic examination suggested that she had been placed in the tree before *rigor mortis* had set in, perhaps even while still alive. A shoe, some clothing and a gold ring were also recovered.

The date of her death was estimated as approximately October 1941. The affair was made even more mysterious when in 1944 graffiti began to appear in Birmingham which asked, 'Who put Bella in the Wych-Elm – Hagley Wood?' or 'Who put Luebella in the Wych-Elm?' Similar graffiti appears sporadically to this day – an example has been daubed on the Hagley Monument on the estate itself. Bella's skeleton vanished, along with the original autopsy report, and neither have yet come to light.

Who Put Bella in the Wych Elm?

Wych Elm Bole.

Margaret Murray, while she was obsessing about the Charles Walton affair, pointed out that there may well have been a pagan ritualistic element to this other murder too. The detached left hand for instance; the 'left-hand path', or *Vamachara*, represented Black Magic in the Tantric tradition. Murray noted that there were also powerful magical traditions in our own culture concerning severed hands, the so-called 'hand o' glory' for example. Although Tantric practitioners were not exactly common in 1940s Worcestershire, 'gypsies', who derived from India originally, were.

Murray suggested that the poor woman may have transgressed the strict mores of gypsy culture – and paid with her life. This author sees nothing inherently implausible about such a theory. In native Celtic culture entombment in a tree while still alive was a known punishment for treachery. Owain Glyndwr, the 15th-century Welsh insurgent, executed a relative who attempted to assassinate him in this way, for instance.

In 1941, there was ample opportunity for treacherous activities, especially espionage by enemy powers. There were some very high-value targets in the vicinity. Haile Selassie, the exiled emperor of Ethiopia, lived in nearby Broome throughout the war years. Charles de Gaulle's Free French officers were based in Ribbesford near Bewdley following the 1940 debacle, and he was often in the neighbourhood. Winston Churchill himself, so it was claimed by locals, was often to be found isolating himself on the Hagley Hall estate during the period of maximum crisis, and his protection officers, who worked a shift system, were sometimes seen in the Lyttelton Arms pub nearby. But these were not the only targets. The key industrial regions of the Black Country, Birmingham, and secret new industrial sites in the Worcestershire countryside were of special interest to the Nazi spy-network, the *Abwehr*.

In January 1941 a Nazi spy, Joseph Jakobs, parachuted into England but turned his ankle on landing and was soon captured by the Home Guard. When he was interrogated by British counter-intelligence he was presented with a photograph of a woman he had on him. Jakobs claimed that she was his lover, and fellow Nazi agent, Clara Bauerle. Bauerle was supposed to have parachuted into England in spring 1941 and was expected to contact Jakobs through her handlers. Bauerle was said to have toured pre-war Britain as a cabaret artiste, and to have become so familiar with Birmingham and the Black Country that she had picked up the distinctive local accent. Bauerle sounds superficially similar to 'Bella'.

126

Jakobs was trying to lead the British intelligence officers on a false trail to waste valuable time and resources and his ploy was soon discovered. His photograph of Bauerle was actually a postcard which was widely available in Germany. Clara had been something of a minor movie star in Germany in the 1930s and a successful cabaret singer. She certainly never parachuted into England and died in Berlin on 16 December 1942 of a lung disease. Jakobs became the last person to be executed at the Tower of London, by firing-squad on 15 August 1941. Rumours persisted, however, that there was some truth in Jakobs's claims, but 'Bella' would have been five feet tall or thereabouts, whereas Bauerle was almost six feet in height. The distinctive dental pattern of the skull bore no resemblance to Clara's either. This, however, was not the only espionage theory.

In 1953 a lady named Una Mossop of Claverley in Shropshire claimed that her deceased ex-husband, Jack, had made a confession of his involvement in the murder prior to his death in a Stafford asylum. He claimed that he had met up with a Dutchman called van Ralt, and they had taken a woman for a drink in the Lyttelton Arms pub in Hagley. This lady had become drunk (or she was possibly drugged by van Ralt) and he asked Jack to help take her to the tree in the wood, where they placed her inside 'to sober her up'.

Jack said that van Ralt was a member of a German spy-ring, and that unwittingly he had become a party to the woman's murder because 'she knew too much'. Subsequently many people have speculated that she was Clarabella Dronkers, wife of another Dutchman and a Nazi spy, Johannes Dronkers. In fact, no such 'Clarabella' ever existed. Dronkers wrote a letter to his real wife before he was executed at Wandsworth prison in 1942, which still exists.

Jack Mossop became increasingly disturbed by the incident (whether real or imagined); he would wake up screaming, after having nightmares about the trapped woman entombed in the tree-trunk. He was certified insane and sent to the asylum where he later died. Interesting though this story is, the account does not tally with the discoveries made by the police – nothing was said about the detached hand, for instance. For this reason, more prosaic explanations seem preferable.

For instance, a Birmingham prostitute who regularly worked the Hagley Road area claimed to the police that a girl called Bella had gone missing in the blackout during the autumn of 1941, precisely when the murder took place. Such work, taking place at night and in semi-secrecy, has always been fraught with dangers. A barmaid at the Chequers pub in Stourbridge also disappeared without trace at this time.

But like the Charles Walton case, no conclusive answers have ever been forthcoming, despite ongoing speculation. Books, plays and even an opera have been written about the Hagley Wood murder, but of all the theories the one which has been most blithely dismissed is actually the one which seems to me to have most credibility – the Margaret Murray hypothesis. If there is a spiritual world, as she believed, I hope she will forgive me if I put some flesh on the bones of this by recapitulating her general argument – and supporting it with new evidence – which, had it been available in her time, may well have supported her incipient theory.

Modern witchcraft has its origins in the mood of Romanticism and anti-clericalism which gripped France during the 1860s, and in particular a work by Jules Michelet entitled *La Sorcière* (1862). In this book, Michelet claimed 'the provisional death of Christianity'. This stance, he thought, was vindicated by what he took to be the underground survival of the witch-cult, which had kept alive the flame of liberty, passion, and 'the old religion' all through the dark age which had ensued with the dominance of the Roman Catholic Church. Christianity was presented as the cornerstone of the *ancien regime*, which legitimised the oppression and persecution of a supposedly 'democratic' social structure that had gone before. Although in historical terms it was arrant nonsense, the book was a great success. One of Michelet's admirers was an American scholar and writer called Charles Leland. A revolutionary by nature, Leland took part in the 1848 uprising in Paris as a student radical.

Following military service in the American Civil War, Leland toured Europe and it was in Italy that he met a peasant woman, Maddalena, who was a local soothsayer. So convinced was he of her extraordinary psychic powers that he pressed her to reveal details of what he believed to be a secret pagan organisation which underlay conventional Italian society. Eventually, Maddalena presented Leland with hand-written offerings something along these lines. Italy is the 'home' of the Goddess, as it were.

In the Alban Hills outside Rome at Nemi, 'Diana's Mirror' a small volcanic crater-lake was the centre of the worship of Diana Nemorensis, 'Diana of the Wood' – the ancient goddess of the hunt. This goddess was, according to Maddalena, something much more powerful and significant – she was, in fact, *the* primordial deity, a concept which subverted the entire edifice of patriarchal religion.

In 1899, Leland published Maddalena's revelations and his own speculative interpretation of them as a book called *Aradia or the Gospel of the Witches*, which soon attracted a cult readership. In fact, this 'gospel' was a melange of material Maddalena had produced in the full knowledge of Leland's predilections, combining Michelet's theories and Leland's own romantic interpretation of occult history. But two strands had been introduced which had a profound influence on modern witchcraft and paganism.

The most important, perhaps, was the elevation of the female principle as the ultimate creative force in the universe, Diana, the goddess to whom the peasantry of all medieval Europe had allegedly secretly adhered. The attraction of such an idea to a new generation of radical feminists may be imagined.

The other strand was a profound anti-clericalism, which presented Christianity as the enemy of 'true' religion – a 'heresy' in itself, inverting the previous order. Diana was alleged to have mated with her brother, Lucifer, to produce a daughter, the 'Aradia' of the title – whom she had sent to liberate humanity from the wicked Christ-god. Such notions were to culminate in the Thelemic religion of Aleister Crowley, and Anton LaVey's Church of Satan in the 20th century.

They were not only entirely spurious, but also disregarded the fact that medieval witchcraft, insofar as it had ever really existed, tended to ape the Church and its rituals, rather than denigrating them. But dangerous and wrong-headed ideas find their time just like any others, and as a new century dawned, many people were eager to explore alternative and radical belief systems, including Margaret Murray.

Murray aspired to be exemplary throughout her long life (1863-1963). She became an Egyptologist – the first woman to dissect a mummy, for example, and the first to lecture in archaeology in Britain, at University College London, and was one of the first female anthropologists. She had always had a fascination for the exotic and mystic, and while visiting Glastonbury in Somerset she had the epiphany that the witch-cult, so-called, was actually the remnant of a primordial fertility religion which long preceded Christianity.

According to this insight, the 'natural' religion of Old Europe had been based on sexual polarity, just as many ancient oriental religions, such as Tantrism, still promulgate. Murray's ideas, though superficially similar to Leland's, are somewhat more sophisticated in that they were at least evidence-based to some extent. Murray studied trial documents from the Inquisition which revealed some of the primary elements of medieval European witchcraft. She concurred that the principal goddess-form of the cult had indeed been Diana, but that a male consort, 'the horned god' or 'the Devil' had also been an indispensable participant in the rites. This 'god' she took to be a man dressed up in animal-skins of horned beasts such as goats. The key to the practices was the harnessing of the sexual energy of the two principal participants, male and female.

These ideas, with their frisson of sexual titillation, radical mysticism and bearing the imprimatur of apparently respectable scholarship, began to permeate the consciousness of a great many people who wanted to be entertained as well as informed. Gradually, Murray's ideas fell into considerable disrepute because she chose to concentrate on the entertainment aspect, abandoning all pretence of serious scholarship. But for all that, her intuitions, and the general tendency of her thinking were not quite as wide of the mark as modern critics sometimes claim.

Central to Murray's thesis of the survival of the witch-cult was the notion that secretive practices had continued in rural areas throughout the medieval period with the full knowledge of the Catholic Church. This was not to say that the practices were condoned – merely grudgingly tolerated. The Protestant Reformation, however, was a reversion to what Robert Graves called the more masculine religion of the 'thunder-god'. Sexual sin came to be seen as an especially female province from which all other wickedness followed.

Witchcraft was, therefore, the enemy of humankind – an evil to be rooted out. This radical change in consciousness lay behind the commissions of such men as Matthew Hopkins (1620-1647), who appointed himself as the 'Witchfinder General' during the civil-war years. He and his colleague John Stearne trumped up charges against hundreds of alleged witches, virtually all of whom were executed.

But when the puritan revolution subsided, an atmosphere of greater sexual freedom and tolerance returned with the restored King Charles II, who was himself a notorious rake and libertine. He begot so many illegitimate children that he became known by wits as the 'father of his nation'. The restoration of the supremacy of the Church of England by the Clarendon Code was merely notional. As the agricultural and industrial revolutions transformed England during the eighteenth century, the new working class increasingly turned to Methodist and other non-conformist chapels. But in the hellish and inhuman slavery of the worst industrial slums, little religious instruction or ministry was to be had, often there were, as yet, no parishes. In such places, ancient folk-superstitions were rife.

Those who filled the vacuum left by religion were by no means sophisticated practitioners of magic, but this was not necessary. The function of these people, mostly women, was to provide practical solutions to everyday problems. They could charm away warts, prepare love-potions, divine the sex of an unborn child, act as a midwife (or layer-out), predict the weather for the harvest, alleviate toothache – but most importantly, they could provide defence against malevolent witchcraft directed against a person by casting a counter-spell, so-called 'Reversal Magic'.

The process of industrialisation introduced conditions which had generally coarsened the manners of the English working class, such that they have never really recovered. So, I would argue that there was definitely the potential for a more vulgar type of 'craft' among the 'lower orders', and that the British ruling class – including the established Church – looked the other way, as with slavery.

But Murray's thesis argued for a much deeper, primordial connection, to a pre-Christian goddess-worshipping cult, bound by a secretive covenant. For many scholars, such speculations were just that. Murray's ideas have been repudiated by academics since her death, and her intuitions rather cruelly denigrated. This seems particularly unfair on her, since the poet Robert Graves (1895-1985), whose ideas about such matters were similar in essence to hers,[15] is rightly celebrated for his genius. Murray's hunch that the cult was still a living active reality in the mid-20th century West Midlands would be contingent upon evidence of a well-established culture of pagan goddess-worship in the area beforehand. If such evidence could be discovered, the idea of pagan ritual murder in Warwickshire and Worcestershire would not then seem so far-fetched.

In 2008 an Oxford archaeologist, Stephen J. Yeates, published a remarkable book called *The Tribe of Witches: The Religion of the Dobunni and Hwicce* and the next year saw a follow-up study, *A Dreaming for the Witches*. Yeates's theories are contentious, but there is no disputing their basis in genuine and thorough archaeological research. The book was an extension of his doctoral research studies at Oxford where he was supervised by the famous Sir Barry Cunliffe. In essence, his thesis is that a pre-Christian goddess, Cuda, was worshipped as a personification of the entire tribal landscape, especially the valleys of the Severn and the Wye, but also the Cotswolds, which region is still named after her.

It is perhaps significant that 'Godda', the goddess of the pagan
Mercians to the north not only sounds similar – but that an
entire region, *Goddeu,* approximating to modern Shropshire,
was similarly named in her honour. This region had a special
magical significance. The original meaning of the word *Hwicce* is
disputed. Professor Sims-Williams in his *Religion and Literature
in Western England 600-800* thought it may be a kind of mocking
self-tribute meaning 'the cowardly ones'. The *Dobunni* probably
meant something like 'the victorious ones' so that might be the
origin of such a 'joke'.

Much more likely, however, is that it meant a 'meal-ark' –
that is the large tub or trough from which animals were
fed. Viewed from the surrounding high ground such as the
Cotswolds or Malvern Hills, there is a clear impression of such
a vessel, which the inhabitants perceived as a 'sacred vessel' or
Holy Grail.

This area, and the sacred deified rivers which flowed through
it were for many centuries some of the most productive
agricultural areas in all Britain, lush and rich, those rivers
brimming over with fish. This abundance was the blessing
of the Lady Cuda, the *Matribus et Genioloci* 'the mother
goddess and the genius of (this) place'. The name of the tribe
is pronounced 'witch-a' and is related to the Anglo-Saxon
word 'witch'. It survives all over Worcestershire, at Wyche in
the Malvern Hills, Wychavon, Wychbold, Wychenford and, of
course at Wychbury Hill near to where 'Bella' was discovered
in the Wych-Elm. The northern frontier of the tribe, in fact,
was coincidentally in the neighbourhood of both of the murders
discussed in this chapter.

A few years before the book came out, I was obsessed with
exactly the same idea, and was considering writing an historical
novel which included just such a goddess. I was astonished when I
came across Yeates's book, which seemed to me a sort of magical
confirmation of all I had already begun to suspect. But what was
the nature of this deity?

We saw earlier on how the megalithic monuments served
as a means for focusing the tribal consciousness onto the
landscape as a whole. For these ancient folk, every tree, rock,
knoll, spring and river was a living being, inspirited and sacred.
Natural phenomena were studied closely, for they revealed
the 'signature' of the gods, and their 'behaviour' suggested the
divine intent. Of all such phenomena water was of supreme

import. On it, human and animal life and the production of crops ultimately depended.

Almost all tribal boundaries were marked-out by water-courses or sources. The rich alluvial soils of the Severn, Avon and Wye ensured prosperity for the Dobunni tribe which was the envy of their more pastoral and warlike northern neighbours – the Cornovii of Staffordshire, Shropshire and Cheshire. But the land of the 'sacred vessel' was home to another spectacular demonstration of the power of the natural deities. One of the 'Wonders of Britain' was the Severn bore, a tidal surge which acts as a shock wave, funnelling water upstream, particularly on new and full moons at the equinoxes. The wave moves rapidly inland, rising to a height of over nine feet. The symbolism associated with the spectacular display was yet another powerful cultural bond which set the 'people of the sacred vessel' apart, marking them as a 'chosen' folk of the goddess.

This cult of a sacred goddess endured for many centuries, and there is no reason to suspect that it was eradicated by the Roman intrusion, which lasted a mere 400 years, and precariously during much of that time. Indeed, at Bath, also within the tribal region, *Sulis*, a Celtic goddess of the thermal springs there, was deliberately equated with their own equivalent goddess, Minerva. The Romans named the place after her, 'Aquae Sulis'.

All over the Cotswolds, stone reliefs of the goddess have been excavated, including some depicting her in a triple form, much like the Germanic *Norns*, the three divine aspects which inspired Shakespeare's 'weird sisters' in his play *Macbeth* for instance. Yeates proposes that not only did this cult survive the Roman occupation virtually intact – but more remarkably that there had 'not only been a major survival of British people but that there was also an influx of Germanic people … who may have held senior positions in society, who were trying to comprehend the native religion within their own traditions.'

This 'influx of Germanic people' came in the form of the *Hwicce* tribe. Unfortunately, we are in the dark about the origins of this strange people. It has been postulated that they were related in some way to the *Gewisse*, a tribe who had been settled as mercenaries to protect the valley of the upper Thames shortly after the final Roman withdrawal. As professional warriors they were in a strong position to consolidate and then extend their territory, which eventually became the foremost Anglo-Saxon kingdom of Wessex. The Hwicce may have been a small war-band occupying the forest still named after them – Wychwood in Oxfordshire. By AD 577 the king of the West-Saxon confederacy, Ceawlin, and his son Cuthwine, were poised to invade the rich lands of the Dobunni.

A decisive battle was fought at Hinton Hill in Gloucestershire, one of the many ancient hill-forts which overlook the region. The Battle of Dyrham or Deorham ended in disaster for the Romano-Britons, and their three kings, Condidan, Conmail and Farinmail were all killed, presumably trapped inside the hill-fort or slain in a desperate rout. These 'kings' were, in fact, the last descendants of the Roman civic governors of Aquae Sulis (Bath), Glevum (Gloucester) and Corinium Dobunnorum (Cirencester) – the tribal capital. Such meagre forces as they could have mustered would have been poorly trained and equipped militia, no match for the Germanic warriors.

The result of this easy win was, perhaps, a compromise – which may explain how the cult of the goddess was transferred to the incoming Germanic aristocracy virtually intact. The idea that the Romano-British aristocracy was simply annihilated but the lower classes spared is supported by folklore from the northern frontier of the region. The Dobunni divided their kingdom into two sub-kingdoms, one ruled from Gloucester, the other from Worcester.

The most outlying northern tribe, called the *Husmerae*, presumably retired to Wychbury hill-fort to make a stand, as their southern comrades had done at Hinton hill-fort. Legend implies that the result was the same and tells of a fierce battle at Wychbury with many fatalities – including 28 Germanic warriors who were allegedly buried under yew-trees there.

These theories are speculative, admittedly, but in essence what we may infer is that a goddess or 'witch' cult survived the Roman imperial colonisation, was 'culturally appropriated' by an incoming Germanic aristocracy and endured into the Christian era *at least*. By the 8th century, the name of the goddess, Cuda, had become a personal name, implying that she had degenerated into a diminutive deity, folk-superstition, or fairy-tale character. But the obdurate survival of such a cult throughout the centuries and millennia must beg the question – could it have persisted into the present day?

Might the strange goings-on at Hagley Wood and Meon Hill be somehow related to an ancient religion so recondite as to be impenetrable to all outside investigation – predicated upon terror of the direst consequences should its secrets be revealed? It is not implausible, for the loving goddess of creation is also

> ... a goddess of death and regeneration. She represented the full cycle of the life continuum. Representations of death goddesses imbued with the promise of new life remind us that the cycle was a totality. They are represented in both the prehistoric and the early historical eras. In the Greek Cycladic Islands were found stiff, nude death figures ... and in the Sumerian poem 'Descent of Inanna' the underworld goddess Ereshkigal, groans in childbirth as she brings forth life out of death ... In Old Europe and Old Anatolia, the goddess of death and regeneration is often depicted as a bird of prey, as a stiff, bone-coloured nude, or as a poisonous snake. The bird and snake are complimentary in death and regeneration as well as in life and nurturing.[16]

7

Sabrina Fair

There is a gentle Nymph not far from hence,
That with moist curb sways the smooth Severn stream,
Sabrina is her name, a Virgin pure,
Whilom she was the daughter of Locrine,
That had the Scepter from his father Brute.
The guiltless damsel flying the mad pursuit
of her enraged stepdam Gwendolen,
Commended her innocence to the flood
That stay'd her flight with his cross-flowing course,
The water Nymphs that in the bottom played,
Held up their pearled wrists and took her in...
And underwent a quick immortal change
Made Goddess of the River, still she retains
Her maid'n gentleness, and oft at Eve
Visits the herds along the twilight meadows...
The clasping charm, and thaw the numbing spell,
If she be right invok't in warbled Song,
For maid'nhood she loves and will be swift
To aid a Virgin, such as was her self
In hard besetting need, this I will try
And add the power of some adjuring verse.

John Milton, 'Comus' (1637)

A long time it has been now since I first came here to Redstone, to make my chapel in the sandstone cave by the river, gently – sometimes fiercely, flowing by. The Rector of Martley gave me my commission, for which I will ever thank him. I know not what became of him, and since the Interdict no news comes which is not evil. May our Lord bless and protect him! For a broken-hearted man such as I had sore need of such a place, a sinful wretch as I once was – still am, perhaps? I *thought* I had become wiser, more gracious, humbler over the last quarter-century, but in my final years I have come to see how the serpent is ever lurking. Let me, therefore, take a rest from my usual clerk's labour (my solitary skill) – and recount how I colluded in the great lie.

> Listen where thou art setting
> Under the glassy, cool, translucence
> In twisted braids of lilies knitting
> The loose train of thy amber-dropping hair
> Listen for dear honour's sake
> Goddess of the silver lake,
> Listen and save.

The simple folk hereabouts call me 'Father', though I am not ordained. I sent many folk away at first, for a clerk or lay man as I am has no proper authority, though he *may* bless, and he *may* read book. 'Begone!' I implored them, 'I am but a *lay* man', and that is what they called me – 'Layamon'. I thought they did so in mockery – till I learned of their utter simplicity. In truth, I could not then forbear company, and had buried myself in my books to hide from God. Despite my reluctance, and as it transpired to my eventual great joy, still they kept coming. Not only my own local 'flock', oak-barkers, trow-men and charcoal-burners, but also those from far-beyond who drive the real flocks – Welshmen, drovers, London-bound. All kneel at my jetty, and the men and beasts are blessed as they wait for the ferry. After five years I learned that they thought me a 'holy man', for no accident or misfortune had ever befallen them during the prolonged and complicated process of the crossing. I should add that I am *not* holy by any means – far from it – merely lucky so far.

The Welshmen are actually a great blessing to me, offering more than just alms. The 'Captains' of the drover-bands speak London English, and tell me such tales! When once they knew I sought stories of that mighty Arthur, their hero-king – there was nothing these stalwart men would not do for me, and with every droving my need for parchment and tallow-candles increased so as to record their stories, which they readily supplied. In summer, I write outside in the mornings, for the light (if it be not damp and overcast), and in winter, lit by a candle-lantern, I sit beside the hearth to do what work I can. With the exception of Christmas, in the winter months my visitors are rare enough. In these grim and evil times I dread to see a lonely woman on the track to my cave. It usually means bad tidings, and on this chilly autumn day, so it proved, as I spied Maggie, the wood-collier's wife, wending her way, a full wicker-basket dangling on her arm.

'A good morning to you Father!', she shouts up.

'Dunna' fuss yerself Maggie! Stay down, and I'll shuffle below t'ya!'

Much cussing, panting and grunting supervened. Maggie steadied me on the slope, before looking me over, like a cowman in November.

'I know, I know!' says I.

'Don't croak just yet Father. I bring gifts! Charcoal, four gooseberry and honey tartlets, a flagon of gooseberry spirit, three big tallow-candles, and a fidget pie, your favourite!'

Such lavish offerings after Michaelmas could bode naught but ill, it seemed to me, and I saw Maggie's frame looked gaunt, and said as much.

'You look to me as if you could stand a meal yourself my dear! Come, sit beside me on the jetty now.'

We sat on either side of my writing trestle.

'Ah! You know my weaknesses my Maggie! I watched for the blackbirds on my gooseberry patch, but do you know – the turtle doves swooped down and had the lot! All gone, so I bless you for these!'

So saying, I took a bite into the exquisite pastry, savouring the sour-sweet filling. I looked at my companion and thought how much I had sacrificed to lack such a wife all these lonely years. I looked her up and down as I brushed the pastry-crumbs from my tunic.

'I think you have some trouble Mag. Out with it then, and we'll put the matter before God!'

My instinct proved correct – my visitors are more often troubled than not – but I never expected the torrent of tears and the cries of anguish which now ensued. Maggie was a tough woman, but I saw she was broken in spirit. When the waves of emotion diminished somewhat, she apprised me of the reason of her distress.

'It's Wal Father! I must take the boys and leave him, for he is not the man I once knew! He is a stranger to me now, cold, drunken, cruel, and I truly fear – either mad or possessed by a demon. He spends all his time at the clamps, sitting staring at her grave. He sleeps in the hut and never comes home to the coppice. Any food I take for him he leaves for his drinking cronies. He swears *she* has come to haunt him! I have done everything a loving wife *could* do, but he only pushes me further away, and the boys, it is as if they no longer exist for him. He keeps company with all the scum of the forest, but his own wife and children he has deserted. Well, two can play at that game! I shall go away to Hugh, my brother's, and the twins with me. We have no family life, no marriage! I repudiate him, do you hear! Father, what am I to do?'

At this, the sobbing and convulsions resumed – I had underestimated the case, this was very serious.

'Come, come, Maggie, calm down! I think it is in your mind that you can dissolve the marriage, in the old woodland way – but you cannot! I cannot undo the bond between a man and wife. The fact that I am not a real priest does not mean the ceremony was invalid. It is a sacrament before God, who sees all. I cannot sanction a separation or a divorce, and I know you cannot truly want that.'

She looked hurt but regained her composure. I gave a long-drawn-out sigh before continuing.

'How long has it been now Maggie, two years?'

She nodded, but I could see that for her, those two years must now seem more like two decades.

'Just over two years, aye Father. How cruel a world that he, of all people, should have found her, tangled up in branches swept down by the flood. He saw her lovely amber hair streaming like water weeds, and knew her instantly. She was face-up, staring at him, he said. He carried her to the clamps to bury her – so that the boys and I would be spared the sight of – well, you know.'

I remembered it all only too well. How cruel a world, indeed.

I sent Maggie on her way with my promise of prayers, and a plan to visit her at the coppice in a few days. I'd have to take the coracle. The waters around Blackstone are treacherous – but my knees can't stand the walk on the rough tracks. Then, I would venture out to the charcoal clamps to try to speak with Walter – I felt responsible in a way. It was I who married them, then 'twas I baptised the lass, the old way, in the river. And it was also I who gave her her name, in a strange way – a name not then known around these parts – the Latin form of the name, Hafren or Severna – 'Sabrina'. A bitter irony, to be sure. It seems like yesterday she was born, but it was eighteen winters back now – when even my crippled body was yet healthy.

Every Christmas, Easter and Whitsun, the forest-folk gather around my chapel in the sandstone-rock to take broken bread

and elderberry wine from a pewter chalice I had as a gift from the
Rector. Nowadays, thanks to the Interdict, some quite respectable
types come to kneel before me, but it was not so back then – my
only congregation were woodlanders or river-folk. Mine was the
only communion they knew, and that was but three times annually.
But there was another gathering, where I neither read book or
offered the sacraments, May-day. This was the feast of the old
river-goddess, a raucous revel, with much drinking, wrestling, and
dancing well into the night.

But before the fire died down, and the young couples sloped
off into the woods, I had my other duty to perform – as a *scop* or
storyteller. My poetry I keep to myself, but the telling of tales comes
naturally to me, especially when my speech thickens a little from
drink. Indeed, the common people love nothing more than to see
their 'holy man' in his cups! The river-folk love to hear the story of
the goddess, the one they call Severna, (or the Welshry, 'Hafren'). I
had come to that point in my *Chronicle of Britain* as I call it (rather
grandly) – where the kinsfolk of Brutus the Trojan have divided the
island of Britain between them. So on that evening, I told the legend
of the goddess, Sabrina, as I called her, to the gathering hard by the
jetty. Soon, there was a respectful hush, so that only the fire-crackle
could be heard beside my voice.

'In Britain, long, long ago … beyond the mists of twice a
thousand years, the heirs of Brutus the Trojan divided the island
between them. Three great and powerful kings there were, called
Locrine, Albanactus, and Camber. Locrine took that portion we
know as England, Albanactus took Scotland for his own, and
Camber's share was Wales. All were fiercely proud of their own
nations, and always ready to fight to defend their territories.
But from a far-distant land overseas came a great army from the
east – Huns in a vast fleet of ships so numerous that they could
not all be contained in the wide estuary of the Humber, which is
still named after them. These barbarians intended to conquer the
whole island – as Brutus the Trojan had done. Even though they
were deadly rivals in normal times, the descendants of Brutus
could not allow the island to fall to the invaders, otherwise, the
great prophesy of the Goddess Diana – that the Trojan colony
in Britain, *Nova Troia*, would become the greatest city in the
world, and the centre of a mighty empire – would never come
to pass.'

I took a good swig of cider and saw that my bemused audience
were well-settled now.

'All the men of Britain now marched against the invaders. From the south, Locrine and Camber, their forces combined, came against the Huns who stood close-by their fleet. From the north, brave Albanactus pressed the Huns onto the northern bank of the Humber, so that they were forced to divide their forces. The battle raged for three days and nights, until the Britons broke in upon the Huns' ships and fired them, so that all were burned. The Huns panicked and jumped into the water where they all drowned – all that is, save one survivor.

Hidden beneath her chariot, a Hun princess, the most beautiful woman in all the world, lay whimpering in fear. She was dragged forth to Locrine, and the men of Loegria, his realm, in their battle-wrath, demanded that she be cast into the water beside her slain people. Locrine enquired of her name, and she replied that she was Estreldis, daughter of the Hun king. As soon as Locrine saw this vision of loveliness, he was bewitched by her raven-black hair and her dark-brown slanted eyes.

Instantly, his heart melted, and all his reason left him. Before all the warriors of Britain, he swore that Estreldis was to be his personal trophy from the battle – and that he would make her his bride, and his queen. But Locrine was already betrothed – to Gwendolyn, daughter of the Duke of Cornwall. The duke demanded that the match be honoured, and Estreldis be sent back to her own country. Camber and Albanactus agreed, and it was clear that Locrine must repudiate his beloved – or fight another bloody war against his own kinsmen.'

The sun was well-down now, and the fire roaring as the young couples snuggled together for warmth.

'Locrine was heartbroken, for his love for Estreldis was reciprocated. So, he made a show of sending the princess away by sea in a grand ship. But the veiled lady who went aboard was not Estreldis, only an imposter. So infatuated was the king, that he had underground chambers constructed in secret beneath the royal palace; the labourers were put to death when all was completed. Here, Estreldis was hidden away, even after Gwendolyn of Cornwall arrived to take up residence as Locrine's new queen.

Soon, a son, called Madan, was born to Gwendolyn, and so the line of Brutus was secured – but in her underground network of chambers, Estreldis was also with child. A daughter was secretly born to her, Sabrina, a girl as fair and noble as ever there was. Many were the times when Gwendolyn heard the cry of a new-born, but when she went to nurse her son found him sleeping sound, but still, she suspected nothing.

One day, after many years of this deception, a breathless messenger arrived at the palace. Corineus of Cornwall, Gwendolyn's father, was dead. Locrine was ecstatic, for, at last, he was free to repudiate Gwendolyn and send her back to her own folk in Cornwall. To her joy, Estreldis was released from her underground confinement, and her bonny daughter saw full daylight for the first time. But the Cornish race are quick to anger, and great fighters. Gwendolyn's humiliation demanded swift and merciless revenge, so they gathered a huge army.

The enraged Cornishmen stormed Locrine's palace and killed him. Gwendolyn quickly located Estreldis and executed her. But what to do about her daughter, Sabrina? It was clear that Madan must succeed to the throne, and there could be no rivals – the beautiful young girl, with her hair the colour of Baltic amber, must also die.

So, she was taken down to the banks of this very river here and offered-up as a virgin sacrifice to the waters. Her hands and feet were bound, and she sank into the depths – but be of good cheer – for the wise river nymphs, knowing of her innocence and purity, were not so cruel as to accept such a wicked offering. Instead, they released her bonds, and revived her, bestowing immortal life upon her – so that she became the *living goddess* of the Severn stream, which still bears her name – Sabrina, fairest, purest maiden, and most blessed! That is all there is to tell.'

Among my audience that night were Walter and Maggie, then lately married. They were so young and happy then, in those blissful times before wicked King John succeeded his glorious brother, Richard the Lion-hearted – the days before the world turned sour. They were quite tipsy, truth to be told, but such was the custom, and I myself was by no means unimpaired. It was Maggie that asked me to repeat the name. She had never heard such a pretty name for a girl-child, she said, and tried it on her tongue as if to savour it:

'Sabrina, Sabrina! Father, our minds are made up! We plan to make a baby this very night, and if it should be a little girl, we are resolved to name her Sabrina – for we are, after all, people of the river, so it is only fitting!'

I said I approved and wished them all good luck in their enterprise – for at least they were man and wife, unlike so many couples that had already taken their way into the trees. And so, the following February, with the hope of spring in the air, 'Sabby', as they called her, was born, and grew into a maiden right handsome to behold.

Now I came to think of it, I had missed Wal and Maggie last Whitsun, and Easter, and at Christmas Maggie came with the boys, but not Walter. A father's grieving for a daughter lasts his whole life thereafter – but I considered him a steady man, with a good and kind heart. Maggie's account of his decline just did not ring true for me, for all knew Wal and loved him in this neck of the woods. As I prayed for the family, I asked the Lord to show me a sign, to offer me some clue as to how I may soothe his troubled soul.

That night I dreamed an odd dream. In the dream it was Christmas day, and I was preaching the gospel. The gathering formed into line to approach for the sacraments, and as the communicants knelt down, I recognised each one in turn. I was surprised to see Sabby there among them, and as I looked deep into her eyes, I heard her voice in my head saying: 'Father Layamon, take heed. My father has lost his faith – be careful lest *you* lose your own!' Then, I awoke in an instant, with my cat pawing me for a tidbit, but I was strangely disturbed, for the dead girl seemed so insistent, and so *alive* and real. I felt this was in answer to my plea to God, and I was unsettled all the following day – for I planned my pastoral visit to Walter the day after that.

I recalled some of the talk about the tragedy at the time, and it was not too hard to divine the root of Walter's self-hatred – guilt. There comes that time for every doting father – when he knows his little damsel's affections have wandered to another. Such a time came for Walter, when a young Welshman chanced upon Sabby stacking the billets for the clamps, which she carried in wicker baskets that she emptied next to the piles of turves. She also brought a pasty for her father's midday meal – but he was busy haggling with an iron-factor on the riverbank.

As soon as he saw her, the dark-haired lad from the mountains was smitten – and her eye-beam returned his gaze, until a smile and a pink-blush to her cheeks showed forth her love more than any words could ever do. The lad spoke passable English too, and was well-educated, from a prosperous family. It was his first visit to England. In days, his drovers' band pressed on to London, but the lad promised solemnly that when they passed nearby on the return journey, he would seek-out Sabby again, and he was as good as his word. His visit to the great city had emboldened him considerably, and he sought out Walter and asked for his daughter's hand. She was sixteen now, of an age, and clearly willing – she swore that she loved young Owain so, that she would follow him to Jerusalem if he commanded her.

Walter was impressed by the young man's ardour but knowing young Welshmen as he did. this was only to be expected. He politely refused the suitor's proposal, saying that he already had a match in mind for Sabrina – one of her cousins in Gloucestershire had expressed his interest, and he had as good as accepted. This was the first the young girl had ever heard of such a plan. She let out a howl of pain and anguish such as Walter had never heard before. The lad retired behind a tree in tears and was sick. Young love is the most tender.

But when the spurned Owain turned on his heels, the maiden ran to him and clung to his cloak in desperation – a most distressing scene. Then, he was gone, her handsome young man with his pretty lilting voice and tender lips – never to return. It was spoken all over that, heartbroken and in utter despair, the girl had drowned herself, unable to endure a lifetime without the true friend of her soul. If all this was known to me in my obscure hermitage, then it was clear that Walter must have heard of the rumour also. This, I knew, was what haunted his troubled soul, and there was only one way to salve such guilt. I resolved to comfort Walter, by telling what is commonly known as a 'white lie'.

The next day I sculled down the river the few miles to the coppice in my coracle, on the pretext of arranging to have the vessel re-tarred – which genuinely needed doing, as it happened. Walter always had a ready supply of tar and had done the same job for me a few years before. I am too hefty and arthritic to use the boat much these days, but in salmon-season even I will venture out into mid-stream with a pole and net. I did not want to let on to Wal that his wife had been to see me, lest that stir up yet more ill-tempered behaviour from him. In these domestic matters, even a priest has to proceed with utmost caution, let alone an interloper such as myself. Naturally reclusive, I have never been comfortable with the pastoral role. I only intervene if there is no alternative course.

Maggie had already discussed a plan, which seemed to me reasonable – a way of preserving a marriage and a family, for the sake of a few half-truths – not the greatest sin in the world, you might think? I shouldered the boat up to the cottage where Maggie was expecting me, with a steaming bowl of pottage and some mulled cider, for late October is chill on the river and this was the last day of that month, the night when the spirits wandering the woods would soon be upon us.

Thus restored I wandered over to the clamps, where the charcoal was prepared under Walter's careful eye. The conversion takes a long while and if the right time is missed, all the timber stacked beneath the turf will be ruined and all the labour of cutting it wasted. Many a man has done so, for under the influence of cider, or after a heavy meal it is too easy to doze and miss the time. One such mistake can easily end a wood-collier's career, and it disturbed me to hear that Walter had taken to the flagon. Maggie knew that he would be watching such a conversion all day, so would have no excuse to avoid conversation with me. Indeed, as I strode into the clearing, he did seem startled to see me.

'How d'ya do Father! A stranger in these parts, aren't you?'

I grasped his outstretched hand, which was black as jet.

'I am, I am! But it has been in my mind to ask for your help with my coracle again, if I may? I need it more now, since my bone-ache set-in! May I sit down beside you awhile – for my knees are killing me!'

So saying, I sat opposite him on a log bench beneath the rain canopy he had constructed. Now, regarding him closely, I saw the change. He was thinner in the face, greying around the temples – but the most awful change, was about the eyes – sunken and fierce, where once the light of love and life had shone. I immediately knew that a demon had him in its grasp. He proffered a leathern cup filled with cider in my direction, but I declined – my first slip-up.

'Nay thanks Wal – I have taken a drink already, and it so early in the day!'

He saw that he had me.

'Up at the steading, was it? I thought you may have seen my wife, perhaps?'

'Aye, I did pass by that way and dropped in for a chat. A good host she is too – you are a lucky man, Wal, to be master of such a spouse!'

He took a deep swig of cider, not from the cup, but from the flagon itself before replying.

'I am no man's master, or woman's – and I submit to no mastery over me!'

I gave a mocking chuckle.

'Cider has mastered many a man before Walter! Beware, you know the risk you run – with no-one here to rouse you if you nod-off – I'm surprised you don't have one of the boys with you to make sure.'

He cleared his throat and spat black spittle, then motioned towards the little hump at the edge of the wood-shore, with a cross of hazel-wands implanted in it.

'*She* watches out for me. Many have been the times when I have dozed and felt her touch on my shoulder – just as she did in life. I see you look quizzical, but it is quite true – for all the priestly cant!'

This last comment was made almost with contempt, and I felt subtly undermined. I said as much.

'Well, I am no priest, as you know – merely a makeshift in a hard time. I do not doubt that you *feel* or imagine she is still here beside you, watching over you. Such a loving, sweet lass she was – a loss very hard to bear. Yet I have a licence to preach the true gospel hereabouts – and even on *this* day of days, I cannot condone the idea of a world of spirits.'

Walter reacted with a first hint of the anger to come.

'And yet – I *do* see her, hear her, feel her touch! Am I mad then? Deluded?'

I stared down at the ground, for his penetrating gaze unnerved me somewhat.

'I do fear so, indeed, Wal, and I want to help you. Have I not always been a steadfast friend to your family in times of trouble? I have gone an extra mile beyond what a real priest would do. Why, just for giving a blessing over the grave my licence could be revoked in a case of suicide – though I have good reason to doubt such was the case.'

I had trailed my bait, and he instantly took it.

'Oh! And what makes you so sure?'

My reply took him by surprise.

'Because she came and visited me for a blessing only a few days before – the accident. She was in no mood for suicide, nor anything of the sort. Whatever happened, Wal, was just that – an accident. It was no-one's *fault*, no-one was to blame.'

Walter's hostile glance was the prelude to an impassioned interjection, immediately throwing me off balance. All the love and good fellowship of former years, I saw clearly now, was at an end for him.

'Why do you come to me with this contrived blather! I know why you are here and who summoned you hither – my dear beloved wife, was it not? She paints me as a monster, to you and all who care to hear. Yet she doesn't starve, or the boys. I labour for them and provide for all their needs, and what reward do I get? To be harangued and nagged and my reputation smeared to the likes of you!'

I bristled somewhat.

'The *likes* of me, 'eh? Tell me good Walter, what am I like then?'

'You are *like* an interfering old busybody – sticking your nose into my private business, conspiring with my wife to undermine my authority! But what is worse, you have no authority – you admit you are no priest. You hope that by moralising to me, you may assuage a guilt of your own, perhaps?'

'I come here not as a priest, nor anything of the kind! I come as a friend. I admit it is true that Maggie has spoken with me, and I have never seen her so desperate. She says plainly, that she will be gone before Christmas if you cannot be reconciled. Think man! Is it not cruel enough a fate to lose her first-born child in such a way, only to be sundered from her dear husband as well? No-one can live without love, and certainly not such a woman as she is. You must be a man, and even in such pain, try to be a faithful and just companion, as she has been to you. I beg you, cast out this demon in your soul – before it is too late!'

He turned around and came back under the awning, before releasing his quarrel straight into my heart.

'I hear tell that you are quite the *expert* with regard to such matters Father! That there was once a time when demons and devils were your bosom companions! Is it not so? You see, the river-folk spread their spiteful gossip everywhere, about everyone – not just wood-colliers like me. Pray, tell me, as one who knows, how one goes about the expulsion of a demon – if, indeed, one wishes the imp to depart? For, it is in my mind that *you* stand in need of such exorcism far more than I! It is thanks to your influence that she was named in honour of the goddess in the first place! It was your meddling in foreign books that set the whole tragedy in motion – for they say the river-nymph *takes* a dozen souls to herself each year. How many times did you read the French book to her, even as a toddler, telling her the fate of her namesake? It was just such romantic notions which inflamed her passions and laid her in her grave yonder! So, before you castigate me – look to your own culpability, am I not right?'

Suddenly, my heart sank, as I realised that my own sin was common knowledge all these years – that the respect and love I had taken for granted in the community for so long, was an illusion. Walter wandered off towards the riverbank, as I sat alone in a stunned reverie, in which time itself evaporated into the gathering autumn mist.

It was quite true of course, what Walter had implied. A branch of my family had been retainers of Robert, Earl of Gloucester, during the civil wars – the years when 'Christ and his Saints slept'. My father died when I was a youngster, and provision was made for me to be educated at the Priory of St James, so as to eventually enter service as a clerk. I hoped to leave England and make my fortune in Aquitania, in the wine trade. But in order to do this, I needed to master French, as well as Latin and Greek. Since none of my companions spoke French, this was no simple matter, and I was forced to practise my conversation in the language alone, stretched out beneath the apple trees in the orchard in the castle grounds. One such morning, I heard female giggling behind me, and turned to see the most astonishingly beautiful girl I had yet beheld.

Emma was her name, of Gascony or Vasconia. We were of the same age but for a few months, and under her capable tutelage my French came on by leaps and bounds. Indeed, the very copy of the *Roman de Brut* by Wace which I still own today was her gift to me. We soon became lovers, despite my lowly rank and poor prospects. What was worse, was that she was betrothed, and so our *fin amor* was ultimately doomed. I became so despondent and afraid as the time neared for her to sail, that my studies suffered, so that I was put to the lash as punishment. As she salved my wounds where I had been scourged, I poured out my heart, declaring my undying love – wherever in the world she may wander. I swore I would do *anything* and sacrifice everything, endure the pains of Hell – if only our love could endure. To my amazement, she whispered that providing I was willing to risk all, perhaps there *was* a way – a means of binding our souls together, for all eternity.

So it was, that the Devil insinuated himself into my soul, for my lover was a Melusine, a shape-shifter, a consort of Lucifer – as I had always suspected, but by now I was in far too deep to extricate myself without great harm. Emma's mother had been of the same faith, which was very ancient in the Aquitaine. When we invoked *his highness* we did not mention him by name, calling him by the title 'The Benefactor of Mankind'.

This supreme blasphemy, she explained, could be accounted for in their faith – because the spirits who fell on the second day were themselves angels, whose place in heaven had been taken by mankind. Thus, there was an eternal enmity between Lucifer and his fallen angels and human beings. But it was possible to appease the demonic host – by taking the bold step of entering into alliance with the 'son of the morning' – daring to storm heaven, to 'sit upon the mount of the congregation'. I little thought then, in my callow ignorance, that our stupid games would cast us both into the jaws of Hell itself.

I make no excuses. Looking back forty years I can scarcely recognise the stripling youth, stricken with love-sickness, as one and the same with the pot-bellied crippled old-fart I have become. Yet, it is so. Had she lived, she would have kept her beauty into old age, of that I am certain, for she was truly a paragon in that regard at least. Suffice to say, that we prepared to take our vows to the Father of Lies, the Evil One. There was then established a man in the town by the name of Aaron.

It was widely rumoured that Aaron's patron was none other than the 'Benefactor' himself, for he was utterly without scruple. Although it had long been illegal in England, slavery still went on underground, and a great many young girls and boys were shipped out of the port by pirates to Dublin across the sea. Aaron said that for a price, he would smuggle us to Ireland aboard a pirate ship, and once beyond the pale, thence by ship to Gascony. My beloved pawned her jewels to this end, but when the night arranged for us to elope came, we found our plan had been betrayed. The old man had been taken to the castle dungeons, and soon spilt his guts to the constable.

My Emma was taken far from England, to a castle in the high Pyrenees. I heard years later that she was drowned in a shipwreck. I was expelled from the priory, and became an insane vagrant for four years, a mere hobbledehoy. One day as I was begging outside the old chapel of St Mary Magdalene in Worcester, brother John took pity on me, and cared for me until my sanity was restored. Thanks to his kindness, I was introduced to the Rector of Martley – who installed me at Redstone Rock. So, one who had once conspired with the Devil, became a priest in all but name, in this riverside idyll. Yet now, it seemed, my tenure was at an end – for I could not hope to retain the respect due to me, if all this were widely known – a bitter blow after so many years.

I remained a long time in the past, but I was suddenly roused by Maggie's voice.

'Hey-up Father! Wake up there! I've brought you some pasties. Lord only knows what it was you said to him – but the man I married is back, thanks be to God!'

She was clearly elated, literally transformed. I was intrigued.

'Oh! How so?'

'Well, he just came in, sent the boys off foraging – and we went at it right there and then! Then he ate like a horse – proper food too! By, he's in a fine mood with it, kissing me – all over. He says he will attend to your boat tomorrow and have one of the boys bring it down. Come Father, it gets late early tonight as you know! I'll walk along to the heights with you and then you can follow the track down home before dark. I've cut you a staff. I want to be home early this evening, if you follow? There's thankful to you I am indeed!'

I was too astonished to disabuse her as we set out on the track downriver into the rising mist.

There was a blasted oak atop the cliffs and we parted company there. I was oblivious to nearly all Maggie's babbling, my mind still only half-way into this time and space. Indeed, as I glanced down the track to the riverbank I did become a little giddy. Nor did I look forward to the final few precarious miles trudging home alone, as I returned Maggie's last joyful wave to me. Only one full hour of daylight remained, so very slowly I picked my way over the stones on the track. It had been a strange day – mystifying and also disturbing. Walter's sudden recovery was by the grace of God, and certainly nothing to do with me. In fact, I felt that his angry outburst had succeeded in liberating him, whereas I was now suddenly overwhelmed, by past memories, grief and guilt. Brother John was my gentle guide in former times, and from him I learned the practice of *Examen* whereby at the evening of each day, one meditated upon the diurnal spiritual lessons. My hips and knees ached, so I decided to rest on a little mound beside the riverbank, to pray and open myself to God's mercy and grace.

Although it was approaching dusk, and I was much fatigued, I swear I am not mistaken in this. I glanced towards the bank and saw a frisky looking hound – of a breed I never yet saw, and chasing the hound, a bonny maid. I thought her whole demeanour and attire most odd – until I looked into her face. It was *her* to the very life, not dead, not drowned, but living and casting a stick for her dog to run after. She stopped awhile, for just a few precious moments, and I saw her glance lovingly, fearfully, towards the steady flux of the river. Truly, to speak of the elder gods, is to invoke them, or so it seems to me.

8

The Nail Stone

Coal, iron, limestone, clay, quarry-stone are the foundations of the Black Country. Minerals which the area contains in good supply, minerals which started the Industrial Revolution from 1750 onwards, and which were to become famous throughout the world and set the pace of commercial progress. A crude and merciless area whose traditions are steeped in jumbled mixtures of pride and craft and strength, in exploitation by Gaffers, and poverty to follow.

Archie Hill[17]

As will become clear, the author Archie Hill has become a strange obsession for me in my latter years, but although I would happily concur with most of the statement above, there is one assertion with which I must demur. The Industrial Revolution did not start in 1750, as he averred, but well over a century before that, in the very Black Country he loved – and hated – so well, not least his native village of Kinver in South Staffordshire, where I am living now (though technically, it is in the 'green borderland'). I once met a relative of his in one of the village pubs, but I never thought to enquire of him as to precisely where Archie was born in 1928.

It is a project of mine to try to erect some sort of memorial plaque when I discover the place, for he was a good writer and a fascinating, though ultimately tragic, personality. The Black Country he wrote about was the same landscape I caught a final glimpse of in my boyhood, the one erased during the last decades of the 20th century. It was unique, the first industrialised landscape in the world, but how did it all begin, and where and when?

151

One day in 1966 my father and great-uncle were digging-over the front garden when my father's spade struck a very large stone, a huge boulder in fact. It was so big that it took both of them to lift it out. I cannot remember now what kind of rock it was; I was less than five years old at the time. It was full of holes which had been drilled into it, and we later learned from Dudley Museum that it was a nail stone. This stone represented the humble and extremely crude beginnings of the Industrial Revolution over 200 years prior to 1750. A workhouse of some sort had once stood where we lived, and we surmised that some of those incarcerated there were put to the task of producing crude iron nails by literally ladling molten iron into the holes in the stones.

King Henry VIII built two massive palaces, at Nonsuch in Surrey, and Hampton Court. These required vast quantities, in the hundreds of thousands, of iron nails. Wooden pegs took too long to make and were too expensive. John Dudley, Duke of Northumberland, sought to ingratiate himself with the king by having his tenants rapidly increase the production of nails, however crude, at this time. We were given to understand that our stone dated from exactly this period – perhaps the first artefact of the industrial age, in fact.

Archie Hill was right to point to the dominance of mineral deposits as the foundation of the development of the Black Country. There have been delvers here for thousands of years. The Romans had bell-pits and quarries on these bleak moors. I heard a story as a boy that a few hundred years ago, a farmer was repairing a dry-stone wall on the slopes of Turner's Hill, when he noticed a concealed pot. It contained thousands of Roman coins, which had been stashed away when the legions departed, and remained hidden for nearly 1,500 years.

Miners have always been pioneers and explorers. In the 3rd century BC, the Greek traveller, Pytheas, who gave Britain its name, came here for copper and tin. It has been shown that a particular DNA haplogroup, originating in modern Ethiopia, migrated to Albania, to become copper-miners in very remote times. Astonishingly, this rare genetic marker turns up in one tiny area of Britain – Llandudno, where the Great Orme Copper Mine was excavated 4,000 years ago. Copper and tin were what first put Britain on the map, but lead-ore, which also contains silver, is abundant in parts of Britain, and gold was once plentiful in Wales, at the Dolocauthi Roman gold mine, where slave-labourers toiled.

The region did not make its fortune from precious ores, but from less glamorous mineral deposits. Of all these, coal was king, and the extent of the local coal more or less delineates the boundaries of the shadowy region – more mythical than geographical. But sometimes myth is more true than so-called reality. There is now a new flag for the region, emphasising its industrial roots, and a 'Black Country Day' takes place on July 14 – not to coincide with Bastille Day in France, but with the invention of the Newcomen Steam Engine in 1712. Thomas Newcomen was actually a Devonshire man, but his engine was the motive force behind the Industrial Revolution. The first of his engines was installed in Dudley on that very day.

The Welsh branch of my family were attracted to the region precisely because of the extensive coal-measures, which once lay exposed, literally on the surface or just beneath. A thirty-foot seam ran along the Rowley Fault, the geological feature which created the bleak uplands that became the Black Country. This was soon exhausted by crude and hazardous drift mining, raging underground coal-gas fires burned out of control all over the area. The Rowley Hills also contain dolerite, known locally as 'Rowley Rag', which is used for kerbstones all over the country. The first Earl of Dudley was persuaded that engineers and colliers from Wales could be relocated to sink a deep coal mine – Baggeridge – so as to get at another twelve-foot seam far below the surface. My father, who was a surveyor there, told me that there was enough coal beneath South Staffordshire to last at least 300 years.

The coalfield stretches from West Bromwich and Walsall in the east to Sedgley in the west, and from Halesowen in the south to Bilston in the north. The centre of the region, the 'capital of the Black Country' as it was called – is Dudley, with its ancient castle overlooking all. The American diplomat Elihu Burritt (1810-1879) was astonished when he looked out over the area, 'black by day and red by night' as he observed – for what he saw was not the urban wasteland punctuated by shopping-malls we see today, but a desolate war zone:

Wolverhampton on the extreme left stood by her black mortars which shot their red volleys into the night. Coseley and Bilston and Wednesbury replied bomb for bomb and set the clouds on fire above with their lighted matches. Dudley, Oldbury, Albion, and Smethwick on the right plied their heavy breechers at the iron-works on the other side; whilst West Bromwich and distant Walsall showed that their men were standing as bravely to their guns and that their guns were charged to the muzzle with the grape and canister of the mine. The canals, twisting and crossing through the field of battle, showed by patches in the light like bleeding veins. There were no clouds except of smoke over the scene; but there were large strips of darkness floating with crimson fringes into the red sea, on which the white moon rode like an ermined angel of peace.[18]

It is said locally that when the Queen Empress Victoria travelled through the area en route north by rail, she ordered the carriage-blinds to be drawn down, so that the pollution and ugliness did not offend Her Majesty – a bitter irony, if true. For from the sweat generated in the furnaces and mines of this man-made wilderness, the power which exerted its mercantile and military hegemony over a quarter of the land surface of the planet was ultimately derived.

The urban wilderness replaced its natural predecessor. The great fault or ridge of high land on which the Black Country and Birmingham stands is a cultural fault-line too. Sir Frank Merry Stenton, in his classic *Anglo-Saxon England* (1970) reminded us that this belt of land once divided the Mercians from their Brythonic neighbours, with Teutonic holy places deliberately named to honour the Germanic gods – Wednesbury ('Woden's Fortress') and Wednesfield ('Woden's Plain'), for example. The two miles or so from Wombourne to Sedgley Beacon ought to be a simple stroll, were it were not for the fact that those miles are a steep, relentless ascent, with views to the Welsh border and the Severn estuary, the Wrekin, Cannock Chase and the Clent Hills; an ideal military outpost.

The great forests of the lowlands gave way here to sparse gorse, broom and heather moorlands, thin soils which could not support steady agriculture. To supplement their meagre agricultural output, the inhabitants took to delving for 'pit-cole' and to making leather and iron goods such as horse-tack. Any squatter who could erect a primitive dwelling overnight had delver's rights on the land beneath. During the reign of King Henry VIII, the local Lord Dudley of the Sutton family acquired vast new estates which were transferred to him as a result of the Dissolution of the monasteries. This meant that a huge swathe of the western Midlands was suddenly the demesne of one powerful family, the Suttons. John Dudley, Duke of Northumberland, had even more grandiose designs. He became the effective regent of all England during the minority of King Edward VI, but he had an even higher ambition for his heirs.

Edward VI, the boy-king, was gravely ill, and a plan was made to marry off John's son, Guildford, to Lady Jane Grey, someone we encountered earlier on in these tales. Edward was adjured to bequeath the throne to his beloved Jane, a Protestant, rather than to his sister Mary, a Catholic. The plot failed miserably, and the surviving Dudley family (John and his son were executed, along with the hapless Jane) fell from grace. The Sutton line was destroyed, and in 1643 a fairly humble family, the Wards, one of the Suttons' many creditors, took over the dilapidated estates.

They became owners of a tumbledown castle at Dudley, which they could not afford to maintain, and a rough tangle of heathland, waste and poor villages yielding little by way of rents. Few could have foretold then that in time this uninspiring backwater would become the industrial powerhouse of the greatest empire in the history of the world, the elite residence of one of the most prosperous families on earth.

By the end of the sixteenth century new blast-furnaces were replacing the old-fashioned bloom-furnaces, meaning that cast-iron of very high quality could be produced in much larger quantities. The fast-flowing little rivers which ran off the hills, such as the Tame and the Stour, were ideal for water-powered forges where small metal goods such as horseshoes and nails could be made.

The last Lord Dudley of the Sutton line, Edward, fathered eleven illegitimate children with his local 'concubine', Elizabeth Tomlinson, described as being a 'lewd and infamous woman, a collier's daughter'. But Edward loved her and was responsible about the education of their many offspring. His favourite was Dud Dudley, born around 1599. Edward fondly hoped that this bright young boy would restore the family fortunes which had fallen so low after the events of 1553. Dud was sent to Oxford to receive an elite education at Balliol College, and by the time he returned home in 1618 or 1619 he was well-equipped to take over the family iron-works on Pensnett Chase. Even as a small boy, he gravitated to the iron-workers and their forges. In the grounds of the family mansion, Himley Hall, the aspiring metallurgist was already conducting experiments designed to perfect a process whereby iron could be smelted using the plentiful local 'pit-cole' instead of charcoal. Even as the 17th century dawned, the great woodlands of oak and beech were almost exhausted by the ravages of the wood-colliers, and so the new process was essential if the family works were to survive.

Black Country foundry workers.

Female brick worker in the Black Country.

Many years later, and after many adventures, Dud wrote a book called *Metallum Martis* (1665) in which he claimed to have smelted iron with coke derived from coal on four occasions at various sites, including Askew Bridge near Gornal, Himley, Cradley and Kinver. But although he was keen to take credit for his genius, he was loath to disclose the technical details of the process – which he knew was revolutionary. When he died in 1684, the secret went with him to his grave – or so it was thought, and the last hope of restoring the Sutton line to its former glory was gone.

Dud's memory faded into obscurity, and his book was forgotten, but the local historian Carl Higgs has proven beyond doubt that Abraham Darby, the man credited with being the first to smelt iron using coke in 1709 in nearby Shropshire, was, in fact, a descendant of Dud. It seems therefore reasonably certain that Dud had perfected a process which was later revived by Darby, who had some inkling of how it worked. The World Heritage Site at Ironbridge ought properly to share the honours with the Black Country.

Dud succeeded in obtaining a patent in 1621, and the future looked bright. But then a series of disasters struck. His forge at Cradley was destroyed by floods, and local rivals vandalised his works at Sedgley, for fear it would put them out of business. Then, during the English Civil War, Dud's Royalist sympathies meant he was forced to keep a low profile, especially after the defeat and execution of King Charles I. But at last, in 1660, the now ageing genius saw his chance when King Charles II was restored to the throne. So eager was he to impress the new monarch that he petitioned Charles on the very day he set foot in England again.

But the king had many more pressing concerns to deal with, and once again, Dud's pleas fell on deaf ears. He died in 1684, but one of his former enterprises at Hyde outside Kinver had fallen into the hands of another early industrialist – Richard 'Fiddler' Foley – in 1627.

I share one thing in common with Dud Dudley, Richard Foley, and Archie Hill. As we have seen, I practise my own 'sullen art' in Kinver, the isolated village which had the unfortunate distinction of recording one of the highest number of cases of infection in England during the 2020 pandemic. It has seen many such plagues come and go in the last 3,000 years, one of the oldest villages in Britain. Dud's experimental works at Hyde outside the village had been acquired by 'Fiddler' Foley. He set-up a slitting-mill, and an ingenious distribution system for iron nails which made the Stour Valley the epicentre of the nail-making industry.

Archie Hill soon moved to the heart of the dark region a few miles away, where as a boy during the Great Depression of the 1930s, he sat gazing out over the colossal sprawl of industry which resulted from these early innovations:

> The wall was part of a lane we called the Cliff, because it was high. From it we could see the heart-pulses of the Black Country, although the pulses were now weak and at low ebb. We could see the iron-foundries and glass-works, the strange mutilations of geographical areas where brick kilns and pitheads jostled shoulder to shoulder with small wild patches of natural beauty ... the dark sombre canals running alongside clean streams which sprang from the earth, and often the cough-making tuberculosis in men's lungs clashed with the song of free-winging linnets, high up in the skies. We sat and ... gazed out over a world of sweat and toil and throbbing iron ... a world sometimes of hunger, vice and darkness, and desperate poachers stalking the woods of Wordsley.

The earliest industrial pioneers are now semi-legendary, like Dud Dudley. Richard Foley was no exception. My infant school was named in his honour, and we learned the legend of 'Fiddler Foley' sitting as cross-legged schoolchildren. Foley was a local iron-master and in 1627 he leased some of Dud's furnaces, including the one at Hyde. One day Foley went to Dudley market where he purchased a battered but still tuneful fiddle. Richard was quite talented on the instrument, and before long he had also acquired some ragged old clothes. In this garb he set out for Hull, where he took ship – some say for Sweden, others for Holland. The Swedish version was the one I was told. Disguised as a wandering beggar, Foley wandered up to a revolutionary new slitting-mill he had heard about.

The workers were amused by the travelling fool who entertained them with jolly reels on his fiddle, sharing their food with him, oblivious to the industrial espionage taking place under their very noses. When the fool left them to return to his native England, the entire operation of the complex plant had been memorised down to the last detail.

On his return, Foley immediately set to work to replicate the slitting-mill outside Kinver. It was actually not the first such mill in England, but it was the first to really revolutionise production and distribution processes, a place worthy of a legend. To take advantage of someone using deception is still known as 'a fiddle' to this day. In fact, the story is probably based on the adventures of George Brindley of Kinver, Richard's father-in-law. The tale is of a piece with many other such fables of vagrants becoming fabulously wealthy, such as Dick Whittington, for example.

Richard Foley, like his namesake Dick, became a mayor – not of London, but of Dudley. The nail-trade boomed, and the family moved to Witley Court, a grand mansion in Worcestershire. A gay enough tale, then, but it disguises a much grimmer reality. For the lives of the nail-making communities were blighted by poverty, squalor, ignorance and disease on a truly industrial scale, exploitation which was indistinguishable from slavery.

As the eminent historian E.P. Thompson pointed out in his epic *The Making of the English Working Class* (1963) the nailers, along with the weavers, were the lowest in the hierarchy of trades in terms of earning power. The growing city of Birmingham was already a centre for small workshops producing a wide variety of small manufactured goods – the 'city of a thousand trades'. Thompson lists buckles, cutlery, spurs, candlesticks, toys, guns, buttons, whip-handles, coffee-pots, ink stands, bells, carriage-fittings, steam engines, snuff-boxes, lead pipes, jewellery, lamps, kitchen implements – among many others. But the life going on in the Black Country or the Stour Valley was something different, far from the vibrant excitement of the expanding city:

> Here in the Black Country, the process of specialization in the first three decades of the nineteenth century tended to take the simpler processes, such as nail and chain making to the surrounding villages of outworkers, while the more highly skilled operations remained in the metropolis of Birmingham itself.

The outworkers were, and notoriously still are, paid derisory wages – when they were paid at all. As Thompson cites: 'Capitalistic outwork may be said to be fully established only when the material belongs to the trading employer and is returned to him ... the wool given out to be spun, the yarn given out to be woven, the shirt given out for 'seam and gusset and band', the nailrod to be returned as nails, the limbs to be returned as dolls, the leather coming back as boots.' The nail-makers and their families were truly slaves in all but name, and amidst this iniquitous misery, a contemptuous disregard for decent standards of human existence was the norm.

There had been two mills in Kinver when King William I ordered his Domesday survey in the 11th century. The strange course of the lower Stour made it eminently suitable for fulling cloth, or 'stuff' to enhance the quality of woollen manufactures. These sites were easily converted to forges, slitting-mills and blade-mills, operated by iron magnates like the Foley family or the Knight family of Cookley.

The nailers obtained their nail-rod from nail-masters. The slitting-mills took iron bars and slit them into thin rods, which the nail-workers and their families fashioned into nails. This was done in small workshops outside the cramped family homes. At first, people combined this work with small-scale husbandry and agriculture, but as production intensified whole communities subsisted by iron-working alone.

They were forced to buy their provisions at exorbitant prices from 'Tommy Shops', company stores which gave out goods in lieu of wages at a commission. It was impossible to make a living from piecework unless the entire family was involved, children included. This was one of the reasons why the local people have often been so contemptuous of education. The Education Acts of the later 19th century took valuable productive labour out of poor communities.

These villages were tough places, close-knit, rowdy, lewd and drunken; some would say they still are. Writing in 1868, Dr Ballenden of Sedgley thought the people of the Black Country 'the most immoral people in England'. Grinding poverty combined with squalor, ignorance and a naturally irreverent attitude to religion, to coarsen the language and manners of the inhabitants. To more gentile persons, such as Dr Ballenden, or Her Majesty Queen Victoria, the denizens of the dark region seemed barbaric, little better than savages.

It was small wonder. After 1830 foreign competition and technical innovation began to drive down the wages of the nailers in particular. They earned as little as 7s per week: 'By night and day we toil for little pay' as their banners proclaimed. In 1842, a hungry angry armed mob seized some of the nail-masters in Old Hill and marched them into Dudley where the riot act was read to their militant captors.

Heavy artillery was set up in Dudley marketplace and the yeomanry cavalry were mustered. These disturbances grew more frequent and riots persisted into the 1860s. It could have been worse. In Kidderminster during the 1850s the weaving trade collapsed, and 5,000 emigrated to the antipodes, leaving a 'ghost town' behind. Violence, ignorance, pollution and poverty became the common experience of an entire population over many generations. The artist John Martin, in his painting *The Great Day of His Wrath* of 1854, depicted the Black Country by night as a landscape more baleful than the darkest infernal regions, a hell on earth.

Perhaps more corrosive was that this experience was internalised. The Black Country became infamous for drinking, betting, dog-fighting, 'wenching', brawling, prize-fighting and any other cheap thrill. The womenfolk, especially a 'mon'umon' (a brawny, tough female) were just as 'handy' as their men, often more so. Many were the men who sported black eyes meted out by 'the missus'. Perhaps the so-called 'epigenetic trauma' of such domestic violence, produced the likes of Archie Hill?

The homes of the colliers and nailers, especially the latter, were tiny. Sometimes two large families shared two cramped miserable rooms. By day, all of them would crowd around the forge outside for light, air and warmth. There was no provision for old age but the workhouse, and in sickness the only recourse for the workers was a 'cunning woman' or a quack.

By the late 1760s a complicated network of canals was interpenetrating Birmingham and the Black Country. These quiet highways for trade enabled local industrialists to export goods all over the country – and on to the expanding empire. Barges queued for two weeks to pass through the 7-feet-wide Dudley Tunnel, but once they had legged their way through, they had easy access to the river and maritime network. Now, their labour was no longer confined to small metal goods, such as nails and link chain. The great anchor of the doomed *Titanic* was forged in Netherton. As the network gradually spread, mines, factories, foundries, brick kilns and crowded wharves sprang up next to them. The momentum of industry was unstoppable, and the long ordeal of the Napoleonic Wars spurred the process on. The rough-and-tumble attitudes of the Black Country folk were slowly changing as civilizing influences percolated down to the working people. Not that these were always welcomed.

In 1743, my ancestor Mr Lane, a magistrate from Bentley near Walsall, was confronted by an angry mob who demanded summary jurisdiction in the middle of the night, arraigning the Methodist leader John Wesley for preaching in the area. The magistrate curtly dismissed their demands, but instead of dispersing, the mob dragged Wesley all over the surrounding area in search of a more cooperative Justice of the Peace. Eventually, they reached Walsall itself, where Wesley was forced towards the river-bridge, as the 'wild men', as he called them, prepared to throw him into the fast-flowing waters.

Wesley meekly prepared to say his final prayers – but was miraculously saved by a giant collier, a notorious bare-knuckle boxer – who hoisted the preacher on his shoulders and carried him all the way to Wednesbury. A garbled memory of this incident used to form a local rhyme:

> John Wesley 'ad a bonny 'oss,
> the finest that yo' sin',
> they took 'im down to Hayseech Brook,
> and chocked 'im yed fust in.

Within a few years, Methodist chapels had been established in every corner of the Black Country and nearby Birmingham, and from this unpromising start, the region became a non-conformist stronghold. The days of staunch loyalty to 'Church and King' were fading, to be replaced by the even more fanatical tribal loyalties to local football clubs. Wesley's ideas were not resented so much as the fact that he was an 'outsider' seen to be meddling in local affairs. The people of Walsall took another such 'outsider' to their hearts, so much so, that her memory is still honoured there to this day.

Dorothy Wyndlow Pattison, known locally as 'Sister Dora', was a Yorkshire woman. Her childhood was marred by her father's mental ill-health, and she desperately sought a suitable marriage partner so as to escape her predicament. Neither of her two suitors proved ideal, however, and after a spell as the dame of a village school in Buckinghamshire Dorothy joined the 'Christ Church sisters' to become an Anglican nun. In 1866, Dora as she was now known arrived in Walsall to minister to the poor, elderly and sick. By the time she died only twelve years later she had become venerated almost as a saint.

Just as Wesley was misunderstood and abused in his time, Dora was greeted with initial hostility. Anglican nuns, especially in the Black Country, were a rarity, and so local folk spread the rumour that she was a Roman Catholic. A mob gathered and pelted the hospital with bricks and stones. Dora continued her work undaunted, and when a deadly epidemic of smallpox hit the town she worked night and day in the worst-infected areas, comforting those who were dying. She sacrificed her own meagre food rations, taking them to bereaved families. Smallpox, which disfigured if it was not fatal, was greatly feared, and neighbourhoods were shunned once infection had spread, but Dora continued to perform her duties all through the long dreary months while the epidemic raged.

She lived and worked in a hospital beside the railway-track, and the men of the railway (there were awful injuries, and many deaths, on the railways) grew to love her dearly, even paying for a pony-and-trap so that she could travel to her patients more easily. There was plenty to keep her busy. There were frequent colliery disasters, but the most horrific ordeal was yet to come.

There was a terrible industrial accident when the boiler blew at the furnaces of the Walsall Iron Company. Seventeen men suffered horrific burns from molten-iron and steam, so excruciatingly painful that they went mad and tried to drown themselves in the canal. Sister Dora nursed them all through their terrible ordeal, refusing to leave their side until they nearly all expired. Two of the men actually survived, and all who witnessed her devotion to them knew themselves to be in the presence of a living saint.

But Dora's work in Walsall was almost done. She developed a tumour in the breast but refused treatment, preferring to continue her work on the wards. Her superiors were forbidden to disclose that she was ill, lest it affect patient morale. On Christmas Eve 1878, after a noble struggle over two years, she died. The whole town felt personally bereaved. The railway-workers she had loved so well were pallbearers and formed a guard of honour at her funeral. The entire town came out to mourn her passing. The local hospital was renamed in her honour, and a statue erected. On her birthday, 16 January, the town remembers her to this day – a woman whose like we will rarely see again.

How odd that God had sent two such extraordinary people to this dark region? But they had won the hearts and souls of local people. That they were remembered with such fondness by the benighted populace was a reflection of something admirable in their characters that mirrored the qualities Black Country people used to hold dear. Although they were ignorant and for the most part unlettered, the local folk continued to respect bravery, self-sacrifice, steadfastness and honourable behaviour – the Mercian virtues.

They adore war and will always run towards a good fight. Wesley's calm fortitude in the midst of extreme danger moved the heart of the collier who saved him. The Black Country felt abandoned – by the government, the Church, and even the queen – but a redoubtable woman from Yorkshire had striven with her whole being to bring them succour. This had been the method of the Celtic saints who converted their forebears, and they instantly recognised it, instinctively – for the Black Country folk *are* at heart, religious – but in a queer sort of way.

By the turn of the 20th century the jumble of villages and towns had more or less consolidated into one great urbanised mass, cheek by jowl with the fast-growing city of Birmingham to the east. 'Foreigners', that is anyone from outside the Black Country or Birmingham plateau, are often mystified by this seemingly trivial distinction. This could prove fatal, for no 'Brummie' likes to be called a 'Yam-yam' (a Black Country resident), 'ne'er t'other rode abaht!', as 'we'am-a-sayin''.

In 1884, the author Francis Brett Young was born in Halesowen, right on the border betwixt the two different cultures. He eventually became a medical student in Birmingham nearby. His experiences led him to write a novel which he set in 'Sedgebury', a fictional location based on the Black Country towns. He was incredibly prolific, especially in the production of his popular 'Mercian' novels. The geographical scope of this fictional region – his equivalent of Hardy's 'Wessex', was almost exactly contiguous with the remit of this book – not a contrivance of my own, by the way, but by sheer serendipity. The effect of this semi-factual, semi-fictional backdrop was to contrast the urban with the rural, the 'squalid slums' with the bucolic peace of the surrounding hill-country.

Brett Young lovingly captured the way in which the region straddled both the 'Black' and the 'Green', as Burritt had already observed. At the edge of Derbyshire and Nottinghamshire, D.H. Lawrence, his fellow author and friend, was experiencing just these same contrasts at exactly the same time, just as Tolkien, a few miles away in Birmingham, was creating his own imaginative landscape. It was as if, after several centuries of gradual development, a point had been reached where the process of industrialisation, the 'flight from nature', needed to be examined from the borderland. The psychological relationship between humans, the despoliation of the natural environment, and the condign retribution of the latter, needed to be better understood and faced.

Ten years before he died, whilst the Blitz was raging in the Second World War, Brett Young wrote an epic poetic work, *The Island*, in which he attempted to extend this 'psycho-geography' to Great Britain and its long history as a whole. The entire project seems very redolent of Layamon's *Brut* and one wonders if this was a deliberate homage. Brett Young was quite successful as a writer, *The Island* completely sold out its first printing in weeks, even under wartime constraints.

For an intelligent, observant, educated young man of the early- and mid-20th century, the Black Country and Birmingham provided ample raw material for a literary mind. Brett Young does not now enjoy the fame of his contemporary D.H. Lawrence, but the Francis Brett Young Society organise study groups and other events to promote his works. Literature, sadly, is not one of the many crafts and trades we usually associate with the Black Country, but this unfashionable, unfathomable conurbation produced another author, more obscure, and for me more interesting.

In 1974 there was great excitement in our small village when BBC cameramen arrived to film a canal-side scene. It formed part of a TV series called *Archie Hill Comes Home*. Little did I know then just how close to home he was. My hunch is that Archie was born somewhere nearby. Hill had been away from his native area for 20 years – and very eventful years at that. His most famous book, *A Cage of Shadows*, begins with his account of a childhood spent in poverty, squalor, and misery in the Black Country of the 1930s. These times were hard enough as it was, but Hill grew up in 'one-down, two-up' houses in which the violence of his alcoholic father kept the large family trapped in an all-pervasive atmosphere of fear. Archie was ashamed at the filth of his family home, and sought every opportunity to escape. In the school holidays, there was work in the local foundries – though his father kept most of his pay. Or there was poaching in the woods of Wordsley, with his father's pals 'Konk' and Pope Tolley, and their totemic Staffordshire bull terriers. But his most exquisite release was to visit the makeshift glass-shop of a retired master glass-craftsman, Billy, who fashioned dazzling Birds of Paradise, or a sow with her little piglets, so tiny they could stand on a sixpenny-bit. All this was produced from thin canes of coloured lead-crystal glass. This seemingly rough, uneducated man with 'fingers like sausages' was actually a maestro, an artistic genius. Although a few museum workshops remain, the glass-industry has gone the way of all British craftsmanship, but these impressions of a place whose outward crudity and vulgarity concealed hidden treasures of beauty and art, born of real human suffering, never left Archie in the dark days to come.

Archie Hill, for all his wit, empathy, and literary and artistic gifts, had sadly inherited his father's love of the drink. In fact, he was a tragic alcoholic, a truth he did not shy away from. His last book – entitled *An Empty Glass: Story of an Alcoholic* – is clearly based on his own raw experiences. The pits, glass-shops, drop-forges and foundries of the Black Country inevitably bred thirsty men.

There were pubs, working-men's clubs and off-licences on virtually every street. As Hill observed, Black Country men didn't just frequent pubs, they 'used' them. In good economic times at least, they were always full to overflowing, with men, women, and children outside or in reserved rooms. The landlord of The Old Swan at Netherton, better-known locally as 'Ma Pardoe's' told me that the chain-strikers of Cradley and Netherton regularly drank up to 50 pints of beer per day! Lads started off in the foundries as 'beer-boys', whose task was to run and bring beer to the workplace. This flippant attitude to alcohol, however, concealed a darker, more hideous reality. The Black Country of Archie Hill's boyhood was a violent place, in which alienated, drunken men often vented their fury on their own families:

He came in this time, and mam had got the baby on her lap feeding it titty. She said something to the dad, he snarled back, she shrieked and cussed him, and then he landed her a belter which threw her half-way across the room. The baby dropped from her lap into the fender, and I thought it was dead; but it started to blart and squeal, and my sister picked it up and ran upstairs with it to get it out of the way. Dad had got me mam by the hair, banging her head up and down against the floor, and she wasn't making any noises now, and I knew she was unconscious. But the dad wouldn't let up. I jumped at him, onto his back, but he threw me off.

There was no help for the wretched victims of these vicious assaults in those days, no refuges existed for terrified, battered mothers and their children until the 1960s and 1970s. The only hope was that a policeman could be summoned to break-up the 'row':

'I'll bloody well kill you you Welsh bitch,' he kept saying to my mam, all the time he was thumping her. 'I'll bloody well kill you.' I grabbed the next brother to me, next in age, and told him to belt up the road fast and get the policeman. I knew too well that the neighbours wouldn't come and interfere, they'd never interfere in things like this.

'It's family,' they'd say ... I could see mam was bleeding at the mouth, and I grew really scared that dad was killing her. I looked around for a weapon, saw the poker in the ash-grid. I picked it up, held it high, brought it down towards the old man's head. Instinct told him, despite the beer he'd drunk. He moved, so instead of hitting him on the head, I brought the poker down on his shoulder. He took it from me like you'd take a rattle from a six-months-old baby. Then he hit me – not with his fist, but with his open hand. I felt as if my head had been ripped from my shoulders. He stood over me.

'Ah said ah'd murder any kid of mine who lifted a hand against me', he said, 'and yoh just did.'

His life outside the house was little better. The ragged schoolboy was forced to walk to school through gangs of 'monty-sods', boys from the 'posh' King Edward VI Grammar School:

There were three that I tried to avoid, but I seldom did. They'd get me in the middle of them and play me off one another like a football. Then they'd get tired of it, they'd give me a belt up the earhole or a kick up the backside to show the unemployed working-class where it belonged. This one time ... I lost my rag, and threw a punch into one of the fellers which made his nose spout crimson like a turned-on tap. The other two gave me what for, and I went home battered and ripped but not crying.

These kinds of experiences were not universal of course, but far too common, and for all I know, still are.

Archie Hill committed suicide in 1986. His chronic alcoholism certainly played its part, but that, in its turn, was partly a product of cultural, intergenerational and epigenetic factors. The Black Country had birthed him with its ambiguous gifts – but ultimately, it also claimed his life. In 1974, when he 'came home' for BBC TV, Hill was on the crest of his wave, quaffing pints in Ma Pardoe's, enjoying a traditional 'faggots & pays' supper with the hilarious Black Country comedian Tommy Mundon. There was also great pain in his homecoming. His story of the Black Country was very far from these comforting caricatures – and he had 'strayed', gone away from his roots. His tribe still accepted him, but he could not accept himself, an 'outsider' in his own native land. But not all of Hill's works were dark, just as no-one's life is entirely dark.

It may be thought that Hill's experience was atypical, extreme, but sadly, I know differently. In 1975, due to a series of unfortunate circumstances, I was excluded from school. My parents were content for me to attend to my own education, on the whole, but suddenly the law was involved. There was an educational trust fund which had been set up for my two cousins by my paternal grandmother. My cousins were unlikely to claim on this trust for some years to come, but suddenly I was in an emergency situation. Despite his bitter feud with his own mother, my father saw that if some alternative were not found, I would drift into the Borstal system. To his eternal credit, he swallowed his pride and begged her assistance to educate me privately, on the condition that I should be confirmed into the Church of England and attend an Anglican school. This was agreed, but my grandmother only undertook to pay the fees.

All the expensive uniform, cricket kit, and various other requirements were left to my parents, who were by no means well-off. Fortunately, my maternal grandmother, Alice, stepped in to assist with the uniform, and I went to be fitted for it at 'Dancer's' outfitters in Halesowen one Saturday afternoon. I was taken in my fancy new clothes to visit my nan nearby, so that she could look-me over, and see how her money had been spent.

She was a very quiet woman but seemed well-satisfied with her investment. I was, of course, exceedingly embarrassed, and there were many more such ordeals to come – but when my parents, aunties and uncles all sloped off to the pub, I suddenly found myself alone with Alice for the first time in my life. To my astonishment, she opened up to me in a way I could never have expected, memories to make Archie Hill's childhood seem comparatively idyllic. From memory, it went something like this:

(Nan) 'Nah then me fine young mon! Yo'am a gooin' up in the world, mixin' it with the 'toffs' are ya?'

(Me) 'Ar ma. Ta for the uniform.' (blushes).

(Nan) 'Do'yoh worry abaht that me young mon! *Our side* can allus find a penny if there be good reason. Yoh looks bostin is all as 'as matters! Yoh'l a' the wenches after yer! But yoh miyend what they'm a learnin' ya – doh tek eve' then they'm a sayin' as gospel. Yoh trust warr'n yer own *spirit* is a tell'n' ya to do. Dun ya miyend?'

(Me) 'Yes, ma.'

(Nan) 'Good then! Yoh wo be the fust ta goo up the ladder, n'eer the last mah mon. Yer grandferther was a ranker – bur'ee ended up as an' officer – an' that was in the *praper* war, warr'n we'am a callin' the *great* war!'

169

I was extremely obsessed with military history back then, and suddenly realised that my nan remembered both world wars, and much more besides. I also realised the sacrifice which had been made for my school uniform, and why seeing me in it pleased her so. Soon, my school photograph would be sent, so that she could place it beside those of all my many cousins on the sideboard and mantle.

His photograph once had pride of place, before the depression and 'last' war. She was widowed in 1934, and remarried to Harold, my mother's stepfather. Jack, my real grandfather, was something of a mystery. It was said that in the photograph he looked very dashing in his officer's uniform and Sam Browne belt. A good-looking bloke, charming – at least that's how it seemed. Alice had many suitors, but this returning hero from the war soon won her heart.

'Ee'am, ya mom's dad – 'ee was a *turk* a right'un. Oh, I did 'ave a game with 'im! D'ya know how many babbies he got on me? Thirteen! Yo'er mom was the last 'un. He died just a'fore 'er was born, and 'er's lucky 'er din't know 'im. I wish ta God I never 'ad!'

Jack, my 'missing' grandparent. My mother knew nothing about him, and her many siblings never spoke of him. There was a rumour that he was born in Scotland, his surname was certainly Scottish. He served on the Western Front in the Great War, and was gassed, I think it would have been in the great German March offensive of 1918. So many officers were killed that non-commissioned officers were rapidly promoted, whatever their social class. An officer's uniform cut quite a dash in the immediate aftermath, but his military pension was small.

He could never work, except for light duties, and in the Black Country of the inter-war years there was little such work available. As time went on, his condition deteriorated, but he still managed to produce a large family with Alice. Some must have been 'Irish twins'. He drank heavily, even when the pantry was empty. Alice told me she would walk to Hagley to work as a cleaner in a 'big house'. The soles of her shoes were worn through, and she had to walk all the way back to Cradley in the snow to save the bus fare.

But for this, the children would have starved, indeed, in hard times they did, before the older boys went to work at 15. Wesley, the eldest, saved the day by poaching out on the Clent Hills. He died of tuberculosis, along with three of the other children. When Alice arrived home after an arduous day, all her housekeeping had gone on beer. She had to take the empties back for the deposit money just to buy some sausages for dinner. I think Jack knocked her about sometimes too, or at least that is my impression.

While she was pregnant with my mother, her youngest, he took ill and died. Just before Christmas, my mother was born. Her brother, also called Jack, told me that he went hungry on Christmas day that year so that the 'young 'uns', all girls, could eat. There was a shop in Cradley Heath selling pork sandwiches, but for the poorest, there was the 'penny dip', bread dipped in the gravy for 1*d*. Jack stood outside with his belly aching from hunger gawping through the window. He didn't have a penny.

A widow with a large brood of children was a particular target for the Means Test Board. The children would be interrogated, too. Jack was warned never to let on if they had eaten sausages. Alice took the older children scavenging for 'gleads', cinders and slack-coal, to burn in the grate for warmth. Technically, taking slack from the coal-heaps and pit-banks was theft – but then, so was poaching.

When Wesley died of tuberculosis, and then one of the girls, then another, my mother and the next youngest sister were taken away to the 'Open Air Hospital' in West Malvern for nearly two years. Otherwise, they also would surely have died of the disease. If the family was to survive, they needed some sort of miracle. This was duly provided, in the shape of Harold Harris, one of Alice's old suitors from her youth. A Methodist and a Socialist, he was also kindly, gentle, loyal, loving and sober. I remember my nan's tender care of him as he lay dying downstairs in 1969. Thanks to him, my mother and her siblings survived and thrived.

A dark region then, in more ways than one, but there can be happy endings here too. Archie Hill didn't shy away from the misery and wretchedness, the exploitation and the desolation of the natural environment – but he loved the Black Country with a passion:

It's the men of the Black Country who ever held me in bond, the native born. Between them, in a sort of composite form, they provided me with a substitute father. The simplicity of them, the strength, and sincerity. And their pride of self in personal craftsmanship which nothing, not even the dark days of depression, ever seemed to daunt for long. I always felt that, whenever Black Country men move on, when they have diluted themselves to 'modern manner', the last threads of Anglo-Saxon England will be no more...

That time is not yet – but it is coming soon. The best of our days are gone, and the sun is setting. Ultimately, Hill's testament is neither nihilistic or self-pitying. In *Summer's End* (1976) he shows us something of the joy and humour of the place, too, but he knows it is a vanishing culture, and feels the sadness in his bones:

> Summer's End is about friendships which existed between myself and others before the Second World War: days of mass unemployment, of no television and of no social security other than the degrading charity of the means test. But the book does not dwell heavily upon these miseries. It merely indicates that hardships which once existed, no longer exist. The book explores myself as a boy against a background of people, young and adult, who – I think – were the last exclamation mark of self-independence and integrity.

Hill could not then have foreseen that those dark days would soon return. Let us take our leave of the old Black Country then – and bid farewell to the last threads of Anglo-Saxon England.

9

Britannia Prima

You have learned from bitter experience how different freedom is from slavery! Hence, although some of you previously, knowing nothing of the difference, never having known slavery – allowed yourselves to be deceived by the alluring promises of the Romans – yet now that you have tried both, you know what a great mistake it was to have preferred an imported despotism to the ways of the ancestors – you have come to realise how much better poverty without a master is to wealth with slavery. For what shameful treatment, what grievous defilement have we not suffered ever since they came into our land of Britain? Have we not been robbed entirely of all our possessions, the greatest of these, while for the meagre remainder we pay taxes? Besides pasturing and tilling for them ... they make us pay an annual tax on our very bodies! How much better then, if we had been sold to masters once and for all, than to have to ransom ourselves every year! How much better to have perished than to go about with a tax on our heads!

Speech attributed to Queen Boudica, AD 61

I never heard the troop of horse trot in through the north gate at first light. I was too busy snoring, having taken too much wine in all three hostelries in the *vicus* the night before. It was my deputy Decurion's birthday binge so I had to make a show – though I'd rather have spent the night with Gwyn – I only get one official pass out of the fort each week, but no-one snitches when I bend the rules a bit. I was roused by a comrade just off his guard duty, yelling at me to get washed and dressed quick. There was a flap on at the Praetorium. The Prefect had arrived from Pennocrucium and there was a terrible rumour spreading – the Ninth Legion had been massacred! I blundered past dazed-looking sentries through the square-set alleys, past the barracks-huts and stables to the Praetorium. A knot of anxious officers were already gathering at the foot of the Commandant's stairs. When all were present and correct we paraded for a mass-briefing on the latest situation reports.

So, it was true then. Cerialis had lost the Ninth! It was hardly to be believed – five cohorts wiped out, nearly 3,000 men. The commander, Cerialis, only saved himself by riding hard for a nearby fort like this one. There, in a place just like this, he was holed-up with his cavalry, all that was left of his command. The barbarians took no prisoners – all wounded legionaries were put to death in the cruellest ways imaginable. So grave was the emergency that Suetonius himself, with two full legions, was already riding from the mountains of Cambria to crush the insurgency – if it could still be called that. To destroy a Roman legion was no easy feat. The woman, Boudica, could not be underestimated. No mere mob could inflict such a defeat – we were facing a real army, rumoured to number in the tens, if not hundreds, of thousands. Suddenly, I felt very sobered. We were no longer fighting for the empire, but for our very existence on this accursed island.

Immediately, patrolling was increased and a new prejudice adopted with respect to the natives. The Druidic religion was now proscribed, and one of their holy men was said to be covertly active in the area. We searched around the cave where he normally resided, 'the August Rock' or 'Rock of Aust' as they call it, but of course, he had long since gone to ground. There was precious little hope of finding him in the vast wilderness of trees below the old hill-fort. But another patrol had chanced upon a young boy with an acorn in his purse. This was the sign the priests used to identify their clandestine messengers. The Commandant's usual laziness was now replaced by a ruthless efficiency and paranoia. The boy was taken to a storeroom beside the granary block. After two days of interrogation, it was my turn to stand guard-duty there, and a pitiful sight it was. Seventeen years I have served, much of it fighting Caratacus and his gang – but I never saw them work a kid over like this before. He swore blind he was innocent – the young fool. I wanted to help him – to save him from pointless suffering.

The two guards stood outside chatting to the Commandant's bruiser. Even he admitted to being sick of the work in-hand. Another session, and the lad was done for, that was for sure. I was senior officer on duty for the night, so I tried to intercede for the boy. I put a proposition to our hefty friend.

'Comrade, I think we may get trouble from this. The boy cannot survive another mauling, and if he dies we are all in the soup! Let me have a go at him! I know their native tongue – they have their own dialect hereabouts. Some of them know me. If the lad knew anything he would surely have coughed it up by now. After such ordeals, a friendly word may elicit more from him than another beating.'

This plan being agreeable, we went in to the boy. The big man stood aside as I knelt beside the pathetic huddled figure, nestled in the sacking. His face was red-raw, bruised and swollen, his entire torso was covered in scabs, bruises and weals. I whispered to him gently.

'Boy! Listen to me. I have come to help you – if you will let me – do you understand?'

He nodded in affirmation. I tried to indicate to him what was at stake.

'Look! These men think you are a spy in league with the Serpent-kind. They found that acorn in your satchel, and think it is a secret cypher of the rebels. But *we know* that you were merely out searching for pannage for your pigs. The acorn was just a sample to show your father, in case your pigs got the flux from eating them before they were ripe – that is how it really was! If they beat a confession out of you – and believe me, they will – your folk will all be punished after you are dead, for they will be culpable too – you see that, don't you? If you want them to live, this is the tale we must tell.'

The boy murmured his assent. I returned to the interrogator and put this story to him. I prayed silently to Minerva, goddess of children, that the boy's life should be spared. For some inexplicable reason, I suddenly felt very paternal that night. I have a nephew back home in Gaul just his age, who I haven't seen since he was a baby. The goddess heard me, for the Commandant, hearing my account, grudgingly granted the prisoner his liberty. In the morning, we helped him into a cart, and rolled down the hill out of the west gate, then over the bridge and up the slope into the noisy community of the vicus.

Opposite the bath-house we stopped outside Gwyn's place and helped the boy down from the wagon. One of the girls was up early sweeping-out. She gasped in shock at the state of my mangled companion. I roused her by barking instructions.

'Don't stand there gawping girl! Wake Gwyn! Tell her to find a bed for this one, dress his wounds and take good care of him, alright? Tell her I will be in tonight at the usual time. Meanwhile, keep quiet about this to the others, do you understand?'

I knew this lass to be a simpleton, I can never remember her name, but I repeated my instructions, just in case, before returning to the fort for the noon patrol. I was in for an earful from Gwyn later on, but for now, that was the least of my troubles.

I set aside my oval-shaped clipeus shield and the long spatha sword in its scabbard, then extricated myself from my mail-shirt. These were my faithful companions, ever since I puked over the side of the ship as I first glimpsed the white cliffs of Albion half-a-lifetime ago. I've been here now all my active military life. I fought Caratacus in the great battle and was wounded. Promotion followed, and since I had learned the British language, I was retained, when other comrades were redeployed. I've grown to love the sunsets here. First, pink, then purple, and finally, at sundown, a fiery inferno of scarlet in the west. But then, the dark, and the silent enemy.

It had been a dreary, pointless patrol again with nothing to show. The groom carried my lance to the rack before departing to attend to my horse in the stables below. As soon as I was changed into a fresh tunic, I headed for the bath-house with my two deputies. We talked of the progress of the rebellion late into the evening, but at a certain point, I feigned tiredness and withdrew as if to return to camp. In fact, as everyone knew, I would cross the street to Gwyn's. The upstairs oil-lamp was still burning in her room, so I braced myself. I'm used to rowing with her now.

Seven years now since I first met her – though the word dignifies what was a purely commercial transaction, at least at first. She was a young 'widow' then, though we cavalry are not permitted to officially marry while on active service. But she was as good as a real wife to the Thracian, and when his horse threw him and he cracked his skull, she tended to him lovingly for two weeks before he died. There was no provision for her, of course, but the soldiers all admired her and felt sorry for her. They took a collection, quite a sum was raised among the 500-man garrison. With this she acquired a lease on a down-at-heel tavern, 'The Old Bush', as we called it.

After two years she extended it, and fitted-out closet rooms at the rear, in which she installed six girls. After that, she didn't need to work herself. Four years we've been an item now, and she hasn't had any other men in that time – or so she says. The simple girl takes my cloak, and I climb wearily up the stairs, I come and go as I please about the place. Nevertheless, I feel it wise to knock at her door before entering. As I duck under the lintel and the door slams behind me, I am greeted by profanities to make a Londinium stevedore blush! But soon enough, I calm her, and then we embrace, kiss, go to bed, as always.

Our pillow-talk had grown more prolonged and intense over this last year. Although I was dog-tired, I knew that tonight, I must shoot my ballista-bolt straight to her heart. All Britain knew what peril the Roman project was now in. I could not disclose too much detail, of course, but if our silly dreams of a happy retirement to a farm were to ever become a reality, I had to convince her to obey me now – to sacrifice all she had built up here. She already sensed something was amiss. She cuddled-up tight and purred:

'The Decurion is deep in thought tonight, sulking, grumpy – why so?'

I turned over, held her by her naked sallow shoulders, and looked into those deep brown eyes, darker than a Moor's. I knew then, had known for a long time, that I truly loved her, more than anything in the universe. I would rather have swallowed powdered glass than have to do this thing.

'My love, you must know what is coming. I don't have to tell you. In all likelihood, Rome and its ways will be swept away here, and soon. I will soon be in the wars and may not survive. I have seventeen years' service and have saved a fair-sized nest egg. I want you to take it and go from this place within the week. I have a contact among the trow-men on the river. Once you reach the mouth of the Sabrina a bark will set sail for Gaul. I have prepared a tablet for you to present to my sister there, Flavia, who will take care of you – until I join you, if I am spared. I beg you my love, there will be no mercy for the Romans' whores – they will roast you on a spit! By the gods, I know it is much to ask – but the storm that is coming upon us now will change the world!'

She spat back fire, contempt and fury. Her long nails dug deep into my shoulders.

'*You bastard!* Who the hell do you think you are ordering me around? I am no chattel of yours to be ferried hither and yon! What will your fine sister Flavia think when a British whore turns-up at her villa? What about this place, I've risked everything and given *everything* to build all these years? What about my girls? What about that poor brat you've foisted on me? And most of all – what about *us?* You selfish bastard Romans think only of yourselves – and screw everyone else, literally!'

I sensed it was pointless to reason with her when she was in this mood, but I had to try to make her see sense. I had only two days leave left before we received new orders, so there was little time.

'Listen to me! If the fort were to come under siege, as it soon may, the whole vicus will be razed – we cannot leave shelter and cover for the enemy. This place is doomed, love! Can you not see that? I've heard grave reports. When Boudica stormed Camulodunum none were left alive, everyone was slain, men, women, and children burned alive. They even disinterred the corpses of the Roman dead from their tombs. The depraved things they did to British collaborators – I dare not recount. If we lose Londinium, our way to the southern ports is blocked, our only escape route. Suetonius will need every last Roman soldier for the great battle. I may be gone within the month. For the sake of all that has been between us – don't torture me by staying in harm's way!'

'I thought you Romans were invincible!' she replied, sarcastically.

'So did I – until we lost the Ninth.'

I was weary by now, and also conscious that I was divulging important military secrets – an offence punishable by death. With a heavy sigh, I put a weighty purse full of coins between her hands, begging her to take it. Without warning, she burst into spasms of weeping. When her tears abated, she damned everything Rome stood for, everything I stood for.

'I heard the story about what your filthy butchers did to her – Boudica, that is. They dragged her down from her throne, and flogged her in front of her two daughters, not yet in their teens. To torment the poor woman beyond all endurance – they gang-raped the girls, pure virgins, and royal princesses – in front of the Procurator's officials. They laughed at the spectacle, apparently! You Romans care very little for women. You leave little baby girls outside on a freezing night in hopes they will perish – that's the value *you* put on our lives. We Britons revere our women, treat them as equals, not just objects to be used, like your people. You treat children with equal contempt. Look at that poor boy you brought in to me, he can't be more than ten summers old. It is despicable to violate a little child so! You have sowed the wind Decurion, now reap the whirlwind!'

'Ah, but the storm will blow your house down too! How is the boy, by the way? I saved his life, cruel Roman though I may be! I am no more Roman than you are! My folk were fighting Caesar when Britannia was no more than a legend. But you can't beat the empire – it is too strong. Even if we are wiped out, the eagles will return, one day. I didn't mean to impose about the lad – but I thought your new fisherman-god would approve. I'll take him back where we found him as soon as he is well.'

She parodied me: 'I didn't *mean to impose* ...' but then, she seemed to grow distant, as if she had something important to tell me. She thought better of it, though.

'Oh, he's doing well, considering he has two broken ribs. I've put him in Brid's room.'

I struggled to recall which girl Brid was, but then remembered – it was the simpleton lass.

'I thought you were going to let that one go, the simple one? She gave up working, must be six months back now isn't it? Why do you keep her on?'

I was surprised by the vehemence of Gwyn's response.

'I'll manage my own business and staff, thank you very much! That's another thing you Romans do – you devalue anything you can't understand. Brid is very far from being 'simple' actually, she is just very sensitive. This new god of hers, the one who welcomes whores and tavern-keepers to his table, is of interest to me. But there is something I meant to tell you! There is a strange empathy between Brid and that boy – I can sense it when I see them together, almost as if they are silently conspiring. That leather symbol of a fish Brid wears around her neck, her lucky charm; well guess what? The lad has just the same symbol tattooed on the back of his neck, concealed by his hair – I saw it when I bathed him the other day. But there is another thing, something very important that you need to know ...'

Before her sentence was finished, I was already fast asleep.

The supplicant maiden trudged on over the sandstone outcrop of the Great Edge. It was a spring morning, so she kept carefully to the path to avoid disturbing the adder-kind. On such balmy days they emerged to perform the 'adder-dance' on the heath, a writhing knot of males squirming to fight for the admiration of the females, sometimes rearing up. But some old snakes still lay hidden among the gorse and heather, ready to strike any careless passer-by with their wicked fangs. An adder-sting could sometimes be fatal, but most lived to tell the tale, just like old Nana.

She had been stung as a child when her malicious older brother threw her wooden dolly into a bramble thicket. It fell into an adder's lair, and she didn't even see the serpent as she reached out her little hand to grasp her prize possession. Serpents never retreat from their lairs; that is why they are guardian-spirits. Her brother heard her squeals and summoned her parents from the caves to carry her home. Her wrist and arm turned indigo-blue before she lost consciousness, her breathing so shallow that the cunning-woman advised her folk she could not be saved.

But little Megan lived, and when she was quite recovered, told of her adventures with the snake-goddess in the Other-world. As she grew-up, she uttered strange prayers and prophesies – a sign that she had been favoured by the snake-deity whose holy-place this was. The Ophites or Iberians, from Portugal and Galicia, long preceded the Druids in these islands. Although she was of humble parentage, at twelve years she was admitted into the Order by the Holy Austin himself.

For twenty years the Companion of God educated Megan in the arts of natural philosophy and magic, until the day came when she was initiated as a *Bandrui* – a Druidic priestess. There was a high price for such pre-eminence. She could find no man to take as a husband. Although marriage, even motherhood, was not exactly proscribed, no sane man would dare to approach her. Even to let her shadow fall across one's path could spell death. To lie with her, it was thought, would mean instant immolation by lightning.

So, she had spent her long years alone, in her cave residence, known to all as 'Megan's hole' or 'the fox-hole' hereabouts. But in her latter years, the ageing woman found a new companion, a foundling brought to her by the villagers. The babe had the colic, but with tender care she nurtured him until he was recovered. She was much too old to make milk, but the little one soon started suckling watered-down goat's-milk from an improvised teat she had fashioned. She called the lad Cara, in honour of the great British hero, Caratacus, 'the beloved one'. For surely, no child was more beloved than this cheeky boy with his wild golden locks. He was the apple of her eye.

Austin visited with gifts for the lad and his 'Nana', as she became known. These events, he declared, had been prophesied long ago. A boy-child, with no mother or father, would appear in the place of snakes – to be reared and educated by the representative of the snake-goddess. The great cycle of life was completing itself once more. Just as she had been selected, nurtured and educated by the Druid, now Meg herself must pass on the sacred knowledge to this, her divine son. It was a blessing to them both, and as her bones began to ache with age, how glad she was of her little companion, her *chela,* he who would be the representative of the All-Father in his turn. But for over a week now, the precious boy had been missing. It was rumoured that the red-cloaks had taken him.

Brid approached the cave reverently. In the penumbral light at the mouth of the cave she saw old Nana slowly emerge from the inner recesses. Meg guessed the identity of her visitor long before she could properly see her – nothing could be hidden from her inner-eye. Brid shouted up to her.

'Nana! Megan! I have him! He's safe and in my care, so fear not!'

The old one scrambled down onto the path to embrace the girl, her tears streaming down her cheeks for joy.

'Is he harmed? What did they do to him? If they have injured my boy – I will bring down a curse on that fort – on all the cruel Roman-kind, I will strike them with lightning-bolts from heaven!' Brid tried to reassure her, as best she could.

'He is badly beaten and sore, but in good spirits and will recover in time. Oh Nana, do not punish them all! There are good and bad among the Romans, just as among our own. It was a Roman officer that saved him, and by the grace of our Lord, brought him to me – the only follower of the Christ in the whole camp. It is a miracle! With a fair wind, he will be home before Beltane.'

They ascended the steep rock-cut stairs into the cave. In a hollowed-out shelf in the darkest recesses stood a small wicker cage containing two cooing pigeons. Megan took the cage onto the outside terrace to give the poor creatures one last glimpse of the light, before quickly removing them and wringing their necks. Their little feathered bodies lay still warm and twitching on the stone flags. Nana next produced a small blade and slit open their bellies to scoop out the entrails. These were strewn beside the corpses so that the Druidess could examine their tiny organs in detail – the oval-shaped spleens, kidneys, lights and hearts.

Brid could not bear to look on, for she loved all living creatures, but none more than doves – emblem of the Holy Spirit. Megan despaired of her young pupil, for divination by such means was not for the squeamish. It was as well that the old ways were coming to an end, to make way for the new faith. In general the auspices were good, she thought the boy would recover and be restored to her soon.

Next, she scattered the blood to watch the fall of the pattern. She seemed perplexed and drew down her birch-bark cap over her eyes. Nana retreated into a corner of the cave and dropped down onto the floor, rocking from side-to-side, cooing like the doves. Then she began mewling and growling like an angry cat. Soon, she had entered the *Awen* or dreaming-state. But these were waking dreams, visions of things to come.

Brid grew concerned when the old one suddenly let out a piercing shriek. She collapsed, began twitching like one in a fit of the falling-sickness. She also passed much water. Eventually, she came to herself, but the trauma of her inner journey left her drained. Brid could contain herself no longer.

'What is it Nana? Tell me the auguries! What did you see?' The old one was still trembling.

'The Black Goddess, Andrasta! Heads stacked in heaps, guts hanging in groves! Breasts sewn onto mouths, bodies impaled, horses trampling swaddled babes! And noise! Such noise. Statues falling, pots smashing, glass cracking, dogs barking – and the roaring of flames – yes, flames, and choking billowing smoke – and screaming!'

'What does it portend, Nana?'

Megan cackled her delight. Her magical son was avenged.

'The Roman city girl! Londinium! It burns – *yes!* It burns!'

Brid stooped over the lad's bed to apply a herbal compress. He recoiled from the stinging pain but bravely bore it for the girl's sake, for she replicated his every yelp and shudder. Besides, it was unseemly to show any weakness before a woman. Once she had helped the boy take some deep breaths to prevent pneumonia, she propped him up in his bed and spoon-fed him pottage from a wooden bowl. She had a natural gift for nursing. As she bent forward he noticed the charm dangling around her neck, the secret sign of the faith.

'How long have you worn that sign about your neck? I think it was not placed there on your ninth day, as is the custom. You take a great risk to wear it so near to the camp. It may arouse suspicion.' Brid set aside the bowl and spoon and tried to reassure him.

'Don't worry, I am so lowly no-one concerns themselves. They think me an imbecile, one touched by the gods. My saviour watches over me, so fear not! Now, sleep boy.' Cara protested, for he was miserable and bored. He wanted to return to his Nana.

'No, don't leave me! Tell me more of Nana, and this vision of hers. When can I leave this place? I need to return to my holy place, I need to know what she has seen!'

'You are not yet sufficiently recovered. My mistress will arrange your return with the Decurion when you are fit and well enough.

But the Romans have other concerns just now, do you not sense the buzz around the camp?'

The boy was intrigued, excited. He yearned for news of the outside world, and this girl was his only informant.

'What is happening? While all Britannia is in turmoil, I lie here useless! The rebellion here is just the beginning! Soon, the whole world will rise up against Nero – the Anti-Christ! If you are a follower of the way, you must help me play my part, for I am indeed what the red-cloaks suspected all along – the last of the Druid-kind, and will be a priest of the new faith – God willing!'

Brid tried to calm him.

'Hush! The rumour is, that Londinium has fallen, just as Nana saw in her vision. The whole camp is in shock. But all these things must pass. They do not concern me – I only want to know more of the Christ! Tell me more of the faith, and how it came to you! If it is true what you say, that the old gods are finished forever – then surely *He* will return in majesty, and walk among us on this island again, as He did when he was a boy?' Cara's countenance grew pained, and his words seemed those of one far beyond his years.

'I am not yet qualified to answer, that is why I *must* get out of here! The Holy Austin has gone ahead, to Ynys Witrin, the Isle of Glass – far to the south-west, in the Summer-country. On that sacred island, the Secret of the Lord lies concealed, a community of saints founded by none other than the Christ Himself! The Druidic faith lies in ruins, all but destroyed. The Black Goddess rises in anger – but she cannot prevail!' He pretended to gnaw on a knuckle-joint, lest their conversation be noticed by a maid who briefly wandered in, but then he continued.

'When the Holy Austin returns at mid-summer, I shall be escorted to the heart of the Invisible College for further instruction. There, I shall learn to draw sounds, and other recondite arts. When I have completed the curriculum, I shall become a God-bearer, give birth to the Christ within! The Druidic Trinity established three separate orders, Bards, who had care of the past, Ovates whose concern was the future – and the Druids – the Oak-knowers, those who reconciled time itself. Now, the white-robed, grey-bearded ones lie prostrate, slain on their own altars! But from the ashes of Ynys Mon – the pyres of the venerable priests – a new faith will be born, against which even Nero himself cannot hope to prevail! Serve me well, and you will be received into the company of heaven by the Christ – smiling, radiant as the sun, a diademed king in supreme majesty!'

I was making my way down the Via Principia early one morning to visit the smithy to collect some repairs, when I saw the Commandant's Optio racing over to the Praetorium. He called out to me.

'Decurion, have you heard yet?' I stood looking baffled. He briefly halted before he conveyed the dreadful news.

'Londinium has been totally destroyed – wiped out, and all who could not flee from there. There are no survivors. Suetonius got out in the nick of time, just before the barbarians stormed the place. He reports that the inferno could be seen forty miles away – a catastrophe!'

The Optio hurried on, his astonishment at the news was no greater than my own. I have only visited the city twice, but it was the one place in Britannia where a Gaul could pretend he was back home, a real city with imposing statues, temples, a gigantic forum – and the busy quays and wharves, the mighty warehouses all along the wide river, bustling with traffic from all over the empire. I took my leave there once, before a visit home for a family funeral. I had a wonderful time and some intimate memories of my own.

I heard the Optio's voice again in my head, 'There are no survivors'; it just couldn't be accurate – that would mean 40,000 people dead! But as soon as we convened in the Praetorium, the grim tale was confirmed by the Prefect himself. We all steeled ourselves for the great battle to come – but then, more disappointment – our orders were to remain in camp.

We were devastated, dishonoured, but the high command had other plans. The warrior-queen had contrived to lure Suetonius into a trap in Londinium – but the old fox was too wily for that. Now, he planned to spring a trap of his own, but should it fail, we were his only back-up plan. We were to guard the *Hen Ffordd* or 'Old Road' to cover any retreat of the legions as they crossed the Sabrina. After that, it would be every man for himself, a race to the coast, and hopefully, evacuation by sea from the territory of our allies, the Demetae. We all knew what a slim chance it was, and the knitted brows of my colleagues spoke volumes. Within a week, two at most, the barbarian host, 200,000 strong some said – would be upon us.

I bribed my deputy to take out my patrol the next morning. It was imperative to see Gwyn, to plead with her again to see sense and flee while there was still time. The northern days were lengthening, it would soon be Beltane. I rarely entered Gwyn's while it was still light, from military decorum I suppose – but now I couldn't care less who saw me. This may even be our last night together – and that thought filled me with a sickening dread. She had become my emotional touchstone, my confidante, much more than a whore to me, and I suddenly needed the gods to unite us, to finally make what had been knitted together over long years indissoluble. I knew I must ask her to marry me in secret – according to the rites of our own Celtic people – even if it meant breaking military law.

Some hours later, well after dark, she nuzzled up to me, whispering in my ear.

'What d'ya think my father did for his living, Decurion?' I was perplexed.

'I don't know! What did your father do?' She quietly giggled.

'Well, he was a swine-herd, if you must know, among other trades.' I couldn't see where this was leading.

'A pig-girl, 'eh! Is that why you're starting to grow porky?' Her punch to my shoulder left a bruise.

'Ouch! Careful, pig-girl, I'm all that stands between you and the barbarian hordes! What are you wittering on about?'

'That boy, is what I am on about. Your Commandant must be a mug. No lad goes out gathering acorns in the spring! What a silly story! You made a mistake, the lad *is* in some conspiracy with the underground. I ear-wigged Brid talking to him this morning while I was hidden outside on the landing.'

'Are you certain? He is so young – what harm could he do?' Gwyn cackled with pleasure at my dilemma.

'He managed to outwit you, and your dim-witted Commandant. The Druids are *born into* the faith. His elder brethren may be looking for him, and then you'll be in a fix, and no mistake!' I was mystified by her merriment, thought she had been at the wine.

'My dear, we are all in a fix! It may have escaped your attention but we stand in some danger just now! What makes you so gleeful, if I may ask?' Then she knocked my whole world sideways.

'Oh, I don't know. Could be mood-swings – they say pregnant women get them.'

'Pregnant women? You can't be serious – you must be pushing thirty!' She slapped me, of course, then gently kissed the other cheek before slipping into her robe.

'Oh, I am very serious Decurion – and I'm thirty-one.' She went out onto the landing to piss in a pot, while I lay stunned, staring blankly into the darkness.

In the early morning Brid came to collect the pot from outside the door. Once she had disposed of all the night-soil and other detritus from outside the rooms, she raked out the grates and relit the fires. On her knees in front of the hearth, she was too busy stacking kindling to notice her mistress enter behind her. Gwyn's voice startled her.

'Brid, leave that. Come into the parlour, I want to speak with you over breakfast.'

The girl was uneasy, aware of something ominous in the manner of her beautiful mistress. Gwyn sat her down on a stool while she prepared some spiced fish and watered wine. For a long time, Brid stared intensely at the floor, but finally she could contain herself no longer. With tears in her eyes, she spoke first.

'Oh ma'am, please don't let me go! I promise, I will mend my ways, do more work, for longer hours. I have no-one to go to, ma'am, no people of my own. I could not live!' Gwyn swigged her wine before replying.

'Your father was a debtor, was he not?'

'Yes ma'am.'

'So you were sold into slavery to pay his debts. We all know that story. So, how come you are no longer in bondage?'

'My master's villa was burned down in a fire from the hypocaust. His family moved into the slaves' quarters and we children were granted our manumission. I was free ma'am, but had nowhere to go.'

'And so, you became a whore.'

'No ma'am, not straight away. I found service as a maid to assist an old holy-man in the caves over yonder. He grows grey and stiff-legged and falls into faints. His soul-friend, an old woman in a neighbouring cave, employed me to care for them both, in exchange for shelter, food and clothing. I stayed there two years. But when my holy-man went away to walk his spirit path, I had no choice but to come to you. Oh, please ma'am, I cannot lie with strangers again! It is a sin, a stain on me – no offence ma'am, I didn't mean any judgement on you, it is forbidden in my faith.'

'Show me that charm you wear around your neck.' Brid removed it reverently and handed it across.

'What's the fish sign all about again?'

'I don't rightly know ma'am. Perhaps because some of His followers were fishermen? It is just our secret sign among ourselves.'

'And your god really doesn't despise you, for all that you have been a whore?'

'No ma'am. But the sin He *does* despise.'

'Wench, you speak in riddles! So, your holy-man left you in the lurch, and you came to me. You are a pretty little thing. Rough soldiers like that. But you earn me no money now! Your holy-man took his way to Ynys Witrin did he not?' Brid gasped in horror.

'How do you know that?'

'I know *everything* that goes on under my own roof, my girl. The boy's voice carries – he's very fond of it too! Fear not, I will not betray you! In fact, I need your help.' Brid was only too anxious to make herself useful.

'Oh, anything! Anything at all ma'am!'

'Very well. Now, keep this a strict secret, especially from the other girls. I have sold the lease on this place. We must prepare to move, and in a hurry!'

The tide of humanity, drunken with blood, stretched twenty miles down the Legions' Road heading north. Wagons packed with booty in the thousands, whole tribes on the move. The women rode in carts drawn by oxen at the rear of the gigantic column. Children, even babes-in-arms, travelled with them, and thousands of yelping ferocious hounds snarling for scraps and bones. Further on rode the mounted warriors, thousands of them, for every horse in southern Britain had been taken. The Iceni were travelling in style now.

At the head of the column, the battle-chariots, light, strong and swift, clattered on their way. There were bottlenecks and jams every other mile. Dismounted from her chariot, the goddess reclined on a liberated couch while her generals conferred in the makeshift tent at the roadside. The queen's daughters ran off to bathe themselves, away from the stares of the warriors. Every day, something like this happened. Needless hold-ups, no discipline or organisation – just chaos, and dissembling excuses from the warlords. At this rate the Romans would be more than ready. In war, space can be lost, but time, never. Her anger was barely concealed as her Commander-in-Chief arrived, looking extremely nervous. He knelt before the divinity and made his report.

'I must sadly report to Her Majesty Victoria, that no further progress can be made today. The Trinovantes say they will not continue north until the city of Verulamium has been – eliminated. It *is* a military obstacle ma'am.'

The queen rose to her feet in fury. She was tall, with a mass of wild red hair tumbling to her waist. Her variegated tartan cloak with its ornate golden brooch-clasp, and a diadem on a golden-band around her head, was all there was to distinguish her from the thousands of other Celtic womenfolk in the host – until she spoke. All men fell to their knees when she barked her words of command.

'Enough of this! I know the Trinovantes and their so-called "military strategy"! Ransack rich villas and guzzle the wine, parade around in rich men's togas, rape the children and murder old men hiding in their cellars – anything, *anything* to avoid battle! Tell those cowardly bastards I will lop off all their heads if we do not *press on* and now! The Romans must be destroyed, the Roman *army* that is. You know what an army is don't you general? They have defiled me! Your goddess, Andrasta! I demand revenge – I thirst for blood, but all I hear is pathetic excuses!'

The general knelt at her feet and bared his neck, offering up his own sword to her to strike the blow.

'If I have failed you ma'am, send me to my ancestors!'

Boudica relented. She would need his sword soon enough.

'Stand up man! How long will it take? Is it defended? What is there to take that they haven't already looted from Londinium and Camulodunum? This is supposed to be an army, not a rabble! Alright, tell them three days – no more, mind. I want that place obliterated, smashed out of my way – and then, I want Suetonius, and all those other Roman bastards. I want them *exterminated* do you understand? Now, dismissed!'

The raven, pecking the ground outside the tent, cocked her head, then flapped her black wings, and rose into the sky heading towards the west. Even ravens grow weary. As she flew over the outskirts of Verulamium, the villas in the countryside around were already burning. She alighted on the gatehouse of the largest in the area, as large as any fortress. The west wing where the servants' quarters were was already ablaze. Men were swinging children by their ankles to smash their skulls against the walls. Others held children between them, one pulling on each limb until they were torn asunder. The men were tied to trees in the orchards, and disembowelled, then wrapped in their own entrails coiled around the tree-trunks. The two young daughters of the house were dragged screaming to the formal gardens and defiled. Their corpses were finally thrown into the pig-pens behind the house. The Greek tutor was blinded with hot irons, his tongue torn out with pincers, and decapitated. Finally, the master of the house was led out by a halter. He had been hiding in the stables with his young son, whose decapitated head now hung suspended around his neck. They dragged him to a field and laid him alive, face-down in a furrow – then ploughed him into the earth with a team of oxen, like manure. These sights, a feast for a raven, were too appalling for human eyes. She flew on, far to the west, where she could shift her shape once more.

'Wait here, while I go to fetch the Nana.'

Brid wandered off into the birch-wood beneath the high sandstone rock. Gwyn sat on a tree-trunk beside the well, shivering a little, despite her cowled tunic and shawl. Even in late spring, a sudden cold snap brought tiny flakes of snow on the wind. Eventually, Brid emerged, supporting the old crone as she hobbled down the path using her staff. Could this really be the Druidess, the seer, the keeper of the encrinite, the 'Snake-stone' or 'Adder-Egg'? There was a hole in the middle of the stone, which this woman had the gift to see through, into the Other-world. Gwyn removed her fur-lined cowl and approached the priestess with open palms, and the traditional petitioner's greeting.

'Welcome Nana! I greet you, as one independent-minded woman to another! I humbly thank you for agreeing to this consultation. I've brought – a little picnic, and some wine!' The old one's bulging eyes sparkled with delight.

'Wine 'eh? Well, let's get to it then! Brid, it is too chill here. Let's get up into the fox-hole!'

The three weird women gathered their belongings to pick their way slowly to the cave, which was, once inside, surprisingly comfortable. When Brid had banked up the fire, the wicker hamper was opened, including three flagons of Gaulish wine. Nana indicated these with a pointed forefinger.

'Crack that open then!' The Nana hadn't tasted wine for thirty years, and was already proffering her beaker. She soon glugged it all down and offered up the beaker in her outstretched talon for more. Gwyn remonstrated with her.

'Steady on, Nana! We have business to discuss! Look, I am in a bind. I've got a bellyful of arms and legs – I know I look over-ripe. The father is the Roman trooper who saved your boy. He wants me to flee, to Gaul, but my roots are struck too deep. I want my baby born here, in the Island of the Blessed. I love the father, and I wish to marry – but cannot, because of my – profession.' The old one nodded sagely.

'Aye, 'tis true.– marriage is forbidden to you under Druidic law, though your calling is even older than my own! But, there is always *t'other*, the old way – which none can deny you.' Gwyn shook her head.

'No, my man is too straight for all that. What I want is for our union to be blessed by this new god – he who welcomes whores and sinners. It seems to me that I can marry in good faith on such terms, at least if I understand things correctly?' Nana wiped a dewdrop from her nose. She thought carefully.

'Madam, you misunderstand. I am a priestess of the old faith, not the new. My soul-friend, Father Austin, he may be able to do it. He is no mere scallywag bard or poor-man's Druid! He'll be back in two more moons.'

'No, no, that's too long! The world is in peril! If it must be done in the old way – then so be it. I am looking to settle somewhere around here, and to build a small farmstead with wide paddocks. I plan to breed horses to sell to the Roman cavalry. I'll be needing a good water-supply. Why not that well down below? It would be some company for you, in old age, and Brid would be close at-hand. What do you say?'

Gwyn handed over the flagon, and the crone drained it at a swallow. She stretched out her hand.

'Well, I shall be glad to marry the couple who saved my boy – in whatever way it pleases you. You are welcome to settle, if you will, for I am warmed at heart by you, a woman of spirit, like myself.'

They clinked beakers, drained them, and the deal was done. The hag suddenly sobered herself.

'But now madam – tell me of my boy! When will he come home to me? I pine here and waste away. Please, bring him, before Beltane!' Gwyn chewed on a piece of blood-pudding, considering her reply.

'Mother, much depends on Boudica! That is why I have come. I need to know the outcome of the coming battle. If the eagles fail, that's the end of my marriage plan *and* my business-plan! That's your skill. I ask you to look through the Serpent-stone, to receive a vision of things to come. Can you do this thing for me, as Brid says?' The hag nodded her agreement, extending her cup yet again.

'Very well madam, as you wish – but we will be needing to take something stronger than wine for our journeying – we must first dine on the flesh of the gods.'

The great queen stretched herself prone on the furs and felt, as her daughters gently rubbed a herbal ointment mixed with goose-fat onto her back. The weals from her flogging were still painful.

Ever since the outrage, she had known only drugged sleep – sleep disturbed by nightmares. She was preparing to take her sleeping draught for the night and settle the girls down when her charioteer drew aside the curtain-flap with an important message.

'My Queen, splendid news! The Second Legion, *Augusta*, has refused to march, and remains at Isca within the fortress. Their commander disobeyed a direct order from Suetonius, fearing the same fate as the Ninth. Now, he has only two legions, maybe less. We outnumber them by more than ten to one! We should press on quickly now ma'am, and destroy them as an offering for Beltane!'

Boudica was overjoyed.

'At last! At first light summon all the chieftains. I will speak from the chariot. I want all these women and children and runaway slaves moved off the road! Fighters have priority now, cavalry and chariots must be to the fore. I issue a proclamation. All looters will be executed after noon today, no exceptions. Send out scouts – he can't be far away now, and I've *got* the old bastard by his balls!'

As the sun rose, a vast host assembled to hear the queen address them from the pulpit of her war-chariot, her daughters huddled at her feet. In her right hand, she grasped the spear of liberty, invoking the war-goddess, Andrasta, whose personification she had become. But now, as the crowd hushed, she wanted more than anything for her human suffering to be recognised, not her divinity.

'We Britons are used to being led by women in war, noble women, that is, but I'm not standing before you as your general – no, I present myself instead as a humble woman, just like your own mother, sister, wife or daughter. I strive to revenge my lost liberty, my tortured body, the violation of my daughters, as any ordinary woman would. Roman greed and lust know no bounds! Even old women and children are not left undefiled! But the gods are granting us our just revenge. The Second Legion cowers in its fortress. We have already cut one legion to pieces, and now only Suetonius stands between us and freedom for all Britain! They won't even stand the raised voices of such a mighty host as this one, let alone withstand our spears! Look at our numbers, and then think of the reason why we fight – and be sure that we must now conquer or die. That is what I, a woman, intend to do – you men live as Roman slaves if you like!'

As Boudica stepped down from the chariot she was cheered to the echo by tens of thousands. The decisive conflict could be delayed no longer.

Old Nana polished the hag-stone and held it up between her thumb and forefinger in the firelight. It was slightly smaller than a hen's egg. She gestured to Brid.

'Girl, make up a bed for our guest. We are going on a spirit-flight. You'll watch over the fire and our bodies while we are gone. Now, fetch me the *pookies*!'

Nana prepared her drum and rattle, raven-feathers and various amulets, as Brid handed her a flask containing the woodland mushroom, dried and preserved in honey. She handed the flask to Gwyn for her inspection. She seemed wary at first, but tasting the contents found them less unpleasant than she expected. She had heard tales about these mushrooms as a child and been strictly warned off them, but there was a first time for everything. Nana reassured her.

'Don't worry. The mushroom folk are tricky, but very wise and ancient. The fruit of the mushroom we see, is but a small part of the main flesh, which grows for miles underground, for thousands of years! The pookie-imps will lead us over the threshold, never fear!'

'Are you sure it won't harm the baby?' Gwyn asked.

'Maybe it will give him a few odd dreams!'

'Why do you say 'him'?'

'Because you are carrying a boy-child in you. Any old maid can see that! There is no point in my leaving the body to scout for you. Only *you* know what it is you want to know. Don't worry, I'll fly beside you to protect you – and the little man – from harm! Now, settle beside the hearth. One night in the wild never harmed anyone.' She sat herself down.

Nana turned her rattle, hissing like a snake at bay, as Brid dispensed the precious nectar on a wooden spoon. Then, the old woman began mewling, her voice rising to a high ululating wail as she beat out a steady rhythm on her drum. As the fire smoke spiralled out towards the cave entrance, Gwyn became aware that something in her was also being drawn-out – and she took a deep breath, as her spirit became loosened from its bodily moorings. When she closed her eyes, Gwyn found that she could actually *see* ghostly shades of different shapes and colours. The noise from Nana, originating deep in her chest, became an almost physical force.

When she opened her eyes, she glanced at Brid, the simple serving-girl – but now, not so simple. There was something very *deep* about that girl! The old one's demeanour, so friendly before, seemed suddenly ominous, hostile. Gwyn started to panic and felt the first onset of nausea. She promptly threw up – but the steady rhythm of the drum beat on and on.

The mother-to-be suddenly felt like a lost soul, and she began to weep – for the fate of her unborn child, soon to be thrown into this cruel world. Just as she had been herself not so long ago. She saw her sister and herself, sitting cross-legged in their mother's weaving-shed, watching and learning each warp and weft in the pattern on the frame – the pattern on the frame – suddenly she was no longer observing the pattern, she had *become* the pattern.

By the gods, this stuff was stronger than wine alright! The next thing she knew, she was giggling helplessly, weeping with hysterical laughter. What struck her was the irony, for there was nothing funny about her present situation – it was just, well, ridiculous! She had always been a naughty girl, a *bad* girl! Then, the drumming ceased. Brid knelt down beside her and whispered in her ear.

'Things will become very strange now ma'am, but remember, you cannot go back – only forward. Let your spirit drift where it will.'

The fire grew lower, the light correspondingly dimmer. A fecund assortment of images danced in the smoke … smoke! Must get out! Roof-thatch burning, oxen and ponies trapped in their stalls, Dada smoking too, his clothing on fire – his hair on fire! Must get out, into the fresh, clear air, into the wide expanses of the slate-grey sky … blackened with vast flocks of unkindnesses, all on the wing, bound for the feast of eyes!

It is well-known that ravens foregather at battlefields *before* the actual conflict, not directly afterwards as one might expect. The lesser birds, carrion-crows and kites, like their soul-brothers, the grey wolves of the forest – at least have the courtesy to wait until the slaughter is concluded before swarming the corpses to gorge themselves, but not the raven-kind. It is men's eyes they crave, choicest of morsels, a delicacy of a special kind, for in a man's eye, it is said – is contained all he has seen in his lifetime, the essence of his vision.

We are not 'unkind' – not at all, for when we have plucked and pecked those tender eggs from their sockets, we soar, high on our jet-black wings, heavenwards to the sky-god, bearing our precious plunder. Not that we care if we are kind or unkind. Our black talons and curved beaks give us a bad reputation, but we mean no harm. We only want to eat. The wide indigo sky cannot contain our collective darkness, our ravenous need.

We flew all through the night, blackness on blackness, until at dawn we looked down upon a dense wood behind a narrow gorge. Far below, the densely packed red-cloaks stood-to-arms behind their huge shields, twelve-thousand strong. Some were still digging a trench in front of their position, while on the flanks the Roman cavalry massed, lances at the ready. The old man himself rode out to address them, to great cheering and the pounding of swords on shields. He was a professional, so he kept it short and to the point.

'Don't worry about the racket these savages make! There are more women and kids in their ranks than warriors. They are an untrained rabble. You are the finest soldiers in the world! Don't worry about our numbers, in every battle, it is always a few heroes who carry the day. Think of the glory you will win, when we vanquish such a mighty host! When they come on, just hurl your javelins – then push forward, knock them down with your shields, stab them, and move on. Kill everything to your front until relieved, no mercy – men, women, children, oxen – be sure to kill them all! When they feel our steel and see our discipline and courage they'll soon crack and run for it, just like they always do. Don't worry about booty – just win the battle, and you'll keep all!'

A mile away, the vast British host prepared to assault the Roman line. A dense mass of warriors, 100,000 strong, were cheering and chanting, blowing on their *carnyx* trumpets, or cavorting in wild demonstrations in their chariots, goading the Roman cavalry to break ranks. To their rear, almost as many women and children stood in a huge grandstand formed from their wagon-train, which stretched in a great horseshoe for over a mile. The queen toured the front line in her chariot with her daughters, exhorting her warriors to return with their shields, or dead upon them, before taking her seat on a specially prepared viewing dais. At her signal, the front ranks, the bravest and best-equipped warriors, moved forward at a steady walk. Gradually, they broke into a trot, before they furiously charged, yelling wild war-cries.

As soon as they confronted the Roman trench, the first volley of *pila*, lead-weighted javelins, arced into the British front-rank from thirty yards range. Almost all found their mark, and no shield was effective against them. Those who survived were forced to discard their shields, and without armour, became sitting ducks for another volley, another hail of death. Men were stumbling over the bodies of their fallen comrades, with no room to manoeuvre. Then, to their horror, the red wall began to form up into a gigantic wedge, completely enclosed by their huge shields, and moved steadily forward.

Now, the real butchery began. The legions drew their short stabbing-swords, thrusting into the bellies of the exposed British warriors. They tried desperately to fall back but could not, for the pressure of all their comrades behind them. The shout went up to fall back, so that those in action could have space to wield their long swords – but there could be no going back. They were trapped by the improvised stadium they had constructed, where their womenfolk and children watched the slaughter in horror, including the queen.

The screaming and pandemonium had already commenced, less than an hour into the struggle, but civilians could do little to escape without the wagons they now stood in. Roman trumpets blew, and their cavalry charged.

The effect was instant. The oxen and ponies set out to pasture began to stampede. Women, some with children in their arms, bolted towards the road, first in hundreds, then in thousands. Boudica was incensed, demanding to be conveyed to the front line, so as to rally her men. But without warning, a group of six burly bodyguards seized her by the wrists, and her daughters likewise. She shrieked and spat, writhing like a wild-cat.

'Unhand me you pigs! I am your queen! What do you think you are doing!' Her charioteer slapped her hard across the face.

'Ma'am, we can do this the easy way – or the hard way. The battle is lost. You must not be taken alive – for the sake of the tribe! If you leave now, your *daughters* may yet live, anonymously. It is over!'

The wild-eyed woman was bundled into a chariot with her two girls following, and then escorted at speed towards the Londinium road with a bodyguard of forty mounted men. Her escape was assured because although the Romans had smashed the Britons in less than two hours, their general's grim extermination order meant that the killing continued all day and on into the night, until eighty thousand lay dead in heaps. The legionaries tramped forward through a mixture of corpses, mud, grass and slimy pools of human and animal blood.

When darkness came there was no energy for a pursuit. The red-cloaks withdrew to their start-lines and simply dropped where they stood, without campfires or food – but not without water. They were desperately thirsty, but they also needed to wash the stench of clotted blood off themselves, for every man was drenched. When they awoke on a bright spring morning, the whole vast plain before them was black with ravens and crows, and dense masses of buzzing flies in a visible cloud over the corpse heaps. The smoke from the first pyres was already rising.

It was almost Saturnalia before the first reinforcements arrived from Germania, in the bitterest winter anyone could remember. I stood chatting to one of them, as we warmed our hands over a brazier. It was so good to have reliable news of the outside world. My comrade was not impressed with the British climate.

'By the gods, it's colder than a whore's heart! Worse than Germania! So, you saw no action in the campaign yourself, Decurion?'

'No, not on the battlefield anyway!'

'You must be cursing your luck. The whole empire is buzzing about it. The Fourteenth Legion are lauded as heroes, and you were stuck in this cess-hole with these barbarians.' I bristled somewhat.

'My woman is one of the "barbarians".' The trooper instantly apologised.

'Oh, I'm sorry sir. I'm forgetting how long you've been over here.'

'No matter. Tell me, how are things going in Londinium?'

'Well, they've laid out the plots, and as soon as this blasted frost thaws they begin rebuilding! Incredible really sir, isn't it?'

'It is. I shall see for myself next year. I have a month's home leave in Gaul, so I'll be passing through.'

'Gaul! A place I love, sir! I was stationed there. There's other good news! The *Cursus publicus* is working again! You can write to your folks in Gaul. You must have plenty of news to tell them.' I couldn't help but give him a sardonic smile, before I continued on my rounds.

'Soldier, you are right.'

I arrived at the storeroom beside the granary where I had first met the boy. I wondered how he was getting on now, in his sanctuary far to the south. What a year it had been since then! The last time I saw him was at our wedding-feast, really just a small picnic in the open air beneath the cave. I remember I was standing with him when Brid led Gwyn down the path in her bridal dress and veil. Brid dragged the trussed-up sow forward, and Nana stuck it – our offering, and wedding-feast. We took our vows before the makeshift altar, on which Gwyn laid her lucky charm and her old clothes. She needed no household gods to protect her now.

We dipped the spelt cake in the cup of rich red wine, before I parted her veil and we both took a bite. Gwyn's white dress, fastened with a double-knot at the girdle, was already slightly tight around her swelling middle. She wore a bright yellow cloak over her shoulders, and yellow shoes to match. I took a glimpse at her through her scarlet veil. We clasped our right hands and swore to be faithful to one another, forsaking all others, so long as we both lived. Then Nana pronounced us man and wife, and we kissed. The boy gave us both a gift of a fish charm, such as Brid wore, and prayed for the blessing of the Christ on our union. Perhaps the lad really was holy – for I have a boy of my own now, a son.

In the morning I paid a visit to the metal-worker, with a special request.

'A stylus, sir? Scratching a tablet is it? Well, why not? You have some good news to share, and no mistake!'

I sat looking at the small wooden squares in despair! How to set down all that had happened in such a tiny space? I hadn't written to Flavia in four long years, though she always corresponded annually. In the end, the courier was due, so not wanting to waste my money, I just wrote the first things which came into my head.

Dearest Flavia,
Thank you for the underpants! They don't make them properly here, and they cost a fortune. Please send more, as the weather here is freezing! I would have written before, but we've had a spot of bother here, which you may have heard about. I managed to miss out on all the action, so don't worry. My main news is, that I am now a married man! It is only a *Concubinatus* but we've been together some years now. She is a woman of property, and what is more we have a baby boy! We plan to visit in spring, so prepare for a big surprise!

Wishing you all a happy Saturnalia,
Your loving brother

10

The Land of Lost Content

Into my heart an air that kills
From yon far country blows:
What are those blue remembered hills,
What spires, what farms are those?
That is the land of lost content,
I see it shining plain,
The happy highways where I went
And cannot come again.

A.E. Housman, *A Shropshire Lad*

There is a particular vista, which can only be appreciated from the Severn Valley, of Titterstone Clee and Brown Clee hills, the highest points in England south of the Pennines. It has become my favourite pastoral scene, quintessentially English, 'God's own country'. But for me, there is something deeper about the county of Shropshire than its Englishness. As we have seen, it is disputed as to whether Shropshire should be classed as England at all. The last attempt at reuniting it with Wales, in 1405, ended in disappointment for Owain Glyndwr's invading Welsh army, but Merlin's prophesy of its repatriation, like the bard himself, only lies sleeping. Ultimately, although the scars from centuries of conflict have left a legacy – the castles, the battlefields – there is a soothing beauty and peace, a contentedness, about the area. It feels like one of the last such sanctuaries in England, and as I enter old age, I gaze out at those 'blue remembered hills' and imagine myself there.

The scholar and poet A.E. Housman (1859-1936) was not himself a 'Shropshire Lad'. He was inspired to write the poems by memories of gazing at the Clee Hills from the east as a boy, from his home village of Fockbury in Worcestershire, and he too, felt a mysterious empathy with this high country. It is said that he rarely visited Shropshire, his fabled land, if ever, though after his death his emotional resonance with the landscape he had envisioned was so celebrated that this atheist's ashes were buried outside St Laurence's Church in Ludlow, whose great tower was made so famous by the poem. People still travel from all over the world there to venerate his memory. His beloved cherry tree stands ready to blossom nearby.

Housman, unlike Thomas Hardy, his near contemporary, did not think of himself as a poet first and foremost. He was a classical scholar, and like his sometime tutorial student, Enoch Powell, he was known to be personally severe, rude, testy and abrupt – and took delight in a sometimes spiteful pedantry, his exemplary intellect notwithstanding.

He lived a solitary, circumscribed, and emotionally unfulfilling life – perhaps occasionally relieved by visits to male prostitutes when he was abroad, although this is only alleged. His poetry, with its themes of military service, an orderly empire and class system, and the glories of the English landscape, combined with an all-pervading sense of premature death and loss, seems to encapsulate a certain sort of Englishness, but it would be too easy to graft onto it notions of national identity. The poet's emotional immaturity and lack of lived experience does come across.

That there is a strange magic about *A Shropshire Lad* few would deny, although many have parodied and disparaged it. At first, the poems struggled, Housman had to underwrite the first limited printing. But by the time of the outbreak of the First World War, in August 1914, the poems were such a success, so deeply ingrained in the public mind, that many soldiers carried a small version designed to fit inside their battledress-pocket with them as they entered the carnage of the Western Front.

As George Orwell, a former Etonian commented, the public schoolboys who formed the officer-cadre of the British Empire were all in awe of Housman's poetry – it was after all, designed for 'lads'. Orwell claimed that they recited them in their dorms, as if they were almost mystical. Many saw in these 63 poems, published 18 years before, a prophesy of the horrors they were soon to witness – and the imminent death of the very England which is now being evoked in the early 21st century. For Housman, poetry was merely a hobby, a diversion, 'a morbid secretion', as he called it. How could such a man have produced such poems?

For me, the man is not so much the issue as the poetry, for it is this sadness, longing, pessimism, gallows-humour, this 'English melancholia', what the Welsh call *hiraeth*, which defines it. Schopenhauer posited a state he called *eudaimonia*, a sort of positive unhappiness, which Housman's work exemplifies. It is, once again, that old song of keening, loss, grief and mourning we have heard echoing across these hills and dales before down the ages. The Lost Lands are the Land of Lost Content. But the mainspring of the poems' extraordinary emotional energy, was our old friend, unrequited love – the poet's most enduring and precious gift.

To be an 'emotionally immature' poet sounds damning, but in this, as in many other cases, I prefer the verdict of biographers to that of reviewers and literary critics. Perhaps the latter should consider the position of a 12-year-old boy, the eldest of seven, with many siblings reliant upon him, when his beloved mother suddenly died during his exceptionally demanding scholarship examinations to an esteemed school – and whose father's ability to cope was compromised, to say the least. What if such a lad were to gaze wistfully to the west, to those carefree hills, to see the faraway lamps from their villages by night – and to wish himself there? For, in his native hills, he was struggling – alone and unsupported for the most part – with the pain of ultimate grief. For the young Housman, no loving God could have inflicted such pain. For him, the death of his mother was the death of God. There was, however, an escape, into his beloved classics and ultimately to Oxford, where his prodigious intellect must surely redeem all. But it was not to be, for the very love he was so determined to eschew in the universe was about to confront him.

In 1877, Housman won a scholarship to St John's College Oxford, where he had fond hopes of proving his precocious genius in Classics. His room-mate there was a young man called Moses Jackson, a renowned athlete. Jackson studied sciences, then considered intellectually inferior. The motif of English public school homosexuality is now worn-out and irrelevant. John Knowler, in his superb *Trust an Englishman*, examines the tradition in more detail than I can do here. But, essentially, close study of the classics immediately makes one aware that heterosexuality, though the most prevalent and conventional now, was in classical times considered as being inferior to male homosexual love, which was thought to be less carnal, and more intellectual and spiritual.

The attraction between a young man with exemplary intellectual gifts and another with a classical physique, but a somewhat inferior mind, was, in these terms, a perfect match. Housman instantly – and irrevocably – fell in love with Jackson, a heterosexual, who was completely unaware of Housman's infatuation. But there comes a time when love must speak its name, whatever the cost – perhaps especially when there is absolutely no hope of its being requited.

When Housman flunked his Oxford final exams, despite his evident genius, he went to stay in rooms with Moses Jackson and his brother Adalbert in London, where he gained humble employment as a civil servant at the Patent Office. Although he was, perhaps, the world's foremost expert on Propertius, the famous Roman poet, he had almost deliberately sabotaged himself by neglecting to study other poets in the 'Greats' curriculum. While Housman was in London, he set out to make up for his failure by diligently studying Latin and Greek poets in the library of the British Museum. These long evenings of private study eventually bore fruit. When his work was published, he was soon offered a chair at University College London, and in 1911, a chair at Trinity College Cambridge.

That he had so much time to spare in the evenings suggests the tensions that were growing. It is a torture to be exposed to a beloved, when one is forbidden to speak of that love. Likewise, to be parted, even for a little while, is an agony too. What can one so stricken do? We cannot know the precise details, but Tom Stoppard's version in his 1997 play, *The Invention of Love*, seems likely to me – in which Jackson suddenly enquires of Housman: 'You're not sweet on me, are you?' Realising that, like his beloved mother, and God, love too must die, Housman soon decided that he had to move out of their shared rooms. Jackson travelled to India in 1887, before returning to England to be married. Housman was not invited to the wedding, or indeed informed until the married couple had already returned to India. Shortly afterwards, Housman's father died. In this personal Dark Night of the Soul, he composed *A Shropshire Lad*.

All this is quite well-known in literary circles, of course, but for many, the Housman of their imagination is someone very different to the reality, usually because they have conflated the man with his poems. The first time I became really aware of his Worcestershire roots was when I arrived in Bromsgrove in the last few weeks of the last millennium, as recounted in the first of these tales. The first thing which drew my eye as I walked through the town centre was the imposing statue of the town's most famous son.

My rural 'patch' included his birthplace in the hills to the west of the town, and I saw the Clee Hills as he saw them in his boyhood.

Those Blue Hills, Shropshire.

Broad Street, Ludlow.

After the emotionally devastating separation from the Jackson brothers, in 1895 Housman took up residence at Byron House in Highgate, where he wrote his most famous poems in the space of a year. Still in the bitter aftermath of bereavement, rejection and humiliation, his days began to slowly settle into a routine:

> Having drunk a pint of beer at luncheon – beer is a sedative to the brain, and my afternoons are the least intellectual portion of my life – I would go out for a walk of two or three hours. As I went along, thinking of nothing in particular, only looking at things around me and following the progress of the seasons, there would flow into my mind, with sudden and unaccountable emotion, sometimes a line or two of verse, sometimes a whole stanza at once, accompanied, not preceded, by a vague notion of the poem they were destined to form part of.[19]

As if he were not already melancholy enough, the first publisher he approached rejected his masterpiece. But literary works undertaken during times of such excessive emotional strain often come to feel talismanic to the author, a compensation, perhaps, for lost comradeship, and shattered illusions. Housman was determined to get 500 copies into print, even at the risk of losing a substantial sum of his own money. The gamble paid off more than handsomely, but no amount of money or fame could ameliorate his heartbreak.

Within ten years, the poems were inspiring some of the foremost composers, such as Ralph Vaughan Williams. So, we could say Housman was a pioneer of 'art-fusion', but he was becoming, according to one critic, 'a detestable and miserable man'. The most exquisite misery was yet to come.

Moses Jackson had fallen on hard times and then been diagnosed with terminal stomach cancer. In a final burst of 'sudden unaccountable emotion', Housman sent out what he called his *Last Poems* (1922) for Jackson to read before he died in Canada the following year. Now, there was nothing left but to wait out his days as stoically as he could, without the comforts of religion, until he, too, expired.

So, Housman's imagined Shropshire was a kind of screen, onto which he projected his own chronic emotional torment. But for another non-native author, his experience of the county became very real, a nurturing haven of peace and rest, like the 'Rivendell' of Tolkien's *Lord of the Rings* trilogy. He was known as 'The Postman Poet', and like Housman's, his mortal remains now rest amidst the glorious landscape he claimed for his own – Simon Evans (1895-1940).

Evans was a native-born Welshman, from a large farming family. As the family grew, it became clear that his father's smallholding was too meagre to support them all. The father decided to move the family to Birkenhead to start a new life, little knowing the mockery his 12-year-old son would be forced to endure at school because of his Welsh accent and lanky, awkward gait. An outsider from the get-go, Evans retreated into a love of reading.

As soon as he left school he found employment with the GPO as a postman, but in August 1914 the First World War broke out, and he immediately volunteered to join his local Cheshire Regiment. He served in the trenches throughout the duration of the conflict, rising to the rank of sergeant. Just as allied victory was almost assured, Evans was seriously wounded in action in 1918. He was badly wounded in both legs. The army surgeons wanted to amputate them, but Evans pleaded with them to relent, arguing that a postman without any legs had a pretty bleak future. His wishes were, thankfully, respected, and his legs were saved. Gradually, painfully, he learned to walk again, but Evans had sustained other injuries. He had also been poisoned with mustard-gas and his lungs would never recover. There seemed every prospect that he must resign himself to a life limited by his disability, and in all likelihood, a premature death. But then fate, in the shape of a kindly GP, intervened.

Uniformed services, such as policemen and postmen, were among the first to volunteer for General Kitchener's volunteer army. Indeed, there was such a shortage of military uniforms for them all, that many were still drilling in their blue postman's trousers when they arrived in France. All these men volunteered en masse, often organised into so-called 'Pal's Battalions', composed of men from the same town or workplace. Those who returned were treated honourably and their old jobs were retained for them as they convalesced.

All this took a considerable time, of course, but Evans was determined to get back to his Merseyside postal round. A doctor examined him and suggested that he needed to get out of the smog-bound urban area and take a walking holiday in the fresh air. The doctor even had a suggestion, Cleobury Mortimer, in Shropshire – where he took his own walking holidays.

Evans contacted the boarding-house the doctor suggested, and went to stay in the little town, birthplace of the great writer

William Langland. A memorial to him is to be found in St Mary's Church, on Church Street, with its famous crooked spire. Evans got chatting with the local postman and to his surprise, found that he was anxious to move out of Cleobury – to somewhere more exciting, like Liverpool. There was a job-exchange scheme in the post office in those days, and eventually the two postmen exchanged rounds. In 1926, Evans moved to Cleobury, soon to be joined by other members of his family. After so much suffering and pain, something rather magical now took place.

The postal service workers had their own trade union, which provided correspondence courses in literature provided by Ruskin College, an Adult Education College in Oxford with strong links to the Socialist and Labour movements. Evans obtained a scholarship to the college in 1928, the year of Thomas Hardy's death. The idea that bright working people, with an inborn determination to 'better themselves', should be excluded from the elite universities purely on the basis of their class, was repugnant to some of the more enlightened dons. In 1899, Ruskin College was founded by former American alumnus Charles Beard, Walter Vrooman, and his generous wife, Amne, with the noble intention of helping people just like Simon Evans and to provide educational opportunities at a reasonable price. Correspondence courses could be studied for as little as 1s per week, with another 1s entrance fee. At last, Evans received the intellectual nourishment he needed. He was free to turn all these new ideas over quietly in his mind, as he walked his dazzlingly beautiful round. In those days, postmen in country districts were provided with a comfortable shelter at the furthest point on their round. Evans converted his into a cosy study and then later, his writing room.

Diogenes is said to have refuted a proponent of Zeno's philosophical paradoxes, who claimed the unreality of motion, by simply standing up and walking away. St Augustine of Hippo's pithy phrase *Solvitur ambulando* ('it is solved by walking') was never more apposite than in Simon Evans's case. He was a great admirer of Housman, and surely empathised with this sentiment of his:

> Clay lies still, but blood's a rover;
> Breath's a ware that will not keep.
> Up, lad; when the journey's over
> There'll be time enough to sleep.

It was now, literally, his job, to walk beneath Housman's 'twelve-winded sky', down the enchanted vale of the lovely River Rea, and up from the pristine dingles to the lonely hill-farms, to deliver mail to grateful, friendly people – all of whom he came to love, and all of whom grew to love him:

> A rainbow like a jewelled arm,
> And Moses Cadd of Detton Farm.

As he walked on the remote tracks, all the time his mind was working, and with each stride, every step in his beloved brogues (he wrote an essay, not a poem, praising brogues), he was nearer to his cosy rest-hut. Though Evans loved poetry, and studied it in great depth, his calling as a writer was prose. But there is one line, deeply felt, which he did leave us:

> The sun, the stars, the wind, the rain,
> Gave me back my life again.

People on his round were delighted when Evans began to publish small articles and pamphlets, and many asked for signed copies, which he would inscribe, often with little verses or couplets relating to the person or place, thus he became known to history, for good or ill, as the 'Postman Poet'. When one continually walks in a landscape in this way, one becomes a part of it, in a way our modern culture has made virtually impossible. News of this wayfaring writer reached the ears of the BBC Midland Service, and he began submitting articles to be read out on the radio.

Shannie Cranton, daughter of a publisher, heard one of the radio broadcasts and persuaded her father to meet with Evans. This resulted in his first book, *Round About the Crooked Steeple* (1931), which was an instant success. Considering that he was a working man, Evans's brief literary output was prodigious, culminating in a full-length novel called *Applegarth*, which won him an appreciative and loyal readership. One reader, Doris Aldridge, also worked for the BBC, as the children's radio presenter 'Auntie Doris'.

She wrote to Evans, asking if he really was a country postman? She could not quite believe in this rural idyll, but when she met Evans she immediately saw her mistake. Soon afterwards, the two married. Doris moved to Cleobury, into a house they had built to their own specifications. For the young man who had lain paralysed and bleeding in the mud and tangled barbed wire of no-man's-land, gasping for breath from his gas-corrupted lungs now,

> The world-wide air was azure
> And all the brooks ran gold.

Their happiness was to be short-lived. In 1939, Evans was forced by ill-health to give up his beloved postal round. The following year, he died on the day before his 45th birthday. His ashes were scattered from his beloved Abdon Burf, on Brown Clee Hill, overlooking Nene Savage, Catherton Common, the Rea Valley – all the places he had made his own. The Simon Evans Way, a 17-mile circuit along Simon's daily round, is now a favourite local countryside walk.

My parents were lifelong walkers, by choice, and I too will keep the faith till death – as Evans inscribed in one of his books: 'To Hell with motor-cars and vans!' Now with much reduced mobility., it is walking I miss most because, as my father inculcated, real thinking can only be done when walking, preferably alone. It was natural in my youth, I suppose, that when I felt the need most powerfully, I headed due west into Shropshire, a place it has always been a privilege to visit.

The distant Clee Hills were what first drew me, for a rather macabre reason. Between 1937 and 1975, there were 19 air-crashes on the hills, claiming 43 lives. During the Second World War, 34 aircrew were killed, mostly British, but there were also a few Germans, Americans, Canadians and a solitary New Zealander. Brown Clee is slightly higher, and so was correspondingly more deadly; 11 of the fatalities were on Titterstone Clee, but both peaks are over 1,700 feet above sea-level. Looming up suddenly from the Shropshire plain, they are deceptive to low flying aircraft, particularly at night.

The Shropshire Hills are renowned for the suddenness with which the mist and fog descends, a particular hazard for walkers, and in those days, aviators. The Royal Navy had stockpiled ammunition for heavy naval guns on the eastern side of the hills, a primary target for the Luftwaffe. For security reasons there was no warning beacon atop Brown Clee – this was well before the modern radar installations which dominate the peaks in our times. There were nine fatal crashes in 1941 alone.

The most spectacular of these took place on 2 April 1941, near Burwarton, on the estate of Lord and Lady Boyne. A German JU 88 bomber had lost its way over Birmingham and in thick fog it went into a steep dive through a plantation of conifers before exploding on the summit of Brown Clee. The bombs it was carrying exploded too, and the local schoolmistress was so concerned that she dismissed the village schoolchildren for the day (it was just before 10 am). Some of the boys were city refugees, and a few of them decided to climb the 2 miles to the summit. They were the first to arrive on the scene, which was one of utter carnage. They ignored the charred corpses of the aircrew in a desperate bid to extract some souvenirs before the police and army turned up. One of the boys saw the German bodies being taken down the slopes by a tractor as he was on his way home. The unfortunate young fliers were interred at Bridgnorth cemetery.

In my youth, I was always searching for such stories, and in those days there were plenty of eyewitnesses still around. As a keen aficionado of that noble institution, the pub, I spent many happy hours listening to such memories. I had a map as a teenager with all the crash-sites marked on it, and I'd hitch-hike out to Ditton Priors or Burwarton to search for the crash-sites, some of them marked by touching memorials to the lost aviators.

Before the turn of this present century, the pub was, along with the Monarchy, NHS, the BBC, National Trust and the Church of England, one of the institutions which defined British life. True, the Irish have pubs, but they are quite different, though no less charming. Like all that is valuable in our culture, the British pub has been 'trashed' – there are approximately half the number of pubs in the UK now than when I started drinking in them in 1976. I could (and probably will) write a book on this subject alone, but the numbers speak for themselves. The entire character of these places has changed – they are now on the whole geared-up for passing food-trade from cars, rather than for local people.

Hardly anyone in the trade knows how to keep British beer, which is extraordinarily expensive nowadays. The British pub and brewing industry will one day be a thing of the past. The cultural vandalism says everything about the saboteurs who now govern us, but in Shropshire, a few precious gems still remain – for now. One is the Cider House at Wootton Green. One of only three cider-houses left in England, this exquisite spot is only fractionally within Shropshire. The border with Staffordshire is only a mile away, at Six Ashes, where the pub of the same name stands. Few people now realise the value of pubs as interfaces with the past. Over the years, I have gathered countless ghost-stories, tales of murders, and other anecdotes. It is with deep regret that I see all this being swept away. But of all the strange stories, the one about Six Ashes was the most extraordinary, prompting me to do some historical research.

As a boy, my paternal grandmother would take my father and I to meet Mabel, her cousin, for lunch at the Six Ashes. Mabel lived in Claverley nearby, and the luncheon was an annual event, at Whitsun. My father got chatting to the publican and asked if he knew of the origin of the pub's name. He knew very little, unfortunately, but my father was really fishing for local confirmation of a legend he had heard as a boy. According to him, the inn where we sat eating our lunch had once been a battlefield – and one which had been forgotten by history.

For here, in this tiny hamlet, Merlin himself had prophesied a great Welsh victory over the Mercians and their fearsome pagan king, Penda. The Welsh name for the place, had been *Onennau Meigion* or 'the ash-trees of Meigion', a great tract of forest which extended over much of southern Shropshire. But who was the man who defeated Penda, the most dreaded warlord of his age? The mention of Merlin made me prick up my ears. Could it have been Arthur himself? The truth, however, was even more interesting.

As we saw in an earlier tale, the legendary wizard, Merlin, was derived from a genuine bard, Myrddin, who acted as a seer for one of the independent Brythonic kings of the 'Old North', in what is now Cumbria. When his pagan king, Gwenddoleu, was defeated and slain, Myrddin was so desolate that he fled the field. So, the real model for the mighty Merlin was actually rather a failure as a magician, compounded by his apparent cowardice; bards were supposed to die with their lords. To live in such a case was a disgrace, worse than death. Myrddin escaped his enemies to wander in the Caledonian forest, living off bird's eggs, berries, roots and the likes, until autumn.

Forced to scrape in the dirt for beech-mast with the swine, the 'wild-man' finally went insane. His desperate pleas to the 'swan-white woman' – the land-goddess, went unanswered – the necessary psychic and telepathic link had been severed. But despite this disintegration, the bard survived, adapting himself to life outdoors, in nature. Gradually, he healed himself, and emerged with a clairvoyant gift superior to any, indeed, it is my belief that the myth exemplified in his personage contains the very last vestiges of the ancient practices of the Druids.

According to the 12th-century churchman, scholar and author, Geoffrey of Monmouth, who appropriated the character of Myrddin to create 'Merlin' (the original sounded too much like *merde*, the

French for excrement) the famous wizard had a twin sister. When the wild-man became famous as a prophet, she sought her brother out, to see if his alleged miraculous power to see across time was true. The test involved a complex series of mnemonic feats, including reciting the names, in order, of all the kings of Britain said to be descended from Brutus, the grandson (or possibly great-grandson) of Aeneas of Troy.

Myrddin successfully recited all the monarchs, but then continued beyond his own day – and on into the future. As a supplementary question, his sister then begged to know the fate of the free Britons. Her brother replied that a new dawn for the Britons was coming – under a mighty warrior leader, a 'Great Eagle'; the Britons still used Roman military symbolism. This king would gather a mighty army and subdue the Mercians at *Onennau Meigion*. Now, the whole concept of 'Merlin' was literally an invention of Geoffrey of Monmouth, but Merlin was a euhemerism, that is, based on a 'real' historical person. The obscure information about the prophesy did not just come from Geoffrey's rather fevered imagination.

This poem, called *Cyfoesi Gwyndydd a Myrddin ei Chwaer*, is quite possibly the oldest written document in Welsh. It could have been copied down from Geoffrey's work, and then interpolated by monks at a later date, but many respected scholars in Old Welsh think that the process was actually inverse – Geoffrey must have embellished his work from some lost Welsh or Breton account of these events. There is simply no way of knowing which theory is right, but the supreme importance of bardic prophesy in Welsh culture in the period meant that they were inspired to liberate the 'Lost Lands'.

The ancient prophesy appears to have been fulfilled, for in 630 or 631, Geoffrey mentions a battle at 'the ash trees of Meigion', in which Cadwallon, king of Gwynedd, defeated Penda, who was then forced to become his ally. This unlikely duo went on to liberate Wales and to ravage Northumbria, killing its king, Edwin, in October 633. The memory of this shadowy battle, though little-known and unremarked in England, continued to circulate among the Welsh bards for almost 800 years.

In 1400, a national uprising took place in Wales, led by its self-proclaimed prince, Owain Glyndwr. The great Welsh poet R. S. Thomas describes the moment:

> Then he spoke, and anger kindled
> in each brooding eye;
> Swords and spears accused the sky,
> The woods resounded with a bitter cry.

This prosperous Welsh lord was actually a direct descendant of two of the principal Welsh royal bloodlines. A wandering bard, Iolo Goch, convinced himself that Glyndwr was the long-prophesied Welsh messiah, the *Mab Darogan* or 'Son of Prophesy', and composed poetic eulogies implying that he should seize his rightful inheritance. The Welsh are indeed 'a people bred on legends'. English boroughs within Wales as well as border towns and garrisons were immediately attacked, ransacked and burned. This bitter war raged for fifteen awful years, before Glyndwr disappeared into the mountains. He was never found.

The high tide of the uprising came in 1405, when with allied French reinforcements Glyndwr invaded England with an army of about 10,000 men. Henry IV rode out with his army to meet them in battle, and arrived in Worcester as the Franco-Welsh army were burning St John's, just over the Severn. Glyndwr's main army withdrew to a strong position at Woodbury Hill near Great Witley, 9 miles to the north of the city. Henry marched to confront Glyndwr, but his forces were not sufficiently strong to assault the hill on which the enemy were encamped. For some days, the armies sat in the sunshine, taunting each other or engaging in mass jousting tournaments, in which 400 men were killed.

Finally, after 8 days, Henry saw that the enemy, in hostile territory, must soon starve and be compelled to retreat. Further bloodshed was, therefore, strictly unnecessary, and the English turned about and marched away, leaving the exasperated Welshmen and Frenchmen to it. Glyndwr's men attacked Henry's baggage train as it was leaving, in desperate hopes of finding food – but there was none. It was a remarkable, virtually bloodless English victory, won by a Fabian strategy, but for the despondent and hungry Welshmen, one last ritual remained.

Earlier that year, on 28 February 1405, Glyndwr signed a pact with Edmund Mortimer, a powerful border lord, and Henry Percy, Earl of Northumberland. Henry IV was regarded by them as a usurper, and the trio resolved to combine their military assets, with the object of overthrowing him. Once this had been achieved, the kingdom would be divided into three – the so-called 'Tripartite Indenture'. Percy was to receive all of northern England, Mortimer the south and east of England and Glyndwr was to receive Wales – plus the 'Lost Lands' in England, defined by a line running on a north-south axis east of the Severn, with its easternmost border fixed at Six Ashes, as had been prophesied by Merlin himself.

As the disconsolate Welshmen marched wearily home, they were reported to have crossed the Severn bridge at Bridgnorth. Six Ashes is only 6 miles away, and it is supposed that Glyndwr's men made a pilgrimage there. Although the names on the tombstones in the local churchyard remain Welsh to this day, Six Ashes has been anglicised ever since.

At a moving ceremony a few years ago, I had the honour to be present as a monument to this lost history was unveiled, thanks to the work of the Owain Glyndwr Society. The text is in both English and Welsh, and the author hopes that both it, and the pub, will survive for many years to come. This is our sacred task now, it seems to me, to reinvest or re-enchant the land, before the very faculties of thought and memory – essential to any meaningful history – are obliterated in a new barbaric age.

The god Odin had two pet ravens, Huginn and Muninn, 'thought' and 'memory', who acted as his spies in the world. But of these, Muninn, memory, was most precious to him. Without this faculty of memory, true thought, history – meaning itself – disintegrate, as anyone who has cared for a relative with Alzheimer's disease can attest.

Senility seems to have overlooked parts of God's own country. A canard was rife at one time that the salubrious air and pure spring-water of the area conferred protection from ill-health and extraordinary longevity. The most celebrated such case is the strange story of Thomas Parr (1482?-1635) of Alberbury, in the hills west of Shrewsbury. 'Old Tom Parr' was allegedly 152 years of age when he passed away in far-off London. When news reached Thomas Howard, Earl of Arundel, of Old Tom's venerable age, he dispatched envoys to Shropshire to seek him out. The story goes that they rode into the village where he lived and encountered a decrepit, shambling old man, supporting himself with a staff. 'Would you be Old Parr?' one of the visitors enquired. The old-timer shook his head; 'Oh, no your honours', he replied, 'Old Parr be my grandfather!'

When the grand old man himself was located, the visitors were even more astonished. He seemed in good enough health – he had become a father at the age of 100 when he had an affair with his housemaid. The child was born out of wedlock, according to the church records. The secret of his longevity, he claimed, was his meagre diet – bread and rancid cheese, milk, and whey. This strict dietary regime never varied – except on one infamous occasion. When Tom's wife died when he was 110, he waited 12 years to take another bride, Jane Lloyd, when he was 122. The story of Tom's penance for fathering an illegitimate child at 100 became known at the royal court of King Charles I.

The Earl of Arundel visited Parr and persuaded him to meet the king himself, where a huge banquet in his honour would take place. When the by now quite frail Parr arrived in London he was feted everywhere. Portraits of him were painted by Van Dyck and Rubens. Tom could not see the sights of the great city, his eyes were failing him, but the abrupt break with his long-established routine – the rich food and foul air – caused him to expire before his time on 13 November 1635. An autopsy was performed on Parr's body by the famous William Harvey, who discovered the circulation of the blood. He found all his organs to be in rude health and attributed his demise to his intolerance of the rich food he had been introduced to during his brief visit. By the king's own command, Old Tom was buried in Westminster Abbey. On his tombstone it is inscribed that he lived in the reign of 'ten princes' (monarchs) –Edward IV, Edward V, Richard III, Henry VII, Henry VIII, Edward VI, Queen Mary I, Elizabeth I, James I, and Charles I. Modern sceptics mock these claims, of course, but Shropshire is a place of oddity and strangeness. If the secret of long life, if not happiness, is to be found anywhere – then perhaps these secret hills are that place.

Another legendary local eccentric (and infamous rake) was 'Mad' Jack Mytton (1796-1834) of Halston Hall, Whittington. It became clear that he had some sort of behavioural disorder when he was expelled from a number of disciplinarian schools, including Westminster. Home tutors were engaged for him, who had to endure pranks such as Jack leaving a horse in their bedroom.

When the Napoleonic Wars ended abruptly at the Battle of Waterloo, Jack left the army in search of a new career in politics. To ensure his success, he incentivised the eligible voters of Shrewsbury with £10 each – a very substantial sum indeed back then. Once he was in Parliament, Jack stayed for just 30 minutes of one debate before abandoning his new career. He thought his colleagues pompous and boring. To be fair, Mad Jack had a low threshold for boredom. On one famous occasion, for a wager, he rode into one of the grandest hotels in Royal Leamington Spa on his horse, trotted up the staircase and out onto the balcony – then, still astride, jumped over the diners sitting below. Jack also allowed his horse the freedom of Halston Hall, where it would lie in front of the fire like a hound.

He also kept an incredible 2,000 dogs, many of them dressed up in bespoke costumes bearing the family arms, who were fed on rump steak and champagne (this was during the 'hungry' 1830s). Jack was a pioneering naturist – he wore no clothes when he was hunting, even in bitterly cold weather. He was also utterly fearless, no doubt fortified by the gallon of port wine he consumed every day. He would furiously ride his horse or a gig at dangerous obstacles, such as toll-gates, just to see what would happen.

After he developed a severe bout of hiccups, he decided to cure them by setting fire to his nightshirt, which he happened to be wearing at the time. When a notorious brawler trespassed onto his estate, Jack challenged the local miner to a bare-knuckle boxing fight, rather than go to the magistrate. The man thought he was in luck, for he was a local boxing champion. Mytton went twenty rounds with him toe-to-toe, until the astonished collier threw in the towel. The family fortunes were ruined by all this of course, but 'Mad Jack' Mytton's memory will not fade anytime soon. A local pub, the Mytton Arms commemorates the man, and a local countryside walk, the Jack Mytton Way.

One grows more credulous with age, of course, not less, as every petty crook and huckster knows. As the old Britain I remember begins to disintegrate, culturally, spiritually, and soon politically and economically, it is a comfort to gaze out towards the Clee Hills, the Stiperstones and Wenlock Edge – to dream of an English Shangri-La. But I know there is something to it. As soon as one crosses west of the Severn, the land rises. Beyond the Clee Hills, the great tower of St Laurence's Church in Ludlow is visible for miles around. From Craven arms the road through the Onny Valley makes anyone with a martial background instantly wary – perfect country for ambuscades. This was where Edric the Wild fought his dogged guerilla war, and Caratacus before him. But the natives are friendlier now.

The old fortress town of Bishop's Castle, with a population of less than 2,000, is a delight to the eye and a tonic for the soul. Little wonder that so many artists have sought refuge here, in this last redoubt of a vanishing England. One such refugee, was Ronnie Lane (1946-1997), of the rock group the Small Faces. In 1973, Ronnie moved to Fishpool Farm at Hyssington, which he used as the base for a 'Rock & Roll Circus'. 'The Passing Show', as he called it, actually had a big top, with the legendary Viv Stanshall as ringmaster. Many famous musicians worked with Ronnie on the project or visited him to record at his mobile studio – Gallagher

& Lyle, Pete Townshend, Eric Clapton – to name but a few. But Ronnie wanted out of the hectic world of celebrity. As the landlord of a local pub put it: 'He just wanted to give it all up, to live like a gypsy.'

Sitting with a pint in front of me at the Miner's Arms at Priestweston, where Ronnie is still fondly remembered, I can't blame him. For right here, at the very edge of England, I find that I finally feel at home in it. A short walk over Corndon Hill brings the rambler to Stapeley Hill, on which stands Mitchell's Fold stone circle. There was a busy stone-axe factory here in Neolithic times, and despite much damage by farmers, vandals and idiots, some of the dolerite stones are still standing after more than 4,000 years. The spectacular view west to Montgomery Castle is breathtaking, and as the sun sinks behind the Welsh mountains, it is not discontent I feel – rather something like true communion.

11

The Shire

The heart of man is not composed of lies,
but draws some wisdom from the only Wise,
and still recalls Him. Though now long estranged,
Man is not wholly lost or wholly changed.
Dis-graced he may be, yet is not de-throned,
and keeps the rags of lordship once he owned:
Man, Sub-creator, the refracted light
through whom is splintered from a single White
to many hues, and endlessly combined
in living shapes that move from mind to mind...

> J. R. R. Tolkien, 'Mythopoeia'

If we discount the Bible, J. R. R. Tolkien's *The Lord of the Rings* (1954) trilogy is the third best-selling book of all time, with over 150 million copies sold. If we add in the sales of *The Hobbit* (1937), itself in the top ten best-selling books – the scale of Tolkien's literary achievement is simply staggering. Despite the lukewarm enthusiasm of the Oxford establishment and initial reviews which damned it with faint praise, the former book was a publishing phenomenon of the first magnitude. Among readers it consistently tops polls – the 'book of the century', it has been called – even the 'book of the millennium'. It was a work sixteen gruelling years in the making, preceded by decades of intense research by one of the finest minds of his age.

Tolkien changed the literary weather, reviving the almost forgotten Romantic tradition, which the intelligentsia of his time had consigned to the rubbish-bin of history. Not only was the trilogy a best-seller here in the UK, but all over the world – and especially in the US of the 1960s counter-culture.

To be honest, as a boy all this passed me by. My father rather discouraged study of what he considered to be 'childish' or fantastical literature. He thought it a distraction from 'real' history, I suppose. It was this severe and cynical approach which brought me into sometimes savage conflict with him, for I saw things quite differently. I didn't even own a copy of *The Hobbit* but my junior-school teacher, Mr Morgan, would read it out to us in his mellifluous Welsh voice, which did it great justice. I only read *The Fellowship of the Ring* as a boy, I didn't finish the trilogy until I was in my late twenties. But as soon as I returned home at the turn of the millennium, all this changed rapidly. My workplace itself was named 'Rivendell' in Tolkien's honour, and my patch was right on the border of Worcestershire and south Birmingham, where he grew up.

Then, there were the resonances with 'Hobbiton'. Kinver Rock Houses and Drakelow Caves are so like Hobbiton that many have supposed them to be the inspiration for the place. The hobbits themselves are simply scaled-down versions of Englishmen, specifically the inhabitants of the West Midlands (not the metropolitan area which goes by that name) – and 'the Shire', their idyllic homeland, is quintessentially English. Tolkien's biographer, Humphrey Carpenter, is explicit:

> His deep feeling that his home was in the West Midland countryside of England had, since his undergraduate days, defined the nature of his scholarly work. The same motives which had led him to study Beowulf, Gawain, and the Ancrene Wisse now created a character that embodied everything he loved about the West Midlands: Mr Bilbo Baggins, the hobbit.[20]

We have seen previously, how the systematic destruction of Anglo-Saxon culture by the Normans had been resisted most obdurately in the West Midlands, which stubbornly stuck to its ancient Anglo-Saxon dialect. Tolkien, through his assiduous philological studies, became aware of the yawning gap that had been left by this cultural vandalism. The Welsh, Scandinavians, Finns and Germans had retained their myths in their ancient languages. But the primal myths of the *English* people (with the notable exception of *Beowulf*) had been extirpated, not only by the Normans but then by the ravages of the Protestant Reformation and Industrial

Revolution. Tolkien, from his earliest years, knew that it was his mission in life to re-invent this sublimated myth-cycle. Indeed, the time came when he took a sacred vow to do so, in memory of one of his fallen comrades – the models for the 'Immortal Four' of his epic.

So, what he produced was not a modern novel, but a work in the manner of the ancient sagas he studied for a living as a university don, and especially *The Wanderer*. Like those Anglo-Saxon sagas, Tolkien's epic is permeated by a deep sense of decay, melancholia, and the ineluctable forces of destiny. Fate, however, is not a purely external force. For Tolkien, magical help is always at hand, but only for those characters who make themselves worthy of it, by showing bravery, fortitude, self-sacrifice and mercy. It is a return, in spirit, to the heroic age, an aeon of chivalry and valour.

There is no doubt that the inspiration for 'the Shire' was Worcestershire – especially north-east Worcestershire, and the last bit of nearby Warwickshire to escape envelopment by Birmingham. We find ourselves in that same liminal zone betwixt urban and rural, ancient and modern, we have seen before: Francis Brett Young, Archie Hill, A.E. Housman. Although Tolkien always proudly described himself as 'a Birmingham man' to his peers at Oxford, his 'true home' was Worcestershire, in a very deep sense. His mother's family, the Suffields, were from Evesham originally, and Tolkien felt himself to be much more like them than the Tolkien side: 'Though a Tolkien by name, I am a Suffield by tastes, talents and upbringing.'

The Shire, then, is Nature in its particularly English aspect – and it is in mortal peril. When Tolkien describes the 'Scouring of the Shire', it is his beloved Worcestershire landscape he sees in ruins in his mind's-eye, a desecration of all he holds dear: 'Any corner of that county (however fair or squalid) is in an indefinable way "home" to me, as no other place in the world is.' It is this same feeling which motivated me to write this book, for I too, regard Worcestershire as my Motherland.

There are two great themes of Tolkien's epic. One, the inevitability of death, is the theme of this book, too. But the second theme, and perhaps what provides the story with its extraordinary dynamic energy – is the destruction of Nature by 'the Machine', which the Ring symbolises. By this, he did not mean only man-made technology, but the proliferation of mechano-morphic and mechanistic tendencies in modern thought and social-organisation – the need to dominate, compel, and control.

During his service on the Western Front during the First World War, the young Tolkien witnessed the calamity of modern technological warfare at first hand, the unequal struggle between steel and flesh-and-blood. But Tolkien had a message too, for in what he called a 'eucatastrophe' – it is our destiny to prevail, to win through, against all odds – as he did.

This man who came to exemplify Englishness was born in Bloemfontein, South Africa, on 3 January 1892. His father, Arthur, was a bank manager there. Although he obliterated the incident from conscious memory, as a toddler he had the extremely unpleasant (and potentially fatal) experience of being bitten by a tarantula. He screamed and ran through the tall grass to his black nurse, who immediately sucked out the venom. The unconscious terror of spiders was to emerge in his stories many years later. He had a vague memory, too, of paddling in the warm waters of the Indian Ocean – and another fleeting image, of his father writing his name on his suitcase as he prepared to board the ship to go to England when he was only three years old – his only memory of him. By then, Ronald, as J.R.R. was known, had a little brother, Hilary.

Mabel, Tolkien's mother, found the African climate oppressive, and her health began to deteriorate. She and the boys left for a respite in the homeland. But while Mabel and the boys were staying with her family in Birmingham, Arthur Tolkien died of a sudden haemorrhage 5,000 miles away; he had been ill ever since his family departed for England. Just before he died, young Ronald had written his father a touching letter. It was never sent. The telegram informing Mabel of Arthur's death arrived the following day.

Everything now depended upon Mabel, a young widow, a single parent with two very young boys. She was left in dire straits, for Arthur Tolkien had not been wealthy, his investments yielded only 30s a week income for her. Fortunately, Mabel was a remarkable woman. She was extremely well-educated, knew Latin, French and German, and she was also a keen artist and musician – but above all, her dignity and graceful bearing in the face of adversity, attracted people only too willing to help her. As well as this, she found that in her grief, her religious instinct intensified. She became a devout Roman Catholic, rather to her family's surprise. Mabel was also determined that her boys should receive a Roman Catholic education, and Ronald remained firm in the faith until his death.

In the late summer of 1896, Mabel took the boys to live at Sarehole, a country village a mile outside Birmingham. Thanks to urban encroachment, Sarehole is now in a suburb of the city, but in those days it was quite detached and unspoiled. Sarehole Mill, on the River Cole, where Ronald and Hilary played so happily in boyhood, is now a museum, which thankfully preserves something of the lost rural idyll Tolkien experienced as a child. By now, J.R.R. was almost 6 years old, with a vivid imagination. His first and abiding happy memories, then, were of this unspoiled, gentle, pastoral place – his first real home. From this place of safety and relative comfort, Mabel made plans for her boys.

Thanks to her own privileged education and with help from a friendly Catholic priest, Father Francis Morgan, the boys were able to take advantage of the educational resources of the Church. In 1849, Cardinal John Henry Newman had founded the famous Birmingham Oratory. The Oratory had its own grammar school, St Philip's, and in 1902, Mabel and the boys moved to a house in Edgbaston which was attached to the school. But the really elite school in Birmingham was King Edward VI Grammar School, in the city centre. Mabel tutored the boys personally and in 1903 Ronald gained a scholarship there.

Unless some unexpected event supervened, Ronald was definitely on his way to Oxford. Considering the predicament she faced, Mabel had made great strides in securing the future for her boys, but the damage to her health had been quietly taking its toll. Quite suddenly, on 14 November 1904, she sank into a diabetic coma and died. The boys had now lost both parents. Ronald was just 12 years old.

The boys moved into a room in an aunt's house, who lived around the corner from the Oratory, in Stirling Road, Edgbaston. On their walk to school in the mornings, they passed Edgbaston Waterworks tower, and further up Waterworks Road, Perrott's Folly, another tower, built as an 'observatory' in 1758 by John Perrott of Belbroughton, which, at 96 feet tall, dominated the local skyline. These towers became the ultimate inspiration for 'The Two Towers', the second volume of his trilogy, just as 'Old Joe' the clock-tower of the University of Birmingham, was to be the imaginative seed of the 'Eye of Sauron'. There was a reason for this imaginative recreation of his new home in the city – the sublimation of extreme emotional pain.

Just like Housman, and his later friend, C.S. Lewis, Tolkien was devastated by the loss of his mother. He felt that she had sacrificed her own life so that her boys should thrive, and a deep responsibility to make good. He loved her deeply, and he came to associate her with the happy carefree days in a rural idyll he had now left behind. For him, the countryside of the English Midlands and his mother became emotionally synonymous.

For the rest of his life he remained faithful to her beloved Roman Catholic Church, for his faith too, was synonymous with his memory of her. For such a boy, the busy industrial sprawl of Birmingham was utterly alien to his spirit – and the same was true of his brother Hilary, who eventually became a farmer.

Father Francis Morgan had been appointed as the boys' legal guardian. He was a kindly and generous man, with considerable private means. Although Mabel had left him £800 in trust for the boys' education, Father Francis augmented this from his own pocket in secret. In 1908, he arranged better lodgings for them with a Mrs Faulkner in Duchess Road.

Just below the boys lived another orphan, Edith Bratt, an intelligent and pretty 19-year-old. J.R.R. was three years younger than her, but they fast became friends. She would smuggle extra food to the boys, knowing how hungry they sometimes were. Soon, friendship became love – a lifelong romance, in fact – for Tolkien was determined to marry her one day, come what may. His dream, his 'eucatastrophe', was to come true, but just as in his stories, there were to be many challenges along the way.

Although they took elaborate precautions to keep their liaisons a secret, following a cycling tryst in the Lickey Hills, their 'friendship' was revealed to Father Morgan when they were spotted together in a tea-house in Rednal. Tolkien's kindly guardian was furious. The boys were moved from Mrs Faulkner's house immediately, and Ronald was strictly forbidden to see Edith again whilst he was still his ward. This was harsh, but Father Morgan had invested a great deal of time and money on the boys. He perhaps had an inkling too, that Tolkien was destined for great things – if only he would apply himself more seriously to his studies. He was only weeks from his Oxford entrance examinations, which he proceeded to fail.

The affair with Edith had indeed taken a toll, and in his heart-of-hearts, Tolkien knew this. Perhaps it was ultimately for the best when Edith went to stay with relatives in Cheltenham. With temptation out of the way until his 21st birthday, three long years away, Tolkien buckled down, acquiring a reputation at King Edward's as a prodigy in languages, especially Old English. In 1911, he passed his Oxford examinations and was accepted by Exeter College to read Classics. Oxford, except for his wartime service in the military, and a brief spell at the University of Leeds as a teacher, was to be his academic home for the rest of his life.

This is not a biography of Tolkien, but this brief background to his early life will prove germane to what follows. Ronald had suffered much loss and heartbreak in his adolescence, but it is a mark of his strength of character that he not only rose to the challenges but overcame them. He had many gifts besides his keen intellect and vivid imagination. He was self-disciplined, devout, and physically healthy and strong – he was a respected rugby player. He was handsome, and clearly attractive to the opposite sex, he had already wooed a girl who was three years his senior, but above all, he was amusing, popular, and clubbable. It was a natural reaction to his inner grief to sublimate it, to seek 'fellowship' – and it was male, intellectual company he especially sought.

Whilst at King Edward's Tolkien had helped form a group known as the 'T.C.B.S.', whose purpose was to share literature and poetry, read from the classics aloud, and to encourage intellectual enthusiasm in a more general sense. The members of this group became close friends, the model for his famous fellowship. They went on mountain-climbing and rambling holidays together, including to Switzerland. The breathtaking mountain scenes were unconsciously filed away in Tolkien's imagination for later use. But all good things must come to an end, and when Tolkien left for Oxford, the comrades went their separate ways.

But nothing could ever part 'the Immortal Four', the core group of these friends – as in the mythic times, they would be faithful brothers unto death. These romantic notions may seem quaint to our tastes, but they were typical of the generation which was about to be devoured.

Newly arrived in Oxford, it was natural that Tolkien should play to his strengths. He immediately sought out a similar select, male, intellectual club – a group of comrades whose purpose was to hone the mind, and especially to share new ideas. Oxford was, in those days, a bastion of class privilege and elitism.

A large proportion of the undergraduates were not especially intellectually gifted, as Tolkien clearly was, but were scions of rich and noble ancient families, for whom college was simply a continuation of public-school life before they went on to occupy hereditary sinecures in the imperial service, civil service, politics, industry – and of course, the Church of England. These entitled people looked down on 'poor scholars' – that is people who had won scholarships, and Oxford was grotesquely snobbish. Thomas Hardy's trenchant critique in *Jude* was no caricature.

Fairly early on, Tolkien became a protegé of Joe Wright, a working-class man from the north, and a philologist of exceptional talent. In 1913, Tolkien took a decision that would change literary history. He had not been really enthused with Classics, and the Master of Exeter College persuaded him to read English instead. Tolkien was steadily finding his own level, but on his 21st birthday, as if by a magical spell, everything fell to pieces again. No longer bound by his promise to avoid all contact with Edith, Tolkien immediately wrote to her in Cheltenham – reaffirming his undying love and indicating his desire to marry her. Edith's response was more paralysing than a tarantula bite. She was already engaged.

As we have seen, Tolkien was no faint-heart. He immediately arranged to travel by train to meet Edith in Cheltenham. She waited anxiously on the platform for him. When he caught sight of her as his train pulled in, it was the first time for three years. She was 'Lúthien' to his 'Beren'; these names are inscribed on their tombstones. This was no ordinary love, but a medieval *fin amor.*

By the time the couple parted later that January day in 1913, the business was settled. Edith would send her engagement ring back to her fiancé and marry Tolkien, what would become a lifetime union of souls. Ronald had faced his worst fears and now he applied his extraordinary mind to what he knew to be his life-task – the study of Anglo-Saxon, Welsh, Scandinavian and Finnish literature, specialising in philology. If he were to support a wife and family, his career must come first. He resolved to become an Oxford don himself, an ambition commensurate with his abilities. But then, the world was changed, on August Bank Holiday, 1914.

The so-called 'Great War for Civilisation' was actually the beginning of a descent into barbarism; the ruin of ancient empires, the great Christian apostasy, loss of integrity in high finance, nihilism in the arts, the proliferation of pseudo-sciences, the breakdown of the nuclear-family – among many other modern ills. But young men were all too eager to rush into it at the time. Tolkien was concerned that he would not be able to take his degree before enlisting in the army for officer training, but a scheme run by the universities enabled him to complete his finals and his basic training simultaneously.

The gallant members of the 'T.C.B.S.' were itching to get into the fight as soon as possible, and the 'Immortal Four' hoped to meet in France before the war was over. Some optimists said it would be finished by Christmas. They had always kept faithfully in touch and felt themselves in the grip of a strange, shared destiny – Tolkien, G.B. Smith, R.Q. Gilson, and Christopher Wiseman, Ronald's oldest friend from King Edward's, after whom his first son was named.

Together again, it seemed as if their intellectual capacity was increased by a factor of four – as if they were no longer four mere individuals – but somehow *one*, a collective entity. In this first, and most important fellowship, Tolkien began to dimly realise the potential in this spiritual bonding for something magical, a solution, perhaps, to the crisis of our age. But by 1916, the death-struggles of Verdun and the Somme were imminent. Ronald hastened to Warwick where Edith was staying, and on 22 March they were, at last, married. After a brief honeymoon Tolkien returned to duty and in early June, he embarked for France.

For over six months, the British and Imperial forces had been preparing for what they called 'the Big Push', an assault by 1,500,000 men along the entire 90-mile section of the Western Front then held by the British. The extensive preparations had to go on in strictest secrecy. There was much to do. Wells had to be sunk, roads, tramlines and railways constructed, field-hospitals and medical clearing-stations built, ammunition and food for hundreds of thousands of men and fodder for horses stockpiled. The main assault required 300,000 men to expedite the attack, along the River Somme. Thousands of heavy guns would bombard the stunned Germans for an entire week before the main assault went in on 1 July. It was the German general Erich Ludendorff who is supposed to have described the British army as 'lions led by donkeys'. In February 1916 this was proven beyond all reasonable doubt.

Orders went out to clear villages of civilians in the rear of the assault, which would be obliterated by German counter-battery fire. In one village, Meaulte, local dignitaries objected to being forcibly moved by a foreign authority. They petitioned King George V himself, who passed the matter on to Sir Douglas Haig, the British Commander-in-Chief. Haig granted the villagers permission to remain, but also advised them to shelter in cellars for 'three days from 1st July'. In a small village, gossip soon spread, and German spies were everywhere. Thanks to Haig's bungling, the German high command now knew, four months in advance, exactly where the 'push' was coming, and exactly when. They reinforced the area and dug deep underground bunkers immune to the heaviest artillery fire. Machine-gunners and barbed-wire would survive the initial bombardment intact, meaning that the men in the British first wave would be committing mass suicide. So, this was the time, and this the hour, for the 'Immortal Four' to prove their mettle.

Tolkien's unit, the 11th Lancashire Fusiliers, went into action on 11 July, after the initial attack had made only meagre gains at the cost of horrific casualties. On 1 July alone, 20,000 were killed and another 40,000 wounded, many fatally. On 14 July, Tolkien's company went out into the wilderness of no-man's-land – the 'Dead Marshes of Emyn Muil' were clearly based on his awful experiences here – dead men, their eyes staring from filthy pools in stinking shell-holes, and rats gorging themselves on rotting flesh. Bloated, putrefying corpses of horses added to the stench. When he returned from the trenches to the rear, a letter awaited him, from his T.C.B.S. comrade G.B. Smith. R.Q. Gilson had been killed on the first day. Soon afterwards, Tolkien was diagnosed with severe trench fever and withdrawn from duty to receive hospital care.

By November, he was home in Birmingham, in a hospital. In December he was allowed a brief home leave for Christmas with Edith, but there was to be no seasonal joy. He received a letter from his best friend Christopher Wiseman, informing him that G.B. Smith had died of wounds sustained under shellfire. The four friends were down to two – and the war was far from won.

Tolkien tearfully re-read Smith's last letter to him: 'The death of one of its members cannot, I am determined, dissolve the T.C.B.S. Death can make us loathsome and helpless as individuals, but it cannot put an end to the immortal four! ... God bless you, my dear John Ronald, and may you say the things I have tried to say long after I am not there to say them, if such be my lot.' Here, then, was a commission, as if from beyond the grave – an exhortation to Tolkien to keep faith with the fellowship and express its ideals to the wider world. Christopher Wiseman urged him on, too: 'You ought to start the epic,' he wrote in a letter. And so, one day, Tolkien picked up a school exercise-book, on the front of which he wrote in capital letters: *The Book of Lost Tales*. The work of a lifetime had begun.

Now, not many are aware these days of the rich and enduring literary inheritance of the West Midlands, one of the deficits this book seeks, in its humble way, to rectify. But Tolkien was very well aware of it. He was, of course, a student of Geoffrey of Monmouth, and Layamon, and so understood the power of literature to reshape and reinvigorate the national consciousness.

I am convinced that his immense project was, for him, his own contribution to this continual chain of mythical transmission. He must have known that to be counted among such august company his myth must be as authentic and compelling as these predecessors, but something extra was required if the saga was to be successful in his own terms. It had to be 'true', to possess its own internal coherence.

For over 20 years, in his notes for *The Silmarillion* Tolkien created a host of mythical creatures, orcs, elves, dwarves and so on, each of which required him meticulously to invent a complex language and history. The landscape in which all this takes place is deliberately similar to England and Wales, Scotland and Scandinavia, but we find ourselves in a different time, a different age, almost inconceivably remote from our own – yet somehow related.

His meticulous study of Welsh and Finnish gave him the basis for entirely new languages, those spoken by the elves, for instance, Quenya and Sindarin, have their own complex syntax and grammar. He was equally obsessive about mapping the imaginary territories. His young son, Christopher, became no mean cartographer. These intricate notebooks provided the raw material for fairy-stories, which he read out to his delighted young children as his family grew. As yet, he had no notion of publishing anything and concentrated on his academic work.

Despite his gradual academic success, an aching void had been left by the demise of the T.C.B.S. Wiseman was too busy with his career to keep pace with Tolkien's increasingly intense train of thought. Moreover, two members is not really a 'club'. When he returned to Oxford as a don after a brief spell lecturing in Leeds, Edith found the snobbish, male-dominated and rather prurient world of Tolkien's peers daunting and annoying.

In truth, Tolkien was somewhat lonely and a little withdrawn, for all his good fortune and apparent happiness – 'survivor's guilt', perhaps – there was a lot of it about after the war ended. But then, by an exquisite serendipity, the fellowship Tolkien thought he had lost was born again, but amplified, as it were – and this time, there were to be no bullets or shells to tear it apart.

In 1926, Tolkien first met C.S. Lewis (1898-1963), known to his friends as 'Jack'. Lewis was a Fellow of the prestigious Magdalen College, where he had spacious rooms. In many respects, they profoundly differed, especially in the matter of religion – Jack was a confirmed atheist. The ancient Celts had a special category of friendship, what they called 'soul-friends', and despite their opposing views, that is what the two men eventually became.

They *loved* the same things, and in the same way. Lewis was, like Tolkien, an expert in medieval English Literature. He was immensely charming and likeable, and Tolkien's equal intellectually. He, too, liked nothing better than a 'gentleman's club', where male companions could toast crumpets and drink beer or port after a walk in the college gardens, times when:

> The whole world, and something beyond the world, opens itself to our minds as we talk; and no one has any claim or responsibility for another, but all are freemen and equals as if we had first met an hour ago, while at the same time an Affection mellowed by the years enfolds us. Life – natural life – has no better gift to give.[21]

Much as he disapproved of Jack's religious position, Tolkien gradually bonded with Lewis. As the older man, he probably felt a misguided responsibility to lead him back to the faith. He knew only too well what lay at the root of his friend's apostasy, for the two men had another thing in common. Lewis, too, had lost his mother, at an even more tender age than Ronald. Yet Lewis always gave the impression of joviality and bonhomie – he was the archetypal Oxford don, most comfortable in an atmosphere which was 'not homosexual, but excluded women', as Carpenter puts it.

Over the years, this 'special friendship' grew into a literary legend – and eventually, like the T.C.B.S., it was to number four core members. In fact, though Tolkien little suspected it, the fellowship which was to dominate the rest of his life had already been formed – 'the Inklings'.

It is important to remember that Tolkien was not primarily an author, but an academic. In 1925, he became a Fellow of Pembroke College in Oxford. The 'epic' was something Tolkien worked on in his own time and for his own amusement, but there was one select group who were an exception, and who were aware of his 'hobby'. Lewis, of course, was the most famous, but Jack hosted meetings in his rooms on Thursday evenings, attended by other creative-minded souls.

Warren 'Warnie' Lewis, Jack's elder brother was always in attendance, along with Hugo Dyson (1896-1975), who taught English at the University of Reading. There were other occasional members – one of the most famous, Charles Williams, had not yet arrived on the scene – but the first member of the group was Owen

Barfield (1898-1997), who had been Jack's close friend at Oxford since they first met in 1919.

Barfield had now left Oxford to practise in London as a solicitor in the family law firm, but he would make his way to as many meetings as possible, and always corresponded, sending in his latest work for discussion if he could not attend. On Tuesdays, a more intimate meeting took place, in the 'Rabbit Room' at the Eagle & Child public house on St Giles' – known as the 'Bird & Baby' to undergraduates. Here, over pipes and jars of foaming English ale, the men discussed their various creative and philosophical projects.

Now, all this sounds rather quaint, but these men were no mere pub bores or hobbyists. They were among the intellectual giants of their age. These meetings were a focus for their private projects, but also, I think, an attempt to find meaning in a world that had just been devastated by one world war and was about to endure another. Their mission was in deadly earnest, for it was clear that humankind now had the power to destroy not only itself, but Nature in its entirety.

No political or materialist solution seemed possible, and religious faith was collapsing. After the Wall Street Crash of autumn 1929, the world economy was ruined. Italy, Germany, Japan, Spain and Portugal all opted for Fascism. Russia had succumbed to Bolshevism. If there was to be a 'eucatastrophe', this could not come about without a radical and fundamental change in human consciousness itself. Of all the four men, it was Barfield who wrestled most with the problem of how to bring about such a change.

For a time he became dreadfully depressed and despondent, suffering a nervous breakdown. But during his crisis, Barfield thought he saw a solution, contained in the history of language itself. His *History in English Words* (1926) was the first in a series of books by this relatively little-known philosopher, certainly now an under-estimated intellectual of the time. But Tolkien and Lewis knew themselves to be in the presence of true genius. This was much more than a twee gentleman's drinking-club in an agreeable setting. These men felt themselves to be on a 'holy' quest to recover meaning for humanity, by changing the way we think about consciousness itself.

But like the shamans of old, they could not hope to cure the world-sickness until they had transformed themselves, recovered from their own disease. Barfield had the worst time of it but received the most profound illumination – a truly mystical experience. Like the Ring, this profound knowledge was a heavy burden, it could not be carried without comradeship and spiritual faith. Barfield had become an Anthroposophist while he was a student at Oxford, much to the dismay of Lewis, who was beginning to have doubts about his own atheism. Rudolf Steiner (1861-1925) was an Austrian-born philosopher, educationalist, and social theorist, who claimed clairvoyance and offered a complete system of spiritual development.

Anthroposophy is not a religion and is open to people of all faiths or none. Barfield was convinced that one of Steiner's theories in particular, the idea of the evolution of human consciousness as a process in historical time, was the key to the rediscovery of meaning for humanity. The intensity of Barfield's writings on these matters began to undermine Jack's atheism, and although he never proselytised, Tolkien, too, was subtly influencing Lewis.

One evening, Jack went for a stroll in Addison's Walk with Tolkien and Hugo Dyson. Lewis, a renowned expert on myth, was passionate about the gods and heroes of his beloved Norse and Celtic tales, but strangely reticent when it came to the Christian story. By now, Barfield had convinced him that there was indeed, a God. But Christ occupied a unique position, he was both man and God, a historical personage and a myth. As Lewis said, 'Myths are lies, even though breathed through silver.' But Tolkien demurred:

We have come from God (continued Tolkien), and inevitably the myths woven by us, though they contain error, will also reflect a splintered fragment of the true light, the eternal truth that is with God. Indeed only by myth-making, only by becoming a 'sub-creator' and inventing stories, can Man aspire to the state of perfection that he knew before the Fall. Our myths may be misguided, but they steer however shakily towards the true harbour, while materialistic 'progress' leads only to a yawning abyss and the Iron Crown of pure evil.[22]

Shortly afterwards, following deep contemplation on the matter, Lewis renounced atheism and returned to the Anglican Church. He was to become one of the greatest theologians of the century, as well as a great author. In 1939, at the outbreak of the Second World War, another thinker was recruited to the Inklings group. This was the poet and author Charles Williams (1886-1945), who worked as an editor for the Oxford University Press. This was actually based in London, but with the Blitz imminent it was evacuated to Oxford and the reluctant Williams with it.

This incredible man was also to have a profound influence on Tolkien. But even though he kept such erudite and discerning company, Tolkien's contributions were always the most eagerly awaited in the 'Rabbit Room', as over a jug or two, the latest chapter of Tolkien's epic was read out to them. Not only did he delight them, but he had also imparted an adamantine idea – that of the 'true myth', and also a method – 'sub-creation'.

So, Tolkien's road to the publication of *The Hobbit* in 1937 had been an epic journey in itself. The seemingly endless task of completing *The Silmarillion* preoccupied him but was still unfinished. A sequel to *The Hobbit* was required, and now Tolkien set himself to deliver up his 'sub-creation', a labour of 16 years, in all, *The Lord of the Rings*. I believe, in the fullness of time, Tolkein will stand beside Shakespeare and Milton as one of our nation's literary exemplars. His powerful warnings against the power of 'the Machine' and materialism will increasingly resonate with the young, as their future is overshadowed by environmental catastrophe. But of all his many stories, there is one which has always fascinated me most – the legend of Numenor.

Numenor, or 'Westernesse', is a great island in the West, which the wicked Sauron conspires to destroy in a deluge, removing the Western lands 'from the circle of the world'. In an unpublished story by Tolkien called *The Lost Road*, the Straight Road to the Ancient West is still to be found for those pilgrims in time who make the effort to search for it. It is the act of faith itself, which works the magic. Tolkien had been familiar with this motif since reading Andrew Lang's *Red Fairy Book* as a child. Numenor, like Hy Brasil or Atlantis, has an odd, numinous quality about it.

In 1908, respectable witnesses numbered in the hundreds swore that they had seen land off the west coast of Ireland, where none had been seen before – which vanished. Remains of drowned settlements are found miles off the coast of Cornwall – Lyonesse, perhaps? Here, at the edge of Britain's Ancient Druid Rocky Shore, the power of 'the Machine' recedes. Signs of the impossible appear, and the supernatural. This Lost Road leads to the final goal, 'Leagues beyond the sunset bar' – and we must all follow it soon enough. But there is yet time to linger in the Shire awhile.

'Bag End' is a real place, in Dormston, Worcestershire, once Tolkien's aunt's farmhouse. It is not just an idle fancy of mine, then, to trace a literary lineage stretching from Layamon, to Shakespeare, to Tolkien, inspired by this landscape, and drawing from it the contours of imaginary worlds so vivid and authentic as to derive from 'a manifold of partially actualized realities'. Tolkien and Lewis – and also Barfield, his *The Silver Trumpet* (1925), was the first 'fairy-story' to be published by the Inklings – both famously wrote epic fairy tales, and what we would call today 'fantasy' fiction, but these were no mere allegories or 'morality' tales. They were 'sub-creations'. Tolkien wrote:

> What really happens ... is that the story-maker proves a successful 'sub-creator'. He makes a Secondary World which your mind can enter. Inside it, what he relates is 'true': it accords with the laws of that world. You therefore believe it, while you are, as it were, inside. The moment disbelief arises, the spell is broken; the magic, or rather art, has failed. You are then out in the Primary World again, looking at the little abortive Secondary World from outside.

We see here the wellspring of the 'fantasy' games industry, 'fantasy-literature', 'Dungeons and Dragons' and so forth, and the implications of that in a future dominated by Artificial Intelligence are mind-boggling. But what does it say about the condition of the 'Primary World', when an entire generation find their spiritual and emotional nourishment elsewhere, in a virtual realm? This objection, however, no longer stands up if the Secondary World is actually *true* and more meaningful than the Primary World: 'Every writer making a secondary world ... wishes in some measure to be a maker, or hopes that he is drawing on reality: hopes that the peculiar quality of this secondary world (if not all the details) are derived from Reality, or are flowing into it.'

If we can create such worlds, imagine such beings, perhaps they have a destiny, to help us transfigure our forlorn planet Earth, and save our fellow creatures from extinction? Perhaps the imaginative flow is not one-way? The exponential growth of Artificial Intelligence may have already vastly exceeded the capacity of human brain-power. We may be the playthings of computer-deities existing outside time, for all we know.

As the power of the Machine grows, its fibre-optic tentacles reaching into every home and every brain, this old world we know and love grows ever more anaemic, hollowed-out, and meaningless. We have become 'zombie-ants', mind-controlled insects hosting a parasitic electronic mycelium. We are witnessing the abolition of humanity – which now seems almost a pre-requisite if other life-forms are to survive. The Scouring of the Shire is a vision of our ravaged, benighted 21st-century world.

And yet, if some demonic agency were to offer me eternal virtual life in a computer-generated universe, I would not trade my brief remaining time in the 'real' Worcestershire in exchange. The motto of the Worcestershire Regiment used to be 'Firm'. The legendary courage and stubbornness of the regiment is celebrated in the Regimental Museum in the Worcester Institute. Nowhere is immune to change, of course, but Worcestershire people are notoriously conservative and, usually, Conservative. Stanley Baldwin was from Worcestershire. If Elgar or Tolkien or the Reverend Geoffrey Studdert Kennedy (better-known as 'Woodbine Willie' and definitely *not* a Conservative) visited Worcester today, they would still find the old familiar landmarks intact, and thankfully, some things can't be changed.

The Malvern Hills contain rocks so ancient that they bear no fossils – no life-forms had yet developed when they were formed. The wide River Severn still follows the same course as when the Roman town of *Vertis* stood here 2,000 years ago. The great spire of St Andrew's, 'the Glover's Needle' still soars nearby with peregrines swooping from its lofty heights, and a little further down Deansway, by the Elgar statue, stands Worcester Cathedral, my favourite church.

Perhaps no prospect is more English than the famous view of Worcester Cathedral from New Road County Cricket Ground. In 1917, a series of stained-glass windows was begun in the cloisters which tells the story of the cathedral since its foundation in AD 680. All the glorious bishops and saints from the see are depicted. St Egwin's swineherd, Eoves, had a vision of the Virgin at Evesham, which is named after him. St Dunstan, St Oswald and St Wulfstan, all bishops here, are shown, and King Edgar, who endowed the monastery school. Lady Godiva was a benefactor and is shown presenting a handsome Bible to the monastic library. Strangely, the fearsome pagan, Penda, has his own window – though it is his glorious death which is the subject of the scene, as he hews around him at the terrified Christian soldiers surrounding him on all sides. William Langland is in another window; although he was a Shropshire man by birth, he beheld his 'Fair Field full of Folk' from Malvern Priory.

Worcester suffered much during the Protestant Reformation and the civil wars of the 1640s, which perhaps accounts for the resistance to change so typical of its folk. The Cathedral Library, which once contained over 600 priceless books, many of them dating from Anglo-Saxon times, was destroyed, along with St Dunstan's Benedictine monastery. Only six books survived. King John's tomb was defaced and Prince Arthur's tomb desecrated when Oliver Cromwell's troops used the cathedral as a stable following the bloody and climactic Battle of Worcester in 1651.

The Lord Protector is not among those memorialised, but the magnificent Guildhall nearby was a tribute from the Stuart dynasty to 'the Faithful City', honouring its loyalty in the Third Civil War of 1651. For ten years, Worcestershire was my home, and I am glad to have had the opportunity to explore the many layers of this exceptional corner of England – its very heart, indeed. This is the England that is fast receding from view. The Dark Riders are gathering, and middle-earth, middle-England, stands in mortal danger – but who will be the Ring-bearer now?

12

Under the Sun

> The thing that hath been, it is that which shall be; and that which is done is that which shall be done; and there is no new thing under the sun.
>
> Ecclesiastes 1:9

Today would have been my mother's 100th birthday, bless her. It is too far now to visit the grave, and too expensive to travel. The roads are unsafe anyway. There was a swarm-attack on Knighton last week, border-raiders using micro-drones. It's Christmas in the Welsh valleys, so the convoys gather for raids. Six dead they say, and many businesses looted and burned-out. Jak, our Polish security-guard, says it took three days for the army to show-up afterwards. I like the guy, but he's only here three times a week for three hours – we are sitting-ducks for raiders. I sleep with a *Kukri* under my bed, when I can sleep. This morning, the 'Age England' 'bus comes to take us Christmas-shopping in Ludlow. With any luck, I'll have time for a pint or two.

Housman was right about this place:

> Clunton and Clunbury, Clungunford and Clun,
> Are the quietest places under the sun.

Not much happens here now the pubs are all gone. St George's church holds a service one Sunday in the month. The playwright, John Osborne, lies buried in the churchyard. My sheltered-housing complex, Osborne Court, is named after him. It isn't the only literary connection. Bruce Chatwin used the village as the model for his *On the Black Hill* (1982). Now, though, the place is ominously rather than pleasantly quiet – the calm before another storm, I fear. The only literary activity here now is my labour *The Fall of Roman Britain*, which I hope to complete by next summer, God willing. It's hard not to see the analogies, of course, between then and now. Did they *know* then, that it was the end, as I do now, I wonder?

I'm looking out of my window towards Flossie's flat. We aren't allowed pets in the complex, but there is a cat we have enticed, which spends its time between us, scrounging food. Sam, I call him. He's usually sitting outside Flat 26 by now, but the light snow flurries have probably discouraged him. I must pick up some food for him today at the supermarket. I'll put it on my list – where *is* the bloody thing? Ah! So, that's chicken-fillet, sausages, cauliflower, potatoes, gravy-mix, sprouts, cheddar, cheese-sauce mix, wine, litre bottle of malt whisky, 8 cans of beer, mince-pies, cream, paper, Flossie's present – and cat food – there. Now, have I got my glasses, my ID card, mask, meds, ration-card, keys – yes, all in order. I'll go and have a shave. I can have my breakfast in the 'Spoons' later. Got my money – yes! Time? Nine-twenty, so he'll be here in, what, forty minutes. Better shake a leg.

Odd, where you end up. I got discharged here from hospital for a rehab, and then this flat came vacant. I was eligible, so applied, and moved in what, three years ago? I lose track of time. I figured it would be safer, out in the wilderness. Urban areas are no-go since the old queen died. Nowhere is safe now though, not since the troubles started. Forty thousand people held in football stadiums, awaiting transfer to the Internment Detention Centres, according to the news. Might as well call it what it is – civil war. They say on the radio that General Woodward will meet the President and First Lady when they land at Brize Norton. They're keeping the king out of the public eye 'until the situation in London stabilises'. Fat chance of that. Woodward only wants money and arms for his 'Home Defence Force', but I expect they'll put on the swank – find some Lifeguards from somewhere, and a gilded-carriage or two for the Potus.

Some radio presenter asked me for 'an historical analogy' the other day, to the current relationship between Woodward and the king. I suggested the relationship of Simon De Montfort to Henry III. The lad was nonplussed. He could not descry my meaning. Bloody mirror's steaming up again. This razor is feather-edged, that's another thing to add to the list – oh, and my library card needs renewing. Good to get out, though, see the hills, but best of all, two whole hours in the pub! I've only been in one twice this year.

The kettle boils and clicks. Just time for a cuppa. The milk's off. They don't do pints now so it always sours half-way down the carton. Never mind. He'll be here in fifteen minutes. The snow seems to have stopped, and the sun's out now. Ah! There's Flossie opening her door to let Sam out. I knock at my window to attract her attention, and wave, then tap my wristwatch. She gives me the thumbs-up and goes back inside. Sam jumps up onto the side wall, and climbs up onto the roof and away, replete with diced liver. Now for the daily ordeal of getting my shoes on – a ten-minute job that, these days. Painful too, osteoarthritis. I put my stick ready by the door next to my hessian shopping-bag. Right, heating switched off, coat and scarf on – time to go. There are nine booked for the bus, more than usual. This is a special outing though. We usually only go to Tuffins in Craven Arms once a week. They're beginning to gather now. Too cold to stand out in it yet. I'll sit in the front room and keep an eye out.

I glance up at the sideboard. There she is! Dear old Ma. I pick the old photograph up and give it a kiss. 'Happy 100th Ma!' It was taken just after the war, I think. She looks so young, so happy and full of life. Oh, he's here. I hoist myself out of the armchair and walk to the front door. The blue bin needs pushing down. There we are. I join the gaggle of women in the queue outside the main foyer. No John again. Dementia getting worse every day, poor chap, and he's going blind. Thank God I've been spared that, at least. Dave, the driver, beckons us on board, and stashes the shopping-trolleys at the back. He has to shout at the new woman to put her hearing-aid in. He gestures to her:

'You need to put your mask on dear!'

She's forgotten it. Flossie has a spare packet and so hands her one. I'm the last on board, I need to use the front seat because of my legs, handy, because I can chat to Dave about the good old days at Molineux while the women all gabble on. Still, we are locked up alone all week, so it's to be expected, I suppose. We're off! Half an hour later the bus pulls up in Corve St, outside the Compasses. I see the Kidderminster bus pull in beside us. It only runs to Kidderminster Station now. There's no on-service to Birmingham these days. I walk slowly down the hill to Tesco in Station Street chatting to Flossie. She's going to her daughter's house in Shrewsbury for Christmas day and is very excited to be seeing her grandchildren. That's one thing I do miss, family. I'm completely alone now.

Forty minutes later, I emerge with my shopping-bags. I bought Flossie a little Koala Bear – she collects dolls and cuddly animals. I struggle up the steep hill to the library. After that, I pop into the Feathers Hotel for a coffee and a breather. The hill and carrying the heavy bags have both taken it out of me. I use my GTN spray in the posh lavatories. Once I am guided to my table, I open today's *Guardian* putting aside the quick crossword for later use. 'Woodward to greet President as crisis in Scotland deepens', the headline says. I look at my watch. Nearly twelve, so time for brunch.

I walk over the Bull Ring to the 'Spoons'. It is cheap, especially for beer, but a real ball-ache to get in. I press the buzzer and order a dining-booth for one, with no screen. I stand still in front of the 'BISIR' (Biometric Identification System for Iris Recognition) – what a rigmarole! The door opens and a pretty girl, at least she has pretty eyes, she's wearing a mask, leads me to my booth. After the usual health and safety lecture, she takes my order – double-egg & chips and a pint of Landlord, for less than £20.00, cheap and cheerful. After I've eaten, I study the paper.

Not that I need to read it. The Stanford Research Institute pay my care-home bills, by the back door, of course. British Intelligence left me in the lurch, as you would expect, after the PsyOps debacle, but hey-ho. The universe *is* non-local, co-inherent, a living intelligence system. I laugh when I (remotely) listen-in to the phone conversations of our 'world-leaders':

(POTUS) 'Arty! Hope you don't mind me calling you that pal? 'Arthur' sounds a little crazy, don't ya think? So 'olde-world' – but that's where *you* folks live! Now, Arty, the US has a whole *lotta* strategic interests in the United – your country – you know that, as well as I do. Now, c'mon, ya been together for all these hundreds – thousands of years! There's the king and all, and *his* family to consider. There's – whaddya call it now – the Commonwealth? There's Europe. Russia's rubbing its hands together – now c'mon! Let's just – get it together. Now, whaddya say Arty?'

(General Woodward, in an Etonian drawl) 'My father named me in honour of the Duke of Wellington, alas. Mr President, if I may make so bold – may I remind you that your *primary* strategic interest here is the security of the nuclear submarine base at Faslane. As you are aware, this has been under siege by irregular Scottish forces for two years. Eighteen Royal Navy personnel have been murdered, and 167 taken as prisoners. Until these prisoners are released, English military operations will and *must* continue to establish their whereabouts. You understand, Mr President, as a former marine, what comradeship is? I urge you sir, do not compromise yourself by mistaking the Scottish uprising for something honourable. It is not. It is a Russian-inspired Communist conspiracy to undermine the transatlantic alliance *at its very heart.* I beg you now sir, as Churchill once said: 'Give us the tools, and we will finish the job.'

(POTUS) 'Well, Arty, I'd just like to know what the king has to say about that? The way I see it, the Irish and Scottish see things the same way we do – and that's OK, right? We gotta lot of Irish and Scottish voters over here, kapeesh? I'm staring mid-term elections in the ass! All I wanna do is meet with the king, shoot the shit – and do a *deal* for cryin' out loud! You get to keep your toy soldiers, the Crown Jewels, Bucking-ham Palace – the whole shit – but lay off of Scotland will ya! That's all I ask.'

(General Woodward) 'Mr President, I think you may misunderstand the situation here. I am *not* a politician, like yourself, but a soldier, born of a line of soldiers stretching back to Waterloo. I will not be intimidated. My name may sound 'crazy' to you, but to us Arthur is the great hero who will save the nation in its hour of need – and that time is now! London is being secured borough by borough and will be pacified by the time you arrive. But we have reliable information that the SNLA intends to strike across the border the moment you touch down. Mr President, we have no choice. Our cross-border operations commence within a matter of hours. They are rebels and traitors against His Majesty, whose true servant, sir, I remain.'

(POTUS) 'Jeez Arty! You're a real hard-assed son-of-a-bitch! Well, you seem to have it all figured out. Now, keep our special advisors the hell out of anything spicy, y'hear? I like your style Arty. See you in Windsor Castle.'

Right, glasses on, let's have a look at the home news section.

FWA Flying Column kills 19 RAF personnel in ruthless ambush. The 'boys' are getting bolder, heavy weapons coming in from Ireland.

A message from an anonymous Free Wales Army (or 'Byddin Rhyddid Cymru') source described the attack as a warning to General Woodward not to replicate his aggressive moves against Scotland in Wales. Since the dissolution of the Constitutional Convention three years ago, the FWA has grown from a tiny, largely symbolic militia, into a highly effective paramilitary force, modelled on the IRA. Intelligence sources estimate it now numbers over 2,000 volunteers, organised into 'Flying Columns' operating in strictest secrecy all around the country, though the most serious incidents have been in Gwynedd, Ceredigion and Powys. The latest attack ambushed two trucks from the RAF Regiment as they were travelling to RAF Valley on Anglesey. All nineteen casualties died, the FWA take no prisoners as a matter of military policy. General Woodward expressed his sympathies for the families of the victims. 'This domestic terrorism – for that is what it is – will be severely punished. When the perpetrators are tracked down, as they will be, judgement will be swift and merciless. There is undoubtedly coordination between all three nationalist terrorist groups, deliberately encouraged by Mr McDonald and the Scottish Parliament. This sad news only reinforces my argument for the establishment of a new Home Defence Force. An auxiliary force such as I propose would take pressure off the conventional armed forces and free them up for other duties. A standing force of say, 200,000 could easily be sustained from National Service provisions,' the General said. 'The key problem is arms and equipment, and also new barracks construction. Urgent talks with the President of the United States at Windsor Castle next week will focus on military aid and assistance. The Democrats in the US Congress have threatened to vote down any military aid which could be used against Scotland, or potentially, Ireland. General Woodward has stressed that the military equipment would be used exclusively by English HDF personnel, and only within England.

More home news. 'Football Association cries foul over sequestration of stadiums'; 'Unemployment at highest levels since 1930s, says ONS'; 'Exiled former London Mayor vows to return "When England is free"'; 'King approves National Anthem for England'; 'Bishop released from detention after 33-day hunger strike'; 'Who guards England's nuclear power stations?'

Let's have a look at the opinion section – if I can find it – Oh God, not Jonesy, I thought they'd have arrested him. What's he saying? 'The Windsor summit: a desperate gamble of a discredited junta.' I'll go with it.

General Sir Arthur Percival Woodward, is not the king – though he fancies himself one. When the President and First Lady arrive next week, there will be none of the usual flummery, none of the red-carpet treatment we used to associate with presidential visits. Instead, the leader of the 'free world' – whatever that is supposed to mean nowadays – will be whisked away amidst tight security and escorted by Armoured Combat Vehicles to Windsor Castle. Up to 8,000 troops and armed police have surrounded Windsor Great Park and the entire area, which is strictly off-limits to the public until the President flies on to Stockholm for talks with exiled opposition leaders.

According to State Department sources, the President's priority is to prevent any escalation of the Scottish crisis, but another key difficulty will be the timetable for the restoration of free and fair elections in England. The king is said to favour a recall of parliament 'at the earliest possible opportunity', but that would be impossible in the current security climate. Urban areas would have virtually zero turn-out, and with the opposition leaders either interned or in exile, there would be no-one to vote for except the Tories and the ENP. Woodward claims his coup was only a temporary measure, but three years later we are still no nearer to anything like a restoration of democracy. The 'Mother of Parliaments' remains closed for business, and when he arrives, the President will be welcomed not by its monarch – but by a latter-day Franco.

Well, Dada, you were right, as usual. Here's to Ma! I raise my pint glass to her invisible presence, and just for a moment, I think I see her coming in through the main security-entrance – but no, just someone who looks remarkably like her, a pareidolia. The waitress thinks I'm calling her.

'Another drink, sir?'

'Why not!' I hand the glass to her.

'Sorry sir, just leave the glass on the side there in the collection-tray. We can't collect them in winter, you see? There's a three-pint per customer limit too, I'm afraid. Public Safety policy, and all that. Would you care to see our dessert menu, perhaps?'

'No, no ta. I'm fine for food. I'll have my *second* pint of Landlord though, if that's OK?' Her eyes smile above her mask, and she is soon back with my beer and receipt. Charming girl. Oh God, the Christmas mob are starting to arrive, office parties. Can't read the paper with all that row *and* Noddy Holder belting it out, nightmare. Crossword? Bugger, no pen.

God only knows what next year will bring – 2035. Should be just the right atmosphere for my new book though. The editor was a bit concerned that we may get trouble from the spooks about the chapter on Carausius, the imposter emperor of Britain in the 3rd century. 'The only difference between Carausius and our current dictator, is that the former was an admiral, the latter a general' – was thought too controversial, and too risky if a defamation notice were issued. They are only a small publisher. God, how did we come to this?

I'm going for Christmas drinks tomorrow in the grounds of Cwm Hall, where Chatwin stayed while he was writing *On the Black Hill*. Clunton is only a couple of miles, but Jak has promised to drop me off and pick me up later – he's a good sort that way. He gets bored just sitting in that office staring at those screens. It seems crazy that they have to hire a Polish ex-commando to guard me from my own countrymen, but that's where we've got to. I have an idea for a book, *Chatwin's Shropshire* I'm researching. With the right photographer, it could sell well, and Bruce is very fashionable again, or so I'm told.

I'm reading a lot of stuff about him, his diaries and letters and Elizabeth, his wife, in particular. When I take my daily walk to the shop, I imagine him sitting outside The White Horse with a pint and his famous rucksack beside him. The pub is up for sale still, but after 5 years, it ain't coming back. What I wouldn't give for just one hour – two would be better – with him! So many questions. But from what I can discern from those who knew him, two *years* wouldn't be enough – too many layers, an ultimate mystery. A good subject for a book, though.

Blimey, I've got a fine thirst on! Three pints isn't enough for a man of my calibre. I've got over an hour to kill too. If push comes to shove, I can always crack a can open under the table and stash the tin. Hopefully, no-one will have time to monitor the CCTV, as it is getting very busy with diners now. Ah, a group of four have taken the table directly opposite. Even if they are pissed, they'll notice my under-the-table antics. I rummage around in the bags, and suddenly realise when I put Flossie's bear I put the cans right at the bottom, it'll be a nightmare to get them out now! I know. The litre bottle of whisky is nicely snug against the side of one of the bags. It's a stopper-top, so I can surreptitiously pour myself a few doubles into the pint pot before the waitress comes back. Come on, it is Christmas – and my Ma's centenary! They say the 'Great Year' of 25,920 years is divided into aeons of 2,160 years, and that, therefore, each degree of an aeon is the equivalent of 72 years on earth – my own age, 'three-score years and ten', more or less. My life-clock is sounding the alarm.

I've still got the knack. I craftily reach my pint pot under the table, unwrap the top, pull the stopper, pour a good-sized dram – and quickly knock it back unobserved, like an alcoholic 'Shadow'. Heck, that was a good measure too! I carefully place the empty glass as far away from me as possible, rinsing it with some slops from another to disperse the smell of liquor. Then, I take out my GTN spray, and squirt it under my tongue, peppermint flavoured. I stand up and beckon the waitress.

Deliberately donning my face-mask, I order a last pint, and ask her to watch my shopping while I go for a 'gypsy's'. She smiles with her eyes, I think she knows my game, but she's a sport. Nice girl, actually, intelligent. I head off to the downstairs disabled lavatories – the 'cripple's shithouse' as someone has helpfully scrawled in one of the cubicles. Christ, it's a bastard to go these days. I could be here five minutes trying to squeeze it out, gasping and groaning – and then I have to turn back on the way out half the time. No, seems OK. Wash hands, lift latch, don mask. As I walk over to my booth, I feel myself floating somewhat, to the strains of George Michael's *Last Christmas*.

Taking my seat, I check under the table. All's well with my Christmas shopping. I take my mask off and pocket my change and receipt from the tray. My final pint of brew awaits. I hold it up and check to see it's clear, before taking a satisfying swig. Ah! *Good*. It is filling up, so up the volume of the music goes, Roy Wood now. Christ, I remember meeting him back in the day! There used to be a no music policy until the great 'Spoons' takeover. A third of the pubs in England now belong to the consortium, according to the company magazine lying on the table. No wonder they are packed. My head does ache though. That whisky was somewhat beyond 'reasonable refreshment'. I'll take it steady – got to be on my best behaviour tomorrow.

I was only reading Chatwin's theory about the collapse of the Roman system last evening before bed. He had a theory about everything, and much of his globe-trotting was related to his need to back his extraordinary hunches; that a now extinct species of prehistoric beast stalked and ate ancient humans, a creature which still lurks in the shadows of the human mind; that a cave in Africa had been excavated, producing evidence of the very first fire kindled by our hominid ancestors; that a network of 'dreaming tracks' or 'songlines' spread out like a vast web all over the Australian outback – a landscape literally sung into existence by the native Australian tribes. As a specialist auctioneer at Sotheby's, he had the knack of instantly recognising the fake from the genuine article, an instinct for finding the rare and obscure oddities lurking unseen in the attics of our homes, and our minds. Only last night I was struck by his insight:

> The same thing happened in the Roman Empire in the third century AD and later. The rich abdicated the responsibilities of their wealth; the cities became unbearable and at the mercy of property speculators. Wealth was divorced from its source. A strong state took over and collapsed under the strain. The rich wore their wealth, and the governments passed endless laws against extravagance in dress. Compare the diamonds and gold boxes of today, and the aura attached to portable possessions. The mobile rich were impossible to tax, the advantages of no fixed address were obvious. So the unpredictable demands of the tax collectors were laid at the feet of those who could least afford to pay.[23]

I smiled when I read one of his earliest letters from the Old Hall School in Wellington in Shropshire, to his parents – a letter surely selected personally by Elizabeth, who knew him best:

> Dear Mummy and Daddy,
> Please could you get me a Romany Book, called Out with Romany by Medow and Stream Because I want it for a friend of mine's birthday. Yesterday we had a lantern lecture on a man's uncle who went to Africa exploring and he took a lot of photographs on big game, and natives. In my book Wild Life there are two photographs. One of some Rock Rabbits, and another of a jackel. It was very nice. I hope you are well. Please will you send me a book called The Open Road. Tell Hugh it won't be long till I come home. Please will you save these stamps till I come home.
> When you see Aunt Gracie next tell her I send my love.
> Love you pieces
> Bruce

There it is, in this early letter home from boarding school – all that was to come, the template for a lifetime's wanderings, physically, intellectually and spiritually. Chatwin, apparently, derives from an old Anglo-Saxon word *chetwynd* – a wayfarer. Nominative determinism at its most subtle. If ever there was a man who followed his fate, Chatwin was he. I glance at my watch. Time flies, I've only got twenty minutes till the bus comes! Best drink up and go for another wee. I've enjoyed it though. There's tomorrow to look forward to, before the day itself – deadly quiet for me. Flossie will be gone, and Jak's at home with his folks. God, this shopping's heavier than I thought! I'll get going.

As I get to the top of Corve Street, I see the bus already there, but none of the 'girls' getting aboard. Strange. Never known Dave to be *early* before. I'm nearly by the Compasses before he sees me. He shouts over:

'Come on slowcoach! You're twenty minutes late!' I don't get it.

'What?', I reply.

'It's quarter past two, we thought you'd been arrested!'

He grabs my shopping and hoists it onto the front seat, before lowering the steps. I check my watch. Sure enough, the bloody battery has packed up! Only happens once every year or two. Too late to get one fitted now, so I'll have no watch till January, bloody pest! Making my apologies, I take my seat up front, with many ribald suggestions about where I've been, and who with, from the masked ladies behind me. Soon enough, we are under way. I take a good look at Ludlow Castle looming behind us as we head out of town. A grand old view, with the tower of St Laurence's in the background. Not long before I'm nodding.

Next thing I know, there's a hand on my shoulder. It's Flossie.

'Wake up sleepy-head! Been in the pub too long again, I shouldn't wonder?' She's not wrong.

'Are we home? Must have dozed-off. I did imbibe a few, yes.' Dave helps me down the steps as Flossie hands down my shopping. Then, she hands me something else.

'Well, you may as well go the whole hog. Here's something to keep you company over Christmas!' It isn't gift-wrapped, and glancing into the bag I see a bottle of whisky – only a blend, mind, but whisky, bless her.

'Don't go running off. I've got you summat as well! I'll bring it over after tea. Christ, I do feel tired. I'm off for a kip!'

Dave helps me up the slope and drops the bags at the side of the bins. We shout our Christmas farewells and I pat my top-pocket for my key-ring. Putting the shopping away, I decide against warming up the Colcannon from last night. I'll have it for supper. As soon as I sit on the side of the bed I start to nod again. There's no time to set-up the CPAP machine before I'm totally gone.

Sleep apnoea. When I wake, it's dark, only the streetlamp shines into the bedroom. Bugger! Flossie's present. I sit up on the side of the bed, feeling rough. Need some water quick! I stagger to the lavatory and run the cold tap. Bending over to put my mouth under the tap there is a bang, a high-pitched noise, and a bright bluish-green light and sparks. The tap is still running. Head hurts, wet. Blood. Crawl to the toilet-bowl and haul myself up. Lean against wall, lurch forward. Throw up. Oh God. Gagging, gasping. Run towards the alarm, pull cord. Stagger to front door, run down path to Flossie's. Knock on window, can't breathe. Flossie comes to her door, looks alarmed.

'I can't breathe! I can't breathe!' I fall. Flossie runs for Jak. The high-pitched noise again. I'm going, going. My vision contracts into shifting geometric forms, like a child's kaleidoscope. Black absence.

Pain! Jak's heavy hands pumping my chest. His lips wrapped around mine. He leans me forward and slaps me hard between the shoulders. He speaks urgently. I hear Flossie on the phone. Jak shouts in my ear:

'My friend, stay with us yes? Breathe in *deep* in, one, two, three, four – then out, one, two, three, four – like so, yes? You been drinking again you old rascal! Now, keep breathing, *good* and *deep*. You spend Christmas in the hospital I think, naughty boy!'

It's no good. I'm done, can't hold on.

13

Remember Not to Forget

If there is to be immortality, there must be another kind of time: one in which past events (i.e., the past in its entirety) can be retrieved – i.e., brought back ... Since time is the true receptacle of being (for the organism) anamnesis equals awareness of the organism as such: a seeing of the more or less complete entelechy; and amnesia equals blindness, since to be seen the organism must be seen under the aspect of time – in terms of temporal extension ... Through anamnesis I could, for the first time, perceive the organism, the one.

Philip K. Dick, *The Exegesis of Philip K. Dick*, Folder 28
(Gollancz, London, 2012)

The novelist Kurt Vonnegut (1922-2007) is most famous for his *Slaughterhouse-Five* (1969) which had a profound influence on me when I first read it in 1986. I had an American tutor then, from San Diego, who was a Vietnam veteran. He had become a lecturer in English Literature, and was on an academic exchange to Yorkshire, where I was then living. He was keen to introduce me to what he thought of as the best living American authors, and Vonnegut's brief but powerful story would, my friend assured me, take 'only an afternoon' to read. I have never really taken to Sci-Fi as a genre, but the author's wartime experiences during the Battle of the Bulge and the devastating allied fire-bombing of Dresden in Germany in the closing stages of the Second World War interested me.

In an entire night, rather than an afternoon, I dutifully read the book. Just as my tutor had said, it was a moving, even life-changing experience. But what was most strange, was that it was just those Sci-Fi elements I had disdained that made the strongest impression on me, and particularly the notion of time-travel, time-slips, and the concept of *non-linear* time, revealed in flashbacks – an experience of being 'unstuck in time'.

These flashbacks are a typical symptom of PTSD, an affective disorder whose psychotic symptoms manifest hallucinations of a very intense and vivid nature. For this to occur, some powerful 'trigger' event is usually required, which quite literally ruptures time, such that Billy Pilgrim, the hero of Vonnegut's tale, is catapulted through time to various locations, including the terrible night of the Dresden firestorm and, in the future, the planet Tralfamadore, to which Billy is abducted by extraterrestrials.

Billy tells us the interesting information that the Tralfamadorians do not see humans as two-legged creatures, but as a 'great millipede' with babies' legs at the one end, and old adult legs at the other, a 'seeing of the more or less complete entelechy', as Philip K. Dick puts it. When I returned the book to my tutor the following week, we discussed it all over a pint at the Black Bull pub in Ripon. Now, Vonnegut was a fine writer, and his reputation is becoming more hallowed as the years pass, but he is not quite in the canon yet. But this little book had moved us both, in its way, and I think there was an unspoken reason for that.

My tutor had experienced combat stress in Vietnam, and the anti-war message of the book was what had first attracted him. He freely admitted that during his medical recovery in the US he had often experienced just this phenomenon of time-travelling. What I did not then reveal, though I wish I had, was that I, too, suffer from a stress disorder. During times of intense emotional stress, I had often been similarly catapulted into the past.

Temporal distortion usually results from deficits or malfunctioning of the left temporal lobe, resulting in various mental health problems and other conditions, such as temporal lobe epilepsy, schizo-affective disorder and Pick's disease. I worked with people who experienced such time distortions for many years, including people with severe dementia whose only valid interactions were with the past – all their short-term memories were wiped.

But although these diagnoses imply 'disordered' or maladaptive thinking, this does not mean that it is legitimate to invalidate what are still conscious experiences – which often contain a profundity and insight, even a meaning. The philosopher-psychiatrist R.D. Laing (1927-1989) suggested that we should compare these experiences to voyages, such as the one he describes in chapter 7 of his *The Politics of Experience*:

Suddenly I looked at the clock and the wireless was on and then music was playing – um – oh, popular sort of bit of music. It was based on the rhythm of a tram. Taa-ta-ta-taa-taa – something like Ravel's repetitive tune. And then what that happened I suddenly felt as if time was going back. I had this extraordinary feeling of – er – that was the greatest feeling I had at that moment was of time going backwards ... I looked at the clock and in some way the clock was reinforcing my own opinion of time going back although I couldn't see the hands moving – I felt alarmed because I suddenly felt as if I were moving somewhere on a kind of conveyor belt – and unable to do anything about it...

The Tralfamadorians 'see time all at once':

I am a Tralfamadorian, seeing all time as you might see a stretch of the Rocky Mountains. All time is all time. It does not change. It does not lend itself to warnings or explanations. It simply is.[24]

Billy finds comfort in this philosophy, which expiates him somewhat of the trauma and guilt which have troubled him since the Dresden inferno, especially his anguish about death:

The most important thing I learned on Tralfamadore was that when a person dies he only appears to die. He is still very much alive in the past, so it is very silly for people to cry at his funeral. All moments, past, present and future, always have existed, always will exist ... when a Tralfamadorian sees a corpse, all he thinks is that the dead person is in a bad condition in that particular moment, but that the same person is just fine in plenty of other moments. Now, when I hear that somebody is dead, I simply shrug and say what the Tralfamadorians say about dead people, which is 'So it goes.'

Billy Pilgrim is aptly named, for his journey through time does, ultimately, have a destination and purpose, a meaning. It is not always clear what these experiences portend, however. Often they are completely random and mystifying.

For hundreds of years, reliable and quite sane people have reported episodes in which they have blundered into history, slipped through time. On the last occasion when I experienced such an episode, I found myself in a pub on the junction of Radford Road and Radford Boulevard in Nottingham. People were playing pool. Music was playing. I could see the flickering lights of the one-armed-bandit and smell the cigarette smoke. I thought that was odd because smoking has been prohibited in pubs for many years. I drank up my beer and left for the main door out onto the Boulevard, but next thing I knew, I was outside my bungalow. I glanced down at the bins outside, which bore the emblem of South Staffordshire District Council. It is true that I was in a hypnagogic state, but this was not what most people would think of as an hallucination. For some completely unknown reason, I suddenly found myself in another time and space, quite as real as this one. This begs the obvious question:

> What is my real relationship to time? I experience the near past, the near future, and the very far past; a lot of my soul or psyche seems to be trans-temporal ... maybe this is why any given present space time seems somehow unreal or delusional to me. I span across and hence beyond it; always have – and the trans-temporal is the eternal, the divine, the immortal spirit. How long have I been here, and how many times? Who or what am I, and how old?

In his monumental *Exegesis* Philip K. Dick interrogated his inner-world in a two-million word thought-journal. In the grip of a mania induced by a visionary religious experience he became utterly convinced that he was in contact with what he called a 'Vast Active Living Intelligence System' – VALIS.

But this voluminous journal was nothing like his Sci-fi novels, it was rather, a spiritual or mystical record, massive and daunting to read even in its abridged version. In that sense, it is reminiscent of Madame Blavatsky and Jacob Boehme, and Dick was greatly influenced by the latter mystical philosopher. His deserved reputation as a popular author of his genre has overshadowed his more serious-minded spiritual and philosophical quest. I believe that if anything of our civilisation survives, Dick's work will one day be treated with the same reverence we now accord William Blake.

As a keen student of the cinema of the golden age since boyhood, it will come as no surprise that my favourite film, *A Matter of Life and Death* (1946), concerns itself with precisely these themes. It is produced and directed by Michael Powell and Emeric Pressburger, 'the Archers', as they were known. An RAF pilot, Peter Carter, is forced to bail out of a burning Lancaster bomber without a parachute but miraculously survives. Lest this be thought fantastical, consider the case of Nicholas Alkemade (1922-1987), an RAF tail-gunner who jumped from a burning Lancaster without a parachute in March 1944. Powell and Pressburger undoubtedly knew of the story. When his parachute burned, Alkemade decided to jump rather than be burned alive, and he went into a free-fall 18,000 feet over Germany. He immediately fell unconscious, but next thing he knew he was lying in deep snow, with a sore back and an injured leg. The heavy snow had come to rest on top of a pine plantation at an incredibly fortunate angle, breaking his fall, so that he was cushioned by the soft snowdrifts below. He whistled for help (all aircrew carried a whistle). The astonished Germans at first refused to believe him, but examination of his parachute harness and the wreckage confirmed his story beyond all doubt.

Squadron Leader Peter Carter also survives, but in an even more fantastical way. Carter is expected in the world of the dead, and a psycho-pomp, a deceased French aristocrat called 'Conductor 71' who 'lost his head' in the French Revolution, is sent to escort the young airman to the other world. But Carter has jumped into a thick fog-bank, so that his escort misses him. Finding himself to be miraculously alive, Carter falls in love with June, the USAAF radio-operator who had originally taken his distress message and who presumes he has been killed.

But the accountants in the land of the dead have already marked him as deceased – the eternal laws of the cosmos cannot be altered. Conductor 71 then appears, stops time, and demands that Carter accompany him to his appointed place in the celestial realm. Peter refuses, on the grounds that in the intervening time he has fallen deeply in love. The amorous Frenchman sympathises and arranges an appeal to be lodged with the cosmic court. Following the apparition of Conductor 71, Peter begins to experience odd hallucinations. June arranges a medical check-up for him, with Dr Reeves, her friend. He diagnoses chronic adhesive arachnoiditis, a potentially fatal inflammatory brain disease, which produces symptoms of time-space synesthesia. An emergency operation is scheduled, and it is while he is in limbo during the complex surgery that his appeal (in fact a kind of trial) is heard before a jury whose members all inherit deep prejudices against Britain and its imperial past.

Carter ultimately wins his case, for 'nothing is stronger than the law in the universe, but on Earth, nothing is stronger than love.' A charming and thoughtful film, there is also a quality of magic about it, for it makes us ask the question Conductor 71 puts to Carter; 'What *eez* time?'

The philosopher Jean Gebser (1905-1973) postulated a tiered structure to human consciousness, consisting of what he called the archaic or original, the magical, mythical, mental and integral. Like Owen Barfield, Gebser was convinced that our consciousness is in a state of transition – not in a graduated way, but in sudden leaps, presaged by periods of world crisis such as the great wars of the twentieth century. Each of the tiers marked an evolution, as it were (though Gebser was careful to avoid the term, perhaps 'punctuated equilibrium' serves better) – an ascent onto new and higher levels of sentient awareness. Our modern mental structure of conscious awareness is contingent on a 'three-dimensional' understanding, derived from geometry, logic, rationality – 'everything is nothing but matter'.

We pretend that the chair that we sit in is solid, when we *know* that, in fact, it is made up of invisible particles called atoms. The transition to mental structure must necessarily render the preceding mythical structure obsolete. With its linear view of time, it has superseded the mythical, cyclical model. Our modern culture despises the 'wise' and sets no value on the immeasurable inner-world, but it will become outdated in its turn. Gebser postulated a forthcoming 'integral' structure, perhaps already inchoate, into which we will transition in the future.

If the outward expression of these consciousness-shifts truly are indicated by periodic world-crises, then perhaps it is time to read the runes. The unfolding of the 21st century has been marked by a steady drumbeat of catastrophe. If we really are to undergo a 'mutation', a hybridisation with AI technology, in which we exchange our frail bodies for holographic avatars, I am glad that my days in this world are coming to an end. My entire upbringing, as I have described, was deliberately designed to inculcate a deep respect for the *cyclical* view of time. I was encouraged to honour the ancestors, absorb the learning and stories of the tribe – and to reject the vapid materialist mental structure. I was a misfit, an anachronism in the declining paradigm – let alone in the forthcoming one. These tales are, therefore, an obituary for a vanishing land – like the legendary spectral islands in the western ocean. It is a good time, my time, to ponder not only what time *is* but what it *means*.

This question has been an obsession for me ever since my prolonged childhood convalescences. Lying awake at night, I dared to ask the question: what happened before time began? If time were linear, it didn't make any sense. My father agreed that it didn't. He explained that the linear view of time was really a human construct, not a natural law. Our civilisation was a Christian one, and this faith envisaged an end-time, and a Judgement. Over time, this eschatological view of time had ceased to be mythical, and solidified into a kind of group-think, but this did not necessarily make it true. Many ancient mystics, as well as modern physicists, rejected and reject the linear view, seeing time expressed in terms of stationary bands through which the spiritual essence transited in order to gain successive experiences.

But then, what was the truth, I asked? My father said to look at nature, and its cycles. It had no beginning, and no end, no Alpha or Omega. It just turned, endlessly, recreating and destroying itself. There were many theories about time, but the closest approach to that of our ancient ancestors, the Druids, seemed to him the most satisfactory. The Druidic bangors or colleges were destroyed by the invading Romans 2,000 years ago, and so it was no simple matter to reconstruct these beliefs. In fact, it has taken me more than fifty years of research.

In my opinion, the restoration of the cyclical view of time as the default human understanding is inevitable. As Christianity declines in the West, the intellectual hegemony which has subordinated the wider world since the colonial expeditions in the sixteenth century will break down. The *Rig Veda*, among the most ancient religious texts in the world, tells us that 'Day and Night revolve as on a wheel.'

In a new millennium where the old assumptions of Western consumer-capitalism, racism, and environmental exploitation are being justifiably challenged, a flawed interpretation of time ought properly to be included among these grievances. The Islamic world is not quite so implicated, it has a hybrid of linear and cyclical time embodied through the incarnation of various prophets.

I believe that all cultures now face a choice. We can either go forwards or backwards. The option of standing still no longer exists. If we go backwards, as I suspect, then the restoration of cyclical time will, I believe, be inevitable for the remnant of humanity which survives the tribulations. If we go forwards, I think AI hybridisation, alongside inevitable transference of political and economic power from the West to the East, will render our present arrangements obsolete. A more rational and culturally neutral system will be designed by AI, to which all will be required to subscribe. In short, one way or the other – we are living at the end of time.

Now, these contemplations made it obvious to me that if time were so culturally contingent, much else about our modern culture may not be actually 'true'. If we conceive of the world as a landscape, full of objects, which has its origin at a receding point – we can only look backwards, as it were. Gazing out at the stars, we are literally looking into the past, seeing them as they were aeons of time ago. We can anticipate something of the future by assuming a logical relation to what has previously been encountered – but even this is really just a leap of faith. What we purport to be historical 'facts', or events, are actually only gossamer-thin memories, insubstantial dreams, even if we were personally involved in them.

The ancient Tantric religion of the Himalayas may incorporate esoteric practices derived from shamanic predecessors who have been experimenting with time for 20,000 years. They saw time as a great monstrous dragon, vomiting forth the events and objects of our material world into existence. But the projection mechanism for this process, they aver, can be reversed, so that it is not located at some vague and distant point in the past, but in the present moment, in each one of us.

By means of elaborate and secret practices, rituals and intense yogic meditations, the Tantric devotee seeks to

> ... reverse the act of Genesis, and stare straight into the continuing act of creation. All the Tantrik practices and art revolve around this process. The key word in Sanskrit is 'Paravritti', which means 'turning back up'. And the attitude of devotion or reverence, which expresses itself in offerings and worship to symbolic images, is, at bottom, a way of keeping this possibility continuously in mind.[25]

Like Owen Barfield in his *Saving the Appearances*, the Tantric devotees consider the material world to be as contingent and semi-illusory as a rainbow. All life is a series of encounters with other apparent energy-fields and conditions, with which we are inextricably intermeshed, and they with us. The Parasamvit, the Supreme Truth, encloses and projects 'all that can possibly exist throughout universes and star-systems as 'numberless as the sand grains in the Ganges'. The object of supreme devotion in the practices is the image of the Goddess Kali, the female personification of time.

This primordial veneration of the female, as Marija Gimbutas showed, is probably the deepest of all religious impulses. Inevitably, everyone on the planet will almost invariably derive their main succour, physically and emotionally, from the mother. It is from her that every human child emerges into this world, and so, therefore, the vagina represents symbolically the monstrous mouth of the dragon of time itself.

Since every creature that is born must also die, Kali, in her destructive aspect, becomes a wrathful and vengeful deity, bedecked with a necklace of human skulls, brandishing a flaying-knife, dripping fresh gore. But if we can succeed, by putting ourselves into rapport with the energies of love which flow through the universe, daring 'the turning-about in the deepest seat of consciousness' – constantly directing the consciousness to the primordial cause of being, we will experience *sunyata*, a revelation which does not come about through discursive thought, intellectual analysis or logical conclusions but rather

> ... through the complete coming to rest and relinquishing of all thought-activities, whereby we create the necessary conditions under which a direct vision of reality can arise, namely the intuitive experience of the infinity and the all-embracing oneness of all that is: of all consciousness, of all life, or however we may call it. For here end all names and definitions of our three-dimensional conceptual world. Here we become aware of an infinite succession of higher dimensions (in which those we know are contained), for which we have not yet found adequate means of expression, though we may sense the existence of those dimensions and feel them with the yet undeveloped organs of our intuitive consciousness.[26]

It is inevitable that the concept of time is intimately linked to *place*. As Chatwin's researches suggested, the indigenous peoples of Australia posited a 'dreamtime' in which past, present and future converged in sacred places, and I have drawn analogies with what I believe was going on in ancient Britain. In his book *Ancient and Modern: Time, Culture and Indigenous Philosophy* (2004), Stephen Muecke emphasises the primacy of place over time in ancient consciousness, and especially in relation to the death of the individual: 'Many indigenous accounts of the death of the individual are not so much about bodily death as about a return of energy to the place of emanation with which it re-identifies.'

In his *The Songlines* Chatwin concludes with two Native Australians returning to their sacred land to expire, grinning at death under the shade of a tree. Strangely, this most ancient, convergent concept of time is confirmed by modern quantum physics. Existence takes place in timelessness, 'the past, present, and future are intertwined,' as my Celtic forebears always taught.

In 1897 fragments of bronze plates from an ancient Celtic lunar calendar were discovered in France. The Coligny Calendar is dated to the first century AD, but the original calculations on which it is based date back to 1,100 BC. It divides the year into months considered to be 'bad' or unfortunate, and those which are 'good' or propitious, corresponding to the dark and light halves of the year. Their ethical ideas were powerfully influenced by this dualism. The function of the Druidic orders was to maintain the cosmic order, a Proto-Indo-European word *rta* seems to be the root for our word 'order'. Right action, or truth, must conform to the fundamental natural laws, or chaos would ensue – the sky would fall in on the transgressor, as it were. Therefore, as in the Arthurian myths, which are steeped in Druidic concepts, night must eventually fall, ineluctably. But the sun also rises, and the sleeping hero-king will be reborn. The sheer power and endurance of these ideas is the reason for the Roman intolerance of the religion. Unless they were extirpated, no real political control could be established over the Celts. Fortunately, the Roman project was not a complete success, and in the western fringes and Ireland the old ways continued into medieval times – possibly longer. The Druids possessed the power to excommunicate anyone deemed maleficent or dishonourable, even if it be a king. Their curses were potent and fearsome, and criminals or enemies of the tribe were sent to the gods under their supervision. That they should be scandalised for this seems odd, considering that prisoners were hanged under our modern jurisprudence until only quite recently.

Each month is similarly divided into a dark and bright half. The calendar's computations incorporate 62 months of 30 days extending over a five-year cycle, with one intercalary month added at the end. This system is so similar to that of the Vedic astrologers of India that this is one among many proofs of a common origin for the Indo-European peoples. The moon sheds its shadow, annihilating and rebirthing itself, captured in the binary opposites of life and death. The goddesses, were, therefore, the personification of time, and were depicted grasping writhing serpents. The blessed light of the moon is a mere emanation of that of the sun, whose light is generated from within itself.

It is speculated that at a very remote time indeed, it was the sun, not the moon, which symbolised the female energy, and the moon was considered male. In fact, in Celtic languages the word *maen* or 'stone' – is etymologically related to 'moon'. On the other hand, menstruation has always been intimately connected to the moon. At any rate, the heliocentric bent in religion had certainly come to dominate in Britain by the time of the Druids, and probably long before that. Pomponius Mela, the Roman geographer who wrote *A Description of the World* around AD 43 had heard of the wisdom of the insular Celts:

> They have, further, their eloquence and their Druids, teachers of wisdom, who profess to know the greatness and shape of the earth and the universe and the motion of the heavens and of the stars and of what is the will of the gods.

Caesar says the same: 'They discourse on the heavenly bodies, the motions of these, and of the size of the universe, and the power and properties of the immortal gods, instructing the young men in these matters.' The first-century AD philosopher Plutarch heard a captivating story from one of his dinner guests one evening in AD 84. Demetrius of Tarsus was a Greek explorer who claimed that the Emperor Domitian (AD 51-96) had given him a commission to visit Britain, and especially Anglesey, to discover the secrets of the Druids.

If true, this proves that some sort of Druidic revival or recovery had taken place since the massacre of the Arch-Druid and his followers by the Romans just over 20 years before. He arrived during terrible storms, which, he was informed, marked the passing of the souls of 'the mighty ones' on their journey to the west. There were sporadic meteor showers and fireballs, which the Druids took to be an intensification of celestial disorder, to accompany the tribulations of the Britons in this world. By this time, the Roman conquest was forty years old, but in the wildernesses of the north and west, the occupation was never completed, the old ways still clung on.

Demetrius tells tales of the awful weather, which sound like any tourist's assessment of Wales. The Druids told him of remote islands further west, and one in particular where Chronos, Lord of Time, was confined. The souls of the dead took the form of geese or swans, and flew far out into the western ocean to seek their final repose. The scholar Procopius tells us that the souls of the Gaulish dead gathered together at the Armorican coast before crossing the sea to Britain. Then they would fly to the houses of fishermen on the western seaboard and bang loudly at the door to demand assistance. The fishermen would then guide them to their ships, where they would wait to be conveyed to the western sea, and final release into the Other-world. Their souls would gather at a place called Bull Island off the western coast of Ireland, with a huge tunnel or doorway in it – named in Gaelic *Tech Duinn* or 'the House of Donn', 'the Dark One', Lord of Death.

To his fellow dinner-guests, these may have sounded like tall tales, but to anyone who knows about Celtic folklore all this sounds very familiar. I am in no doubt that Demetrius definitely visited Britain. In fact, a recently discovered memorial dedicated by a visitor to York around this time bears the name of a Demetrius, who was probably the same man. An Imperial Commissioner was a VIP in this frontier outpost. A 19th-century Scottish clergyman, the Reverend Dr Cririe, postulated that the entire pantheon and apparatus of the 'fairy-folk' was actually modelled on the Druids, and that the legendary 'fairy-women' from the Other-world were originally the *Bandrui* or female Druidesses. Researcher Patrick Graham equated the so-called *fees* or fairy-women, with a folk-memory of Druidism. In his ground-breaking study *The Fairy Faith in Celtic Countries* (1911), W.Y. Evans-Wentz seemed unconvinced by this theory, but I am not so sure.

Something which makes me more supportive of this 'Druid theory' of the origin of the fairy-faith is the story of the famous Mold Cape. In 1833, a gang of labourers digging outside Mold, in Flintshire, were persuaded somehow (the details are unclear) to excavate a local burial-mound, called in Welsh *Bryn yr Ellyllon*, 'the hill of the Fairies'. For as long as anyone could remember, a tale had been told of a ghostly figure which walked in the moonlight, reflecting its rays in a raiment of dazzling pure gold. What they found within took their breath away: human remains, amber beads and a cape of pure beaten gold, exquisitely decorated with hundreds of concentric rings. The original artefact, after much trouble and care, was acquired by the British Museum in London. It was skilfully made 3,000 years ago, probably by the rich tribe who exchanged copper from the Great Orme mine for exotic goods from overseas.

But this 'garment' was not designed for a king, or a warrior – it is far too small, only 18 inches in breadth across the chest. Whoever wore this supremely prestigious ritual garment, therefore, was either a young female, or a child. I am certain that young virgin Druidesses served as direct intermediaries with the gods and goddesses, as they did in many other similar cultures.

The spirits, daemons and discarnate deities were invoked to appear at the burial mounds by night. On certain nights, I have sensed their presence in such places myself. The trance utterances of the young oracle or medium were analysed by the elders, the most venerable of the male Druids, and debated upon until an agreed conclusion was drawn. It is my belief, based purely on 'analeptic' intuition, that the later Druidic culture encountered by the Romans at the turn of the 1st century AD was descended from an antecedent which was much more ancient, in which female oracles predominated, who were literally worshipped as living goddesses – at least for the duration of a year, until another girl was selected. I also believe that such practices survived into the modern era and may still be extant today, not as a pantomime copy but in an authentic form.

The eminent scholar Stuart Piggott, once Chatwin's archaeology tutor, in his classic *The Druids* (1968) explained how, for the classical writers, Britain had become inextricably conflated with other quasi-historical or legendary lands, such as the Elysian plains or the Rhadamanthus mentioned in Homer. These places are blessed with 'a blissful and pleasant temperature'. Pliny the Elder, who was obsessively interested in the secrets of the Druids, described an insular paradise similar to that encountered by Europeans when they discovered Polynesia in the eighteenth century: 'Their habitations be in woods and groves, where they worship the gods both of themselves, and in companies and congregations: no discord know they, no sickness are they acquainted with.'

As Piggott said, it is an easy step from this romanticised history to the poetry of Tennyson:

> Island-valley of Avilion
> Where falls not hail, or rain, or any snow,
> Nor any wind blows loudly.

He thus combines the Homeric and the Hyperborean Shangri-la in his Victorian Celtic Britain. But 'the old order changeth, yielding place to new.' Tennyson's Arthurian poetry was a prophesy of our present dark age.

How are we to reconcile time, to make sense of it, to find meaning in it? Perhaps to try to do so is just 'a waste of time'? At a time of life when every day is a bonus, I do not think I can afford to squander my energies on frivolous speculations. There *must be* a solution to this conundrum.

Perhaps I have been searching in the wrong place, groping about in the dark wearing a blindfold? Owen Barfield said:

> I believe that the blind-spot which posterity will find most startling in the last hundred years of Western civilisation is that it had, on the one hand, a religion which differed from all others in its acceptance of time, and of a particular point in time, as a cardinal element in its faith; that it had, on the other hand, a picture in its mind of the history of the earth and man as an evolutionary process; and that it neither saw nor supposed any connection whatever between the two.

Like him, I think I now see the connection, and agree with him that 'the revelation of the mystery of the kingdom was not turned off at the tap when the New Testament canon was closed, but is the work of an earth-time.'

14

Elysium

Oh, procrastinating one, who thinketh not of the coming of
   death,
Devoting thyself to the useless doings of this life,
Improvident art thou in dissipating thy great opportunity;
Mistaken, indeed, will thy purpose be now if thou returnest
empty-handed from this life.
Since the Holy Dharma is known to be thy true need,
Wilt thou not devote thyself to the Holy Dharma even now?
                    The Tibetan Book of the Dead (1965)

In 1943, the year before Nicholas Alkemade jumped from his
burning Lancaster 18,000 feet over Germany, another young
airman fell to earth, a Luftwaffe pilot flying his dive-bomber on
the Russian Front. Like Alkemade's story, there was something
elemental about Joseph Beuys – the stuff of legend. The affair is best
told in his own words:

> Had it not been for the Tartars I would not be alive today. They
> were nomads of the Crimea, in what was then no-man's-land
> between the Russian and German fronts, and they favoured
> neither side. I had already struck up a good relationship with
> them and often wandered off from the camp to spend time with
> them. 'Du nix njemcky', they would say, 'du Tatar', to persuade
> me to join their clan. Their nomadic ways attracted me, of course,
> although by that time their movements had been restricted.
> Yet it was they who discovered me in the snow after the crash,
> when the German search parties had already given up. I was still
> unconscious, and I only regained consciousness completely after

twelve days or so; by then I was back in a German field-hospital. So the memories I have of that time are images which penetrated my consciousness.

Like Squadron Leader Peter Carter, Beuys has his imagination 'violently shaped by war', and also like Carter, the young German flier is saved by the seemingly miraculous:

The last thing I remember, was it being too late to jump, too late for the parachute to open. That must have been a couple of seconds before hitting the ground. Luckily I was not strapped in – I always preferred being able to move freely, rather than buckling my safety belt. I had been punished for that, just as I had been punished for carrying a map of Russia – somehow I felt I knew the area better than any map. My friend was strapped in and he disintegrated on impact – there was almost nothing left of him. But I must have been propelled through the windscreen as it flew off at the same speed as the plane hitting the ground, and that saved me, although I suffered serious skull and jaw injuries. Then I was completely buried in the snow. That's how the Tartars found me a few days later. I remember voices saying 'voda' (water), then the felt of their tents and the dense and pungent smell of cheese, grease, and milk. They covered my body with grease to help it regenerate warmth and wrapped me in felt as an insulator to keep the warmth in.[27]

This extraordinary story of the man who fell to earth in the Crimean steppe was just the kind of tale which had always obsessed me, of the exotic interface with an ancient and noble race, the efficacy of their wisdom and healing power amidst the wreckage of modern technology and war – their kinship with, and care for, the helpless enemy pilot. Beuys, however had changed one crucial detail in his account.

He *did* crash in a JU 87 'Stuka' dive-bomber. He *was* very seriously injured. But there were no Tartars, no felt, no fat. Beuys was rescued by a German search party sent out to find him. It seems that Beuys invented the myth in order to account for the importance of the materials of felt and fat in his later artworks. Beuys was dismissive about this deception. Whether or not he had been rescued by 'noble savages' in order to transmit their ancient wisdom to a benighted, war-ravaged 20th century was irrelevant. The myth was truer, more poignant, more aesthetically and morally pleasing than the 'reality' – in fact, it was a work of art, an 'action'.

The call to the west is magnetic, ineluctable, always has been. The yearning for the land of sky, woods and water the Welsh call *Cantre'r Gwaelod*, a Celtic Atlantis in Cardigan Bay. The king of these other 'lost lands' was a notorious drunkard. As condign punishment, his kingdom was submerged in a great flood.

I remember standing at the crossroads; my sign reads 'Holyhead Please'. A wagon stops, with a Red Dragon draped in the back of the cab. In a few hours I am moping around the dreary pubs on the dockside of the ferry-port, sheltering from the driving rain. In two hours, the ferry gets underway, and in the early morning, as the last glimpse of Snowdon fades. the lights of Dublin blink into view. We get the bus into town, and I head for the coach station. Soon we are out beyond the pale: Athlone, Roscommon, Athenry. Finally, the descent into Galway Bay, and on the day following, a trip to the Cliffs of Moher, towering seven hundred feet above the wide Atlantic, curving turquoise beyond the Aran Islands, all the way to Newfoundland. Somewhere out there lies *Tir na nOg*, the Land of Eternal Youth.

Easter Sunday, 2021, under social-distancing restrictions, I hobble down into the village to the off-licence. I consume a few cans in the village clock-tower-cum-bus-shelter, some wags call it my 'mead-hall'. The chill evening air has the last of winter in it, and the first inkling of spring. I consider what to order at the Chinese takeaway, then tramp back up the hill, past 'Dracula's Castle' (my former infant school), and on up to Edgecliff High School. I sit on the wall outside for a breather. The security lights throw a shadow of my bulky frame onto the pavement, and the spiked iron-rails immediately behind me. I laugh at my shadow-self, and think: 'Well, old-chap – behind bars again!' But then I remember our old friend, Archie Hill, and his 'Cage of Shadows'. I never did find his birthplace, but no matter, I am not done yet. My live shadow is different from the rails', more agile. I sway in rebellion, and make hand gestures, my shadow-motion transcendent, through the precise, immoveable, timeless rank of rods. At the Foley Infant School, the rails are appropriately made of nail-rods.

All our pasts are shadows, of the tribe and the nation, as much as for the individual person. If we wish to, we can move our shadow-self (or selves) of the past as deftly and subtly between the static iron-bars, as I did then. Perhaps that was what Beuys was trying to communicate to us. It was in the desperate void between the crash and his recovery by his comrades that the young airman had the experience of nurturing and care, hospitality and warmth.

His head injuries were serious. One of the reasons he wore his famous felt hat was because his brain became chilled from the steel-plates in his skull. I cannot call a man a liar because of his experiences under extreme stress. I presume it *was* a pretty stressful experience to be shot down by flak. The RAF pilot Richard Hillary, in his autobiographical *The Last Enemy (1942)* seemed to think so. The book was released in the US as *Falling Through Space*, a title more appropriate, perhaps, to Nicholas Alkemade. The 'Last Enemy' of the original title, of course, is death (1 Corinthians 15-26). After his slow and painful recovery from his horrific burns, including pioneering plastic surgery, Hillary volunteered for active duty. He was killed on active service quite soon afterwards.

Our memories, then, are selective and edited, but although this has been very far from a conventional history, something like the foregoing sort of happened. In art, verisimilitude need not be our touchstone, as it should be in jurisprudence. One of my (perhaps not so subtle) hints in this book is that among the earliest British learned classes, history was regarded as a branch of storytelling or literature. For the Northumbrian Bede and his British predecessor (and valuable source), Gildas, history was the record of God's intervention in the affairs of the 'Island of the Mighty'. Gildas thought that the warlike and heathen Anglo-Saxon immigrants were sent as a scourge from God on his fellow-countrymen, the Britons, for their apostasy and sinfulness.

Bede was quick to note this theme in Gildas and took the concept to the next level. His entire message to the English Church and people is that they must never repeat the errors of the Britons – lest they, too, lose the sovereignty of Britain. If there is a single defining national myth of the British, it is that when the country falls into *dishonour* it will lose its virility and martial eagerness and become prey to invaders. Archbishop Wulfstan took up the theme in his 'Sermon of the Wolf to the English' in the 11th century, but the rot had set-in too deep by then.

The Normans, in their turn, seized the sovereignty of Britain, and did not squander the opportunity. They ruthlessly consolidated their English acquisition, then used it as the springboard for the subjugation of the British Isles and, in time, a large part of the wider world. Now the details of all this are obscure and of very little interest to the majority of the modern population. But the sense of it, the mythology, the 'sacredness' of it – is absolutely hard-wired into the national psyche. Those who seek to antagonise or provoke the British (especially the English) about their history should beware. for although most of them know very little about it, they do not like to hear of their heroes being execrated or belittled – particularly when they are long dead, and unable to defend themselves. In such a sharply divided island as we have now become, no academic discipline has become more weaponised than history.

But just as the English, Welsh, Scots and Irish have every right to preserve and honour, to regret and despise their long histories, the more recent waves of immigrants should also feel that their story is being told, and their ongoing contribution recorded. There *is* a profound disconnect between many black and brown people and 'White British' history. It seems to be *their* history, of how white people raped the world, and got away with it – and how that's supposed, somehow, to be OK now. But the more serious neglect, is of the orientation of recent immigrants in the wider landscape.

Too often, young black people remain in cramped neighbourhoods of the large metropolitan areas and rarely leave the inner cities. Nick Hayes in his *The Book of Trespass* (2020), quotes Trevor Phillips, the former head of the Equality and Human Rights Commission, describing a 'passive apartheid' in the British countryside:

> Figures show that the 9 per cent of Britain's population who are from an ethnic minority constitute only 1 per cent of the visitors to the countryside. Further to this, the stats say that while 10 per cent of the population in towns are from ethnic minorities, only 1 per cent of the rural population are Black and Minority Ethnic. In 2013, Brian True-May stepped down from producing the ITV show *Midsomer Murders* after declaring that 'we just don't have ethnic minorities involved because it wouldn't be the English village with them ... We're the last bastion of Englishness and I want to keep it that way.' ... In the eyes of rural England, black means urban, but the moment these communities cross the line into the countryside they challenge 'the very idea of Englishness itself'.

Of course, this virtual exclusion of black people from the countryside is not *enforced* by anyone. It is a simple fact that immigrants anywhere traditionally prefer to remain in close proximity to each other, for obvious reasons. The British had many such concessions and exclusive quarters all over the world for centuries. But this 'apartheid' has other negative consequences.

'White Flight' from the urban areas into the countryside has been growing exponentially, driving poorer young rural people out of their home communities. The artificial inflation of house prices assumes that only wealthy, older, white people will be potential customers. Agricultural or other workers, travellers, the disabled, the homeless – and black people – must needs look elsewhere.

It is extraordinary that we have overlooked and tacitly condoned this hypocrisy for as long as we have. It is plain to see, we can deceive ourselves no longer. It is perverse that at the precise time when history is so controversial and poignant, there are fewer history undergraduates in our universities than ever before. There is even serious discussion about taking history out of the core schools curriculum. Why? 'History is irrelevant,' young people say; 'History is boring.' What has been done to the education system of this country in my lifetime is the single most pernicious domestic policy disaster I have witnessed, and I prophesy it will lead Britain to its doom. In that sentiment, at least, I stand in the tradition of our two earliest and greatest historians.

In the fourth century AD, Roman Britain reached the peak of its power. Opulent villas, with underfloor heating, some dwarfing Buckingham Palace, were dotted in their hundreds all over central and southern Britain. They were run by slave-power, the entire Roman system was predicated on slavery – the British Empire was proud to carry on the ancient tradition. There may have been as many as 3 million inhabitants of the Roman provinces. Roman London, with 50,000 inhabitants, had the largest buildings in the empire outside Italy itself. Some people were getting very rich in Britain, and they preferred to keep it that way. In the late third century, they decided to attempt an early form of Brexit by seceding from the empire. Taxes which should have gone to the emperor instead went into the treasuries of wealthy magnates who had supported the usurper emperor, Carausius. Britannia had large military forces, by land and sea, and felt more than equal to Roman might, though they eventually succumbed and rejoined the Roman scheme.

Just over a century later – all this was gone. The population had declined by more than half. The economy was ruined – the money economy, coinage, simply ceased to exist. London was a virtually empty, burned-out, rat-infested wasteland. The legions, and the *Classis Britannica* or British navy, had long gone, and the only 'troops' left were unpredictable mercenaries, usually Germanic.

No-one could remember the craft of building in stone anymore. Literacy disintegrated. Christianity was in retreat too, and heresy and paganism rife. Famine and plague and murrain stalked the land. That is how quickly the darkness falls.

The knells have been sounded for our culture and cannot be unrung. This may sound like the jaded pessimism of an ageing 'Celtic Melancholic', and of course, it is. The 'Baby Boomers', myself included, came in on the post-war wave which is now breaking on the shore. Like God, they are now in retirement. In my opinion, with a few notable exceptions, they were responsible for many of the ills of 21st-century Western culture. Their mass apostasy unravelled the Christian values which had underpinned our civilisation for 2,000 years, replacing them with spurious 'isms'. In the optimism of the 1960s, much was promised, but what emerged in the aftermath was banal consumerism, self-indulgence, infantile enthusiasms – and (for some) a vulgar materialism undreamed of since the decadence of Rome.

They were supposed to be the Golden Children, who would rebuild a better world after two global conflicts. By the time they became adults, the world seemed young, too, exciting and sexy, and God, therefore, seemed older – 'square'. Technical know-how, innovation, and specialised computing knowledge replaced the men in bowler hats. The church pews emptied. Everyone 'did their own thing'.

There is no room in such a worldview for the unchanging assurances of faith. Like God, history is too much to take in for a culture with such a short attention span. What is the *use* of it? But here's the rub. Now, it is our turn to scan the prospectuses of care-homes – to feel the pull of the sea lapping at the western shore – but who, or what, will greet us there at life's bitter edge? Not fairy-maidens, but nurses in face masks.

And what then? The Tibetan Lamas, meaning 'way-finders', 'pioneers', or 'pathfinders', have concerned themselves somewhat more seriously than most people of today about these matters:

> Then the Lord of Death will place around thy neck a rope and drag thee along; he will cut off thy head, tear out thy heart, pull out thy intestines, lick up thy brain, drink thy blood, eat thy flesh, and gnaw thy bones; but thou will be incapable of dying. Even when thy body is hacked into pieces, it will revive again. The repeated hacking will cause intense pain and torture.

Jung called this experience, 'a chaotic riot of phantasmal forms'. It is, he said, 'a way of initiation in reverse, which, unlike the eschatological expectations of Christianity, prepares the (dead) soul for a descent into physical being.' For the intermediate or *Bardo* state is 'a terrifying dream-state of a progressively degenerative character':

> The supreme vision comes not at the end of the Bardo, but right at the beginning, in the moment of death; what happens afterwards is an ever-deepening descent into illusion and obscuration, down to the ultimate degradation of new physical birth. The spiritual climax is reached at the moment when life ends. Human life, therefore, is the vehicle of the highest perfection it is possible to attain.

Is this view of human (and all sentient) life as being unique, precious and valuable, consistent with our modern Western view? Of course not. The exiled Lamas have no choice but to share their abstruse wisdom now – but they cast their pearls before swine. At least they can teach us how to die, and perhaps, paradoxically, how to live.

A 'Sorrow Tale'. Long, long ago, 'beyond the mists of twice a thousand years', an Irish king was defeated in battle near what is now Dublin. He sought refuge in the western wilds near Killarney in Kerry, with a few close companions, and his son, Osian. One day, they were all out hunting and the hounds pursued a young doe. As they gained on her, a beautiful damsel, on the finest white steed, her broad-brow diademed, both mount and rider arrayed as befitted royalty – confronted them and begged them to call off the pack. The king enquired who she was, and of what kingdom, for she was clearly of noble stature, and would need to be restored to the protection of her lord and master. She replied that she was Niamh, princess of Tir na nOg, the blessed island in the western sea. 'I have no lord, no master, nor any husband,' she declared.

The pack of warriors drew their breath. No such woman, surely, could be unattached? The king spoke the obvious question in all the men's minds. Were the men of Tir na nOg unworthy then, or 'not fond of women'? Niamh replied that, in vision, she had espied her only true beloved – and that was Osian, the king's own son. She had come from the Other-world into Ireland, to claim him as her own – if that was his own true wish. Osian gawped in awe of this paragon, more beautiful even than the famed colleens of Ireland. His father warned him, seeing the sense dimming in his young eyes. 'It is for my son to choose, whether to abandon his own people, so sorely beset – to journey west across the ocean, into your world, to live among a foreign race!'

Niamh beckoned Osian and whispered in his ear. Her land, she promised, was overflowing with milk and honey, the corn was ripe in the ear all year round, for there was perpetual summer. No sickness or old age, no war or famine, fear or grief, ever concerned the people of her land, where exquisite music and exotic perfumes filled the air – and beautiful people coupled freely in endless ecstatic union. Shortly afterwards, Osian bid his father and companions a fond farewell – but not without a final warning from the king. Tir na nOg might be a pretty fine place, indeed, but it was not Ireland.

The young man leaped up onto the horse behind his new-found beloved, and she spurred the steed on into the western ocean. The sea parted before them and closed back behind them in foam as they flew through the great water at frantic speed. But still, there was no land in sight, even though many days and nights elapsed. But then they sighted dolphins, who led them into an expansive, sheltering bay. They put ashore, and gathered grapes from well-tended vineyards, scooped honey from hives among thriving flocks. A lord and lady rode past, bedecked in finery, and instead of challenging them, bid them welcome, and a hearty good-day. 'Surely, this must be Tir na nOg, and those fine folk, the noble deathless ones you spoke to me of?' the lad enquired. But Niamh merely laughed, and said, 'Oh no! This is not my homeland, just a worthless, mortal country like your own. Those fine folk beyond – would be the lowest *peasants* in Tir na nOg! We must journey onwards, my love!'

Onwards into the western sea they went, until a huge rocky outcrop appeared, with a great fortified city atop, the bastion of the giant king of the Fomorian sea-pirates. Osian learned that a damsel was confined within, in the grim dungeons of the castle, and challenged the giant Fomorian king to armed combat. Osian overcame the ogre, rescued the maiden, and upheld his honour – but this land was not yet Tir na nOg. Niamh and Osian journeyed on and on, until one day – they reached the blessed land in the west itself.

Matilo Roman Fort.

Swan near South Parade, Worcester.

At last, Osian was presented to the king of his adopted land, and the couple were married in a lavish ceremony, which would have been called a holiday in any other country. But in Tir na nOg, there never *were* any holidays, just as in C.S. Lewis's Narnia, 'it was always winter, but never Christmas.' All Osian had been promised to him by his new bride proved true. Their sexual passion never lessened in its ecstatic intensity. Their three bonny children never knew ill-health, nor did they ever know want. Every day of each succeeding year was just as blissfully perfect as the last.

Washing his hair at the pool one morning, Osian regarded his reflection, and saw that it had not changed. There were no grey hairs, no wrinkles, no signs of ageing at all. Yet, he had been in Tir na nOg these many years now! His children were almost full-grown. What of his own father, and his old companions? What of his dear homeland of Ireland? He would give up his immortality, disburse all his treasure, if he could be granted just one precious hour in his own home, to hear the familiar lilt and music of his own folk. 'Whoever has ears, let them hear.'

Approximately every 29 years, the planet Saturn returns to the same position in the heavens it occupied at the moment of one's birth. As I write, I am just completing the second of these 'Saturn returns'. Saturn represents, among other things, time, patient, diligent but immediately unrewarding work, discipline, and restriction. The deity, in other words, is associated with agriculture, always a tedious and risky business. The sign of Aquarius represents humanity, society, communications. Saturn also represents the harvest, that is why he is depicted as carrying a scythe, 'the Grim Reaper' himself. He has been busy this last year. I doubt I will see him next time around – indeed, it has been touch-and-go to get this far.

For sure, it is time to prepare. My plans are forming now. Like the song in the old film, *I Know Where I'm Going!* (1945), another classic romance from Powell & Pressburger. Joan Webster (played by Wendy Hiller) also has a plan, but life, and love, have other ideas. In an epic scene, Joan almost becomes caught in the infamous Corryvreckan whirlpool, to the north of Islay and Jura – the world's second largest. Corry means 'Mother Goddess' or 'the womb of all creation'. Breacan, a Viking prince and mariner, was sucked down into the seething, boiling waters and never seen again. Many more have followed him since. No, I have learned of the uselessness of plans – but at least I now have a direction.

I am well-placed, too, though I should like to be on the right side of the Severn. The sacred Severn, at 220 miles long the longest river in Great Britain (the Thames is the longest entirely in England). In his *The Welsh Marches* Housman's rhyming couplets really weave their magic:

> When Severn down to Buildwas ran
> Coloured with the death of man,
> Couched upon her brother's grave
> The Saxon got me on the slave.
>
> The sound of fight is silent long
> That began the ancient wrong;
> Long the voice of tears is still
> That wept of old the endless ill.
>
> In my heart it has not died,
> The war that sleeps on Severn side;
> They cease not fighting east or west,
> On the marches of my breast.

Once upon a time, Gwyn ap Nudd or Nodens, the ancient Celtic god of the underworld, sat astride a giant seahorse as the famous Severn bore surged upstream. There is an ancient temple dedicated to him at Lydney Park in Gloucestershire. But the supreme river-deity, of course, is Sabrina, Lady of this mighty force of nature, whose destructive power is well-attested. The wild Severn in spate is a truly awesome sight to behold, and every year, lives are lost – people are 'taken by the river', as they say. She is to be feared, true, but none the less loved and adored.

Housman's poems came to him on the wind. Like him, I have lost my muse, but no matter. The beautiful girl, walking along the riverbank each morning, serves just the same purpose. Her simple, innocent grace preserves the perpetual order.

Tomorrow, I will enjoy my beloved view of the Clee Hills, brooding over the Severn Valley, watch the birds flit in-and-out among the exotic trees of the little arboretum, admire the spring flowers lining the lanes of Wootton Green. There may be some early bluebells. I'll pay my respects at the monument at Six-Ashes on the way. It'll be packed at the Cider House, I'm pretty sure, and with the chill spring weather, I'll be needing my warmest coat and mittens. There'll be old comrades there, and good cheer – but sadly, some will be missing. A trenchant reminder that every day above ground is a good day. So, let us drink, and toast one and all, both the living, and the dead:

Ale man, ale's the stuff to drink
For fellows whom it hurts to think:
Look into the pewter pot
To see the world as the world's not.

And faith, 'tis pleasant till 'tis past:
The mischief is that 'twill not last.
Oh I have been to Ludlow fair
And left my necktie God knows where

And carried half way home or near,
Pints and quarts of Ludlow beer:
Then the world seemed not so bad,
And I myself a sterling lad:

And down in lovely muck I've lain,
Happy till I woke again.
Then I saw the morning sky:
Heigho, the tale was just a lie;

The world, it was the old world yet,
I was I, my things were wet,
And nothing now remained to do
But begin the game anew.

Notes

1. Gimbutas, M., *The Living Goddesses* (University of California Press, Berkeley & Los Angeles, 1999)
2. Graves, R., *The White Goddess* (Faber & Faber, London, 1948)
3. Reilly, R.J., *Romantic Religion* (1971)
4. Laing, R. D., *The Politics of Experience* (1967)
5. Carl Jung in Evans-Wentz, W. Y., *The Tibetan Book of the Dead* (Oxford, 1965)
6. Florence of Worcester, *Chronicle* (ed. & trans. Forester, T) (London, 1854)
7. Burnet, Thomas, *Archaelogiae Philisophicae* (1692)
8. Watkins, Alfred, *The Old Straight Track* (London, 1925)
9. Robb, Graham, *The Ancient Paths: Re-discovering the Lost Map of Celtic Europe* (Picador, London, 2014)
10. Heath, Robin and John Michell, *The Measure of Albion: The Lost Science of Prehistoric Britain* (Bluestone, St Dogmaels, 2004)
11. Hoggart, Richard, *The Uses of Literacy* (London, 1957)
12. *The Lion and the Unicorn* (Secker & Warburg, 1941)
13. *Fabian of the Yard* (BBC, 1954–56)
14. Murray, Margaret, *The Witch Cult in Western Europe (1921)*
15. Graves, Robert, *The White Goddess* (London, 1948)
16. Gimbutas, M., *The Living Goddesses* (1999)
17. Hill, Archie, *A Cage of Shadows* (London, 1973)
18. Burritt, E., *Walks in the Black Country and its Green Borderland* (1869)
19. Quoted in Nick Laird's introduction to *A Shropshire Lad and Other Poems* (Penguin, London, 2010)

20. Carpenter, H, *J. R. R. Tolkien: A Biography* (George Allen & Unwin, London, 1977)
21. C. S. Lewis, *The Four Loves* (London, 1963)
22. Carpenter, H., *Tolkien: A Biography* (London, 1977)
23. Chatwin, B., Chatwin, E. & Shakespeare N., (Eds.) *Under the Sun*, London, 2011
24. Vonnegut, K. Jr., *Slaughterhouse-Five* (1969)
25. Rawlinson, P., *Tantra: The Indian Cult of Ecstasy*, T & H, London, 1979
26. Lama Anagarika Govinda, 'Foundations of Tibetan Mysticism' (Bombay, 1960)
27. Durini, L., *The Felt Hat: Joseph Beuys, A Life Told* (Rome, 1991)

Select Bibliography

Barfield, O., *Saving the Appearances*, Wesleyan, 2011

Baring-Gould, S., *Bladys of the Stewponey*, 1897

Beowulf

Bevan-Jones, R., *The Ancient Yew*, 2002

Boehme, J., *Aurora*, 1612

Brett Young, F., *The Island*, 1944

Burnet, T., *Archaeologicae Philosophicae*, 1692

Burritt, E., *Walks in the Black Country and its Green Borderland*, 1869

Canu Heledd

Carpenter, H., *J.R.R. Tolkien: A Biography*, 1977

Chatwin, B., *The Songlines*, 1987

Chatwin, B., Chatwin, E., & Shakespeare, N., (eds), *Under the Sun*, 2011

Chitham, E., *The Black Country*, 1972

Dick, P.K., *The Exegesis of Philip K. Dick*, Jackson, P., & Lethem, J., (eds), 2011

Donne, J., *Divine Meditations*, 1633

Douglas, K., *The Inner Wheel*, 1970

Dudley, D., *Metallum Martis*, 1665

Durini, L., *The Felt Hat: Joseph Beuys: A Life Told*, 1991

Evans, S., *Round About the Crooked Steeple*, 1931

Evans-Wentz, W.Y., *The Fairy Faith in Celtic Countries*, 1911

Evans-Wentz, (trans) *The Tibetan Book of the Dead*, 1965

Fabian, R., *Fabian of the Yard*, 1955

Florence of Worcester, *Chronicle*, Forester, T., trans, 1854

Gimbutas, M., *The Living Goddesses*, 1999

Govinda, A., *Foundations of Tibetan Mysticism*, 1960

Graves, R., *The White Goddess: A Historical Grammar of Poetic Myth*, 1948

Hawkes, J., *A Land*, 1951

Hayes, N., *The Book of Trespass*, 2020

Heath, R., & Michell, J., *The Measure of Albion: The Lost Science of Prehistoric Britain*, 2004

Hill, A., *A Cage of Shadows*, 1973

Hill, A., *Summer's End*, 1976

Hillary, R., *The Last Enemy*, 1942

Hoggart, R., *The Uses of Literacy*, 1957

Housman, A.E., *A Shropshire Lad*, 1896

Hughes, T., & Godwin, F., *Remains of Elmet*, 1979

Kightly, C., *Folk Heroes of Britain*, 1982

Knowler, J., *Trust an Englishman*, 1973

Laing, R.D., *The Politics of Experience & The Bird of Paradise*, 1967

Larkin, P., *The North Ship*, 1945

Layamon, *Brut*

Leland, C., *Aradia or The Gospel of the Witches*, 1899

Lewis, C.S., *The Four Loves*, 1963

Marcuse, H., *One Dimensional Man*, 1964

Markale, J., *The Celts*, 1976

Mela, P., *A Description of the World*, 43

Milton, J., Comus, 1637

Michelet, J., *La Sorcière*, 1862

Monmouth, G., *Historia Regum Britanniae*, 1136

Morris, J., *The Age of Arthur*, 1973

Muecke, S., *Ancient and Modern: Time, Culture and Indigenous Philosophy*, 2004

Murray, M., *The Witch Cult in Western Europe*, 1921

Nennius, *Historia Brittonum*

Orwell, G., *The Lion and the Unicorn*, 1941

Piggott, S., *The Druids*, 1968

Rawlinson, P., *Tantra: The Indian Cult of Ecstasy*, 1979

Reilly, R.J., *Romantic Religion*, 1971

Rhinehart, L., *The Dice Man*, 1971

Robb, G., *The Ancient Paths*, 2014

Sims-Williams, P., *Religion and Literature in Western England 600-800*, 1990

Sillitoe, A., *The Death of William Posters*, 1965

Sillitoe, A., *Raw Material*, 1987

Stenton, F., *Anglo-Saxon England*, 1943

Stoppard, T., *The Invention of Love*, 1997

Sturgeon, T., *More than Human*, 1953

Suso, H., *Horologium Sapientiae*

Sutcliff, R., *The Lantern Bearers*, 1959

Tennyson, A., 'Morte d'Arthur', pub.1842

Thompson, E.P., *The Making of the English Working Class*, 1963

Tilley, C., *A Phenomenology of Landscape: Places, Paths and Monuments*, 1994

Tolkien, J.R.R., 'Mythopoeia'

Tolkien, J.R.R., *The Hobbit*, 1937

Tolkien, J.R.R., *The Lord of the Rings*, 1954

Trioedd Ynys Prydein, 'Triads of the Island of Britain'

Vonnegut, K., *Slaughterhouse-Five*, 1969

Wace, R., *Roman de Brut*

Watkins, A., *The Old Straight Track*, 1925

Yeates, Stephen J., *The Tribe of Witches: The Religion of the Dobunni and Hwicce*, 2008

Acknowledgements

Thanks are due to the many kind people without whose encouragement this work would not have been completed, especially John and Judy Gibbons, Robert Bevan-Jones and Robert Plant, Edmund Simons, Jane, Paul and Lola Meyrick, and Kevyn Gammond. Thanks, too, to John Myers for his permission to use images from his *The End of Industry* (2019) and others for the use of photographs. Every effort has been made to seek permission for copyright material. If, however, I have inadvertently used material without permission or acknowledgement, I apologise and will make the necessary correction at the first opportunity.

List of Illustrations

Index

Also available from Amberley Publishing

'A remarkable book ... an inspiration from
the heart of the Shire'
ROBERT PLANT

THE
MAGICAL
HISTORY OF
BRITAIN
MARTIN WALL

Available from all good bookshops or to order direct
Please call **01453-847-800**
www.amberley-books.com